GERALD M. PHILLIPS, Ph.D., professor of speech communication at The Pennsylvania State University, has written numerous books, papers, and articles on the subject of shyness. He is currently director of the only permanent, full-time program in the United States that trains people to overcome their shyness.

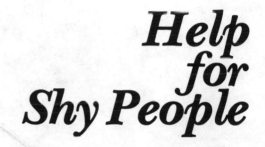

Help
for
Shy People

Help for Shy People

*and anyone else
who ever felt ill at ease
on entering a room full of strangers. . .*

Gerald M. Phillips

A SPECTRUM BOOK

Prentice-Hall, Inc., *Englewood Cliffs, N.J. 07632*

Library of Congress Cataloging in Publication Data

Phillips, Gerald M.
  Help for shy people.

  (A Spectrum Book)
  Includes bibliographical references and index.
  1. Bashfulness.   2. Interpersonal communication.
I. Title
BF575.B3P46   158'.2   81–5187
ISBN 0–13–386110–4   AACR2
ISBN 0–13–386102–3 (pbk.)

This Spectrum Book is available to businesses and organizations at a special discount when ordered in large quantities. For information, contact Prentice-Hall, Inc., General Book Marketing, Special Sales Division, Englewood Cliffs, N. J. 07632

10   9   8   7   6   5   4   3   2   1

Printed in the United States of America

Editorial/production supervision and interior design
   by *Heath Lynn Silberfeld*
Cover illustration by *Rudi Von Briel*
Manufacturing buyer: *Cathie Lenard*

Prentice-Hall International, Inc., *London*
Prentice-Hall of Australia Pty. Limited, *Sydney*
Prentice-Hall of Canada, Ltd., *Toronto*
Prentice-Hall of India Private Limited, *New Delhi*
Prentice-Hall of Japan, Inc., *Tokyo*
Prentice-Hall of Southeast Asia Pte. Ltd., *Singapore*
Whitehall Books Limited, *Wellington, New Zealand*

Contents

chapter **3**
Where Shyness Comes From
23

chapter **4**
What the "Experts" Say
32

chapter **5**
Starting to Change
40

chapter **6**
Communication and Human Relationship
54

chapter **7**
How to Set Goals
74

chapter **8**
Analyzing Situations
93

chapter **9**
Making Sense
117

chapter **10**
Talk and Daily Living
153

Preface

The first reticence class was conducted at The Pennsylvania State University in September 1965. It arose out of research I did earlier at Washington State University with the Reverend Laura Muir. While working in a speech and hearing clinic, we discovered a number of people who came for help and appeared to have no diagnosable speech difficulty. The Reverend Ms. Muir's subsequent thesis research turned up the model of an individual who was apprehensive about speaking in situations that transcended simple stage fright. The term *reticent* was used to designate those individuals, since we had no desire to label them pejoratively. The later theoretical notion was that some people simply choose not to talk much but can do so when they care to. Reticent people would like to talk more and talk effectively but cannot do so. In the last two years, because the term *shy* has become so popular, it has been used to designate the group of people with whom we work.

The original group of reticents consisted of sixteen students who were prepared to leave the university rather than take a required public-speaking course. These students were identified with the help of psychologist Samuel Osipow. A team was composed from The Pennsylvania State University staff, consisting of Larry Steward (now at Portland State University), Tim Hopf (now at Washington State University), David Butt, and Douglas Pedersen. The students, who included one who had been institutionalized for muteness, one who had attempted suicide because of his distress at talking, a third who broke out in hives when required to talk, and a fourth who could begin to talk only after literally banging his head against the wall, as well as those with minor disabilities, were offered a ten-week training program in communication skills. What distinguished this program from others was that each student had a private syllabus of requirements. Individualized instruction remains a main feature of the Reticence Program to this day.

Opposition to the program was strong. Some academics objected because they felt the course was a "Mickey Mouse" way of escaping a requirement. Others were insulted, for they believed themselves able to cope with problem speakers in their classrooms. A third group simply did not believe students could have such problems. An open debate was scheduled, pitting me against Professor Carroll Arnold, a world-renowned authority in oral communication. Professor Arnold grilled me for nearly two hours, compelling me to present justifications and prognoses for improvement. As a result the program was authorized as a regular feature of instruction, and Dr. Arnold became one of its major supporters.

In the earliest days of the program we made an attempt to identify reticent people through the use of a paper-and-pencil test. James McCroskey of Western Virginia University has become a nationally known authority on the problem of speech apprehension through his efforts to discover an instrument to identify degrees of anxiety associated with communication disability. McCroskey's position is that it is anxiety that impedes successful communication and that if anxiety is removed, skill will result. McCroskey remains to this day a powerful antagonist, whose energy on behalf of his own cause has stimulated our own research into techniques for improving communication skills. McCroskey is also a vital friend, whose encouragement and support have helped make reticence a national concern.

Various individuals contributed to the developing technique. David Butt designed programs in environmental management derived from various sensitivity-training techniques. Tim Hopf offered the definition of *reticence* used to this day: Persons elect to be reticent when what they stand to lose from speaking seems to outweigh the possible gain. Larry Steward's research uncovered a vast pool of people disqualified from communication with superordinates and authority figures. Kathleen Kougl, Kent Sokoloff, and Nancy Metzger devised the current training pattern based on goalsetting, planning, rehearsal, and critique. In addition, a generation of faculty colleagues, department heads, and loyal students contributed mightily to the growth of the program. Particular thanks are due to department head Robert Brubaker for supporting the program and to fellow faculty members Herman Cohen, Douglas Pedersen, and Kathryn DeBoer for their efforts in the classroom. Of the students who tried their hand in the classroom, significant contributions were made by Susan Stone-Applbaum, Susan Ackerman-Ross, Paul Friedman, Robert Harrison, Jerry Zolten, Cindy Begnal, Mary-Linda Merriam, Wing Spooner, Daun McKee, Jan Turner, and Marie Bartlett-Stagl. Particular contributions were made by Lynne Kelly and Susan Sorenson in the design of training programs for public school teachers; by Paul Friedman and Mary-Linda Merriam in designing and administering a broad experimental program in the public schools of Alameda County, California; and by Douglas Pedersen of the Pennsylvania State Continuing Education Program and his entire staff in generating and maintaining a variety of public-school programs in Pennsylvania.

Significant research into the nature of reticents and the effects of instruction was contributed by Barbara Wilson Streibel, Lynne Grutzeck, Patti Fox, Nancy Metzger, Kathleen Kougl, Katrin Rittler, Larry Steward, Susan Oerkvitz, Bruce McKinney, Dennis Kleinsasser, and David Sours. Their work will be referred to subsequently in this book.

Research and teaching continue. To date we have served more than three thousand students and adults. Recently a special program for overcoming stage fright was added to the program, and currently research into the possibility of applying the techniques of the reticence program to socialization training for depressed adults is being conducted. The Reticence Program can be contacted through the Department of Speech Communication at The Pennsylvania State University.

G.M.P.

chapter 1

What Is Shyness?

Shy people take a beating! Day in and day out they are pushed, bullied, ignored, and rejected by the aggressive people around them. They are constantly frustrated because they cannot say what they need to. They are further insulted by various authorities who call them "sick," proclaim them to be candidates for treatment, and suspect them of latent violence.[1]

There is nothing wrong with people who are simply quiet because they wish to be, so long as they can speak effectively when they want to. The world might be a bit better off if most of us talked less and listened more. But shy people cannot compete well socially. They are constantly thwarted in what they seek. Most of them need to learn to talk effectively so that they can make more of an effort on their own behalf. We call shy people reticent because that word contains less social prejudice. Reticent people have a choice to speak or be silent. Shy people are often regarded as locked into their "disability."

It is the purpose of this book to help quiet people who want to learn to be more effective socially. We do not regard them as disabled. We believe they need an "equalizer" in order to be more effective with others. People who are not shy all the time can also use this book, for shyness is not a pervasive disorder but a condition that comes upon us when we encounter a social situation that we do not have the skill to handle. We are all shy from time to time. This book is for anyone who ever felt a little sick when entering a room full of strangers, felt butterflies while giving a sales report to the "brass," or broke out in a cold sweat when facing a job interview. This book is not for people who want to defeat others in human relationships. It is for those who seek equity, not victory.

We do not offer the message to people that if they learn to take care of themselves, they will live happily ever after. Quite the contrary! Our message is that personal success depends on sensible consideration of the other. Rather than counseling people on how they can look out for Number One, we offer training in how Number One can enlist the cooperation of Number Two so that they can succeed together. In this book we seek to teach you how to be understanding and how to be understood so that you and others can attain goals important to you. It is a book that offers advice you can apply immediately to your daily life. It is addressed to those who are willing to take action on their own behalf; it offers little to those who believe that merely by reading it their lives will be changed.

This book is based on twenty years of experience at teaching shy people to become more effective socially. The program from which this book was developed has been successful in improving the social relationships for 85 percent of the more than 3,000 people who have participated.[2] We recommend the method to anyone who has ever felt bullied, browbeaten, ignored, or snubbed; to anyone who ever felt fear when talking with other human beings.

THE BEGINNING

"I am sure that many of the people who come to see me really don't have anything wrong with them. Why do they come to a speech clinic?" That question, asked by an imaginative speech clinician,[3] began the search for a method to overcome shyness. Early research made it clear that shyness was not a "defect," but a lack of skill. Shy people are frustrated by their inability to talk when they need to or want to. They often feel tense and depressed or feel they have some flaw because they do not seem to do well with others. They often confuse the feelings they have about what is happening with feelings about themselves as persons. They allow the signs of their problem to make them tense about themselves, and sometimes they become so preoccupied with their inner feelings that they do not pay enough attention to what is going on around them. Their concern impedes their ability to perform. That is why some psychologists regard their problem as an emotional disorder.[4]

Shyness does not behave like a disease, however. When physicians diagnose a disease, they find similar symptoms and similar causes in everyone who has it. They find ways to treat either the symptoms or the cause, ways that have a probability of success in every person who has the disease. Their remedies are directed against microorganisms or tumors that cause the symptoms. Shyness, however, is composed of nothing but symptoms, and there is no common cause. What shy people feel about themselves results from symptoms. Shyness is like the inability to drive a car: You may not be able to drive a car and you feel bad about it, but even if you stopped feeling bad, you would still not be able to drive the car. Shyness is actually a set of incompetencies different for every shy person. Some people are anxious about their incompetencies, and there are many authorities who seek to find ways to measure and remedy the anxiety.[5] It is clear, however, that merely removing the anxiety does not automatically confer skill.

Shy people lack skill at talking with others. Their problem does not stem from a glandular imbalance, germs, heredity, or a fundamental flaw in their character. They simply have not learned how to talk well enough with others, and they have decided that it is probably not worth the effort to try. Feelings can build up around this decision, and many shy people distract themselves from their real problem by focusing on how they feel. Their problem, however, is an inability to perform. They did not become unable because of their feelings.

The Book of Lists reported a survey taken of young people that listed public speaking as the number-one fear.[6] Most humans are apprehensive about performing in front of an audience. But anytime we talk to someone, we perform. We try to persuade that other person that we are worth listening to, perhaps wise and witty to boot. Shy people unconsciously understand the performance nature of social interaction, and this is what terrifies them. Their fear of socialization is often equal to their fear of public speaking. Think about your own life. Even if you do not think yourself shy, you are at least a little apprehensive when you enter a room full of strangers, go for a job interview, or speak up at a public meeting.

That is why this book is not addressed exclusively to shy people. Shyness is often situational. Everyone has experienced the queasy stomach, pounding heart, and feelings of inadequacy that go along with being shy. The methods of overcoming shyness presented in this book can be used by anyone. This book is about talking and how to do it in public. Talking is the human way to enjoy other people; to get our jobs done; to get others to recognize our worth. Talk matters! All of our human relationships depend on it. We learn to base our judgments of others on how they talk. Shy people fear the judgments others will make of them. Rather than risk a negative judgment, they do not try. They feel bad about not trying, but their experience has taught them that they cannot succeed and that they are better off silent. Some claim that talk doesn't matter, and they develop a veneer of aloofness. Others claim that good talkers are born, not made, and that they just don't have the right endowments. Either way, they are not aware that they are not judged by what they feel but by what they do. They seem to think that others can read their inner fears. But we customarily judge others by what they say and how they say it, from which we draw inferences about how they must feel. A person who looks confident is evaluated as confident, and no one inquires about his or her inner feelings.

People who cannot talk decisively are handicapped, for they do not offer enough information for others to give them a fair chance. Because they concentrate so hard on how they feel, shy people evade learning skills of self-presentation. They are content to appear timid, dull, and uncertain, and they put up with being treated as if they are that way. The consequences of shyness are earned by the way shy people behave.

THE CONSEQUENCES OF SHYNESS

If you can't tell your boss to pay more attention to your ideas, you are shy. If you can't complain when you are mistreated, if you lose your job because the boss is not aware of how competent you are, if you stay home on weekends because people don't mind having you around but just forget to call you, you are shy. Women sometimes fail to get promoted not because they are women but because they aren't able to call attention to the quality of their work; they are shy. Men who do the same routine jobs day after day, never advancing in their career, may not be incompetent, just shy. People who form exclusive relationships and invest everything they have in them are shy. Shyness sometimes reflects itself in an inability to tell doctors about your pain or to tell someone you love how much you care. Shy people sometimes avoid doing very ordinary things like shopping or going out to lunch because they cannot handle even the limited contact with clerks and waiters. Shy people sometimes tell their good ideas to confidants, only to see them borrowed, used, and claimed by someone else. You can spot shy people at social gatherings. They stand alone, against the wall, drink in hand, waiting for someone. Shy people suffer!

Shy people are usually resigned to their "fate." They believe they were created to be ignored. They expect people to treat them as if they do not exist or as if something was wrong with them. Once they decide they are shy because they are sick, they may begin to act in sick ways. They drink a bit too much or go to psychiatrists to have their insides examined; they join encounter groups and hope for the best; or they take pills, read self-help books, and join strange religions. Nothing seems to break the pattern of solitary anxiety. Sometimes they justify their silence by claiming that other people are not worth talking to anyway.

In our society anyone who appears to be a little different earns some kind of punishment. It is our custom to regard people who do not conform as sick, antisocial, or stupid. In schools we "remediate" or flunk students who cannot read, write, or do math. Sometimes we do worse, we give them social promotions and try to explain their substandard performance by "understanding their complicated internal dynamics." Guidance counselors are very busy trying to understand "under-achievers," "social deviants," "addicts," "alienated youth," and sometimes they get rid of them by classifying them as retarded or mentally ill. Generally counselors are very concerned about how their clients feel. Their consensus is that people are the way they are because of the way they feel. They assume that if people could just feel better, they would behave better. Shy people are prime candidates for this kind of advice. After all, it is easier to console people who feel bad than to train them to behave in ways that will not permit them to feel bad.

The main service shy people render to folks around them is that they offer themselves as victims. A great number of so-called leaders have built their success on their ability to control the quiet people with whom they surround themselves. Quiet people may have the potential to say a great deal, but if someone keeps them good and quiet, they present no threat. Voluntary silence, of course, is everyone's right, but silence out of fear is not useful. Involuntarily silent people suffer constant frustration from not being able to speak their mind. And, of course, society loses the contribution that these people could make.

People who do not carry their share of conversation are euphemistically referred to as "good listeners." At worst they are seen as dull and stupid. Effective speakers often overlook shy people. They become part of an anonymous audience and are otherwise ignored. This has enormous consequences on the job, where the contribution of shy people could often make a difference. But supervisors are generally not trained to solicit information, and when they try, shy people usually resist responding out of fear of looking foolish. Thus companies often lose the services of competent people, and competent people lose their chance to advance.

There are even occasions where colleagues milk quiet people of their ideas and claim them as their own. They do not necessarily do this with malice. Good ideas demand to be spoken. If the person who has the idea cannot present it, someone else will. People cannot be required to "footnote" what they hear in casual conversation. Thus shy people often experience the additional frustration of not being able to claim credit for their contributions.

A recent study of corporate executives concluded that one of the main criteria for promotion to executive ranks is the ability to communicate well, both orally and in writing.[7] Leadership skills are oral. The ability to argue a case, to report clearly, to make encouraging conversation, to make others feel comfortable, to be interesting and amusing, are all characteristics of the effective leader. If a person has technical skills, the best way to move up through the ranks is to cultivate the ability to communicate well. Many shy people have technical skills but no way to display them. As a result, they remain at low-level jobs. Both their work lives and their personal lives suffer.

The main personal consequences of shyness are loneliness, boredom, and impotence. These are endemic and epidemic diseases among the shy. Loneliness may be inherent in contemporary American lifestyles, but many people make a real effort to overcome it. The superficial relationships formed in social clubs, at singles bars, and through computer dating may provide amusement for an evening, but they do not seem to work out well over the long haul. It is possible to have fun with others on occasion, but it is most important to have someone with whom to face adversity and share joy. Shy people either lack these kinds of contacts or they invest everything they have in one relationship. Thus healers of all sorts, gurus, religious movements, causes, and those who offer panaceas grow strong and wealthy because people seek friends and social fulfillment through them.

The only way to overcome loneliness is through the formation of strong and lasting relationships. Counseling and psychiatry, after all, often constitute nothing more than paying someone to be your friend. Even if you learn to "understand yourself," you may still be unable to make a friend and to share in decisions about what happens to you. Feeling impotent is the price you pay for withdrawing from society. Withdrawal also leads to boredom.

Some sociologists use the term *alienated* to refer to isolated people.[8] Alienated people are sometimes aggressive in their opposition to social norms, but sometimes they just simply avoid socializing altogether. Their isolation removes them from opportunities to participate, which in turn confirms their notion of themselves as unable to participate. The loss of "self-esteem" makes it harder and harder for them to reenter the circle.

Some therapists attempt to improve people by helping them to think more positively about themselves. To think oneself competent when one cannot perform competently is, of course, self-deceptive. No one would want an inept surgeon, no matter how high his or her self-esteem was. The best way to earn self-esteem is to have others regard you as competent. This usually does not happen until you perform competently.

Thus the shy person is trapped in a web of deception and frustration. Feelings do not become more positive until acts are performed that lead to positive results. Those acts cannot be performed until the shy person learns how, and the shy person cannot learn how while dwelling on how bad it feels to be shy. Shy people can learn to make choices and they can learn ways to execute those choices. It is easier to learn how to act than it is to change the way you feel. Once you act well, you will feel good. That is the major premise of this book.

The problem of shyness is most severe when we consider what it costs us to have so many people unable to contribute their share to society. One specialist in shyness has estimated that nearly 40 percent of the human beings with whom we share the world are so shy that it prevents them from doing important tasks of daily living.[9] There is disagreement about precisely how many people are shy, but there is no disagreement about the fact that shyness is disabling, whether you are shy all the time or only on particular occasions.

What is most serious for society is that "loud mouths" and "bullies" sometimes force themselves into positions of leadership because their skill at talk is not challenged. A great many people owe their personal success to their ability to cow shy people into compliance. This means that a great many decisions are made by less competent people who happen to talk well, while competent people remain in the background, unable to challenge or change things.

AN EXERCISE: ARE YOU SUFFERING THE CONSEQUENCES OF SHYNESS?

Answer the following questions yes or no. If you answer more than five of them with even a limp, halfhearted yes, shyness is interfering with your life. If, in fact, you answer even one of them yes, you can improve yourself by overcoming that particular problem.

1. Do you ever go home from social gatherings thinking about intelligent remarks you could have made if you had not been blocked out of the conversation?
2. Have you ever wondered why someone you met on the job or at a party never called you?
3. Have you backed off from defending your ideas because other people who opposed them seemed to be shouting at you?
4. Have you ever been frustrated when a colleague at work passed off one of your ideas as his or her own?
5. Have you ever met a person of either sex whom you wanted to see again but couldn't muster the courage to call and extend an invitation to?
6. Have you ever had a complaint to make in a restaurant or a store but suppressed it because you didn't want to make a scene?

7. Do you often find yourself going to places you won't enjoy because you were unable to suggest an alternative when you were offered a chance?
8. Do you often go to movies or eat out alone because you couldn't ask someone to join you?
9. Do you find yourself standing near the door or away from other people at social gatherings or coffee breaks?
10. Do you find yourself staying home weekends because you don't have an invitation to go anywhere?
11. Do people often finish your sentences for you because you don't talk fast enough?
12. At parties do you cling to the people you know because you are afraid of meeting strangers?
13. Do you have a neighbor you would like to meet but have been unable to respond properly to when he or she greeted you?
14. Do you think about inviting company but feel you don't know how to go about it?
15. Do you find yourself frustrated on the job or in class because you have questions but don't know how to ask them?
16. Do you sometimes play stupid rather than try to answer a question you are asked?
17. Do you prefer self-service stores because you don't like to make conversation with clerks?
18. Do you spend a lot of time watching TV when you would rather be with people?
19. Do you tend to select spectator activities because they help you avoid talk?
20. Have you ever tried to get treatment for your shyness?

If you feel anxious about dealing with others, it is probably out of some frustration you feel over some of the items to which you answered yes. Each yes can become a no when you acquire some skill. Start now to understand your shyness. The first step is to understand that you are shy because of what you do and say, not because of what you feel. Many skillful performers feel anxious before they perform, but they know they are judged by what they do—no one even knows how they feel.

As you read on in this book, you will receive suggestions about things to do. Try them, but don't expect miracles. Remember, it took you a long time to become shy. Improvement will come, but not overnight. The only "miracle cure" for your shyness is hard work.

REFERENCES

1. Philip Zimbardo et al., "The Social Disease Called Shyness," *Psychology Today*, August 1975, pp. 68–72.
2. Susan K. Oerkvitz, "Continuing Effects of a Rhetorical Method of Instruction for Reticent Students" (M.A. thesis, Pennsylvania State University, 1976).
3. F. Laura Muir, "Case Studies of Selected Examples of Reticence and Fluency" (M.A. thesis, Washington State University, 1964).
4. Philip Zimbardo, *Shyness* (Reading, Mass.: Addison-Wesley Publishing Co., Inc., 1977).
5. James McCroskey, "Measures of Communication Bound Anxiety," *Speech Monographs* 37: 4 (November 1970): 269–77.
6. David Wallechinsky, Irving Wallace and Amy Wallace, *The Book of Lists* (New York: Bantam Books, 1978), p. 469.
7. For detailed information on this matter write: Speech Communication Association, 5105 Blacklick Rd., Annandale, VA 22003.
8. Amitai Etzioni, *The Active Society* (New York: The Free Press, 1968), especially the last chapter.
9. Zimbardo, *Shyness*.

RECOMMENDED READINGS

Gerald M. Phillips, "Rhetoritherapy versus the Medical Model," *Communication Education* 26: 1 (January 1977): 34–43.

Gerald M. Phillips and Kent A. Sokoloff, "An End to Anxiety," *Journal of Communication Disorders* 12 (1979): 385–97.

James McCroskey, "Oral Communication Apprehension," *Human Communication Research* 4: (Fall 1977): 78–96.

Robert Weiss, *Loneliness* (Cambridge, Mass.: M.I.T. Press, 1973).

chapter 2

The Faces of Shyness

People use nouns the way they learned to in elementary school. They think that a noun refers to a "person, place, or thing." But shyness is not a place, nor a physical part of a person, nor is it a thing like "streptococcus germ" or "whiffle-ball." When someone says, "Oh, you are shy!" the words sound like a doctor saying, "Oh, you have a broken bone!" The obvious response is, "Can I stay home from school?"

No matter who writes about shyness or what he or she calls it, that person must concede somewhere that "shyness takes many forms." *Shyness* is a word used to describe some people who do not talk very much and who are uneasy about it. *Reticence* is a better word to use because it does not imply that there is anything seriously wrong. It merely describes the behavior. There is nothing inherently wrong with most people called shy. There are few shy people who are physically unable to improve their behavior, regardless of the thickness of the wall of isolation they have built around themselves.

The great variety of faces shy people present to the world demonstrates that shyness cannot be considered an illness. It is hard to distinguish people who are quiet by choice from those for whom silence is a defense against difficult social situations. We must conclude that social behavior is a strategy through which individuals try to do the best they can for themselves. When we look at shy behavior this way, it is logical to suggest that shy people can change their strategies and thereby do a little better for themselves. They can choose to behave differently.

One way to distinguish people who are quiet by choice is to discover whether they can communicate when they need to. People who are voluntarily quiet feel confident of their ability, while truly shy people report frustration and distress because they cannot communicate well when they need to or want to. But above all, shyness is not a diagnosis. It refers to a choice that can be trained. People are shy for many reasons, at different times and places, and in many ways, but the only thing they have in common is that they have been called shy by others. They might just as easily have been called ineffective talkers.

Everyone has behaved in "shy" ways at one time or another. In your own life you can recall situations when you preferred not to talk because you felt that talking would indict you or get you into trouble. You behaved in a "shy" fashion at those times. There are often good reasons for shyness. Some people are unpleasant to be with, and some situations are difficult to deal with. Remaining silent when your only alternative appears to be to lose is sometimes very prudent. However, sometimes our desire to withdraw from trouble keeps us from defending ourselves properly, and we lose because we cannot participate.

Shyness grows by experience. In elementary school we all had to put up with unpleasant teachers and playground bullies. Some of us had a bit of success standing up to these people. Others got slapped around sufficiently to keep them silent. Those who became silent learned that they could control a bit of what happened to them by seeking out situations that did not call on them to talk much. Some of them chose their vocations, their life-style, and their mates because of feelings about how much talk would be required. We all know of elementary school teachers who chose the profession because it did not require them to talk much with other adults, or social workers who took their job because it made them feel superior to their clients, so that they did not have difficulty talking.

A great many prospective accountants and engineers chose their vocation because they saw it as having minimal socialization potential. A great many of them failed in their attempts to learn the job when they discovered just how much human contact was required.

It is not unreasonable for people to be shy some of the time. There are a great many occasions when simple avoidance costs nothing. But if there is no way to avoid dealing with the unpleasantness, shyness may be self-defeating, because refusal to participate may deny you an advantage and even cause you to lose. When you make life choices based on your inability to talk with others, you not only reduce your personal effectiveness but you present a face that others can use to justify avoiding you. You give them reason to call you snooty, dull, stupid, or shy.

The shy face appears in all human activities and in many different ways. Shy people, for example, are not always quiet. There are a number of techniques people use to cover up their shyness. We have all met shy people who have learned how to make aggressive attacks in order to shut off conversation. Still others can converse at length about their personal hardships and suffering or regale us with extended tales of the exploits of their children. Others claim to be good listeners and cultivate the skill of head nodding, but basically indicate approval of the fact that someone else is talking. Some shy people become evangelists. They cultivate skill in one topic to cover up their ineptitude in other topics.

TRY THIS EXERCISE NOW

Find some quiet person who lives near you or works in your office. Start a conversation. Open it by saying, "I am reading a book about talking. May I ask you some questions in order to do an exercise from the book?" If the quiet person approves, proceed with the questioning. If the answer is no, look for someone else. It is painful when someone forces attention on an unwilling shy person.

Ask the following:

1. How did you get this job?
2. What do you like to talk about with other people?
3. Would you like to get a promotion? How would you go about getting it?

Check to see if the answers are long or short. If your respondent is truly shy, you will get very short answers or none at all. You might get a protest that the questions are too personal. You can blame that on the book. The whole business should take no more than a minute. Thank your respondent and leave. Then sit down and figure out the answers you would have given had you been asked those questions.

MYTHS AND MISCONCEPTIONS ABOUT SHYNESS

The most frequent mask for shyness is illness. Quietness is often associated with depression. Depressed people lack the energy needed to make social commitments. However, most diagnoses of depression are based on changes in behavior. Shy people do not change their behavior. If a person changes from talkative to silent, then a diagnosis of depression may be possible. But if a person is naturally silent, it is hard to identify behavior change, unless of course he or she begins to talk. One of the most difficult issues in dealing with shy people is that it is so hard to spot qualitative and quantitative changes in the way they talk. Their silence seems to hide their emotional state. Even when they feel bad, it is hard for them to tell anyone else about it.

Some shy people are given to occasional angry outbursts. Many psychologists have warned us not to trust shy people because they have a tendency to violence.[1] This is simply not true. What is the case is that when shy people express their frustration, the behavior seems so unusual that we find it noteworthy. There are shy people who are potential predators, and there are outgoing people who are equally dangerous.

Shy people are often angry because they are not sought out by others; yet, when people do approach them, they have nothing to say. Shy people often console themselves with the notion that they could talk well enough if they had to. They do not, however, find any occasions when they have to. A clear sign of shyness is never to test oneself just to see if one can do it.

Shy people often convince themselves that they are cured after experiencing psychotherapy, sensitivity training, est, or some other program. For a time they may even look like they have improved, but it doesn't take long to discover that nothing has changed. They may have improved in the clinic or the encounter room, but there is no carry-over into their daily lives. There are, of course, programs with an exceptional record of helping shy people. The Dale Carnegie Courses and Toastmasters International have for years helped willing shy people to overcome their problem by learning skills of public speaking and socializing. Unfortunately these programs must start with a core of self-assurance. Most shy people really don't have the confidence to make an appointment to go to a Carnegie session.

Probably the worst problem shy people experience is the disappointment that comes when they discover that people they care about very much aren't even aware of their existence. Shy people often over-react to acts of kindness by others. One kind word can be escalated into a love affair. Shy people frequently find themselves making strong attachments to teachers, employers, and other authority figures based on a misassessment of the attitude those people have toward them. Shy people continue to hope that others will take note of them, seek them out, discover their worth. They hope for a special person who brings them out of themselves. But because shy people can give little back, they are not noticed. Most of us are too busy with our own lives to seek out shy people. If people do not talk, we read it as a sign that we should leave them alone. We talk to those who can reward us with a response and never even notice the others.

While the behaviors of shy people are widely different, most of them share some common myths and misconceptions about their condition. For example, most believe that people acquire social skills because of some accident of birth; some people have "it" and some people don't. Thus they evade responsibility for improving themselves by claiming that conscious efforts to learn social skills are "manipulative" and therefore dishonest. They make a variety of excuses about how unethical it would be to attempt to learn how to be more effective in talking with others. They also fear the word *performance*. They freeze, claiming that they cannot do public speaking. When they are told that people perform in all social settings, they claim that this is not so, that interaction is a spontaneous event that some folks just naturally do well at.

Some shy people are attracted to sensitivity training in the hope that it will give them interpersonal skill. However, changing attitudes toward others has nothing to do with skill. Social skills must be learned.

Shy people eventually learn to regard loneliness and boredom as parts of their lives about which they can do nothing. They believe they are the way they are because that is the way they are. They regard those who are not lonely and bored as fortunate, but they do not see how differently those people act. Most shy people cannot even describe the behavior they think is effective. It is characteristic of shyness not to be aware of particular communication behaviors but to make global judgments about the social effectiveness of others.

Shy people offer a similar explanation of how some people get to be influential. It is because they have "leadership ability." Shy people do not believe they are capable of influencing anything at all. People who exert influence have money or personality, come from the right family or are gifted. Sometimes shy people ascribe the differences in the effectiveness of people to fate. It is their fate to be shy, while others are fated to be leaders.

Shy people, thus, are not happy people. Their behavior is similar enough to depression for the two to be equated. But they are not necessarily connected. Because shyness can look like depression, shy people often believe that psychiatric help will work wonders for them. But much of psychiatry deals with feelings, and unless the shy person can propose a behavior change, there is little that a psychiatrist can do to improve behavior. Furthermore, a psychiatric diagnosis provides an excuse to the shy person to escape responsibility for changing. One distinguished psychiatrist commented that people would rather be sick than stupid.[2] This is certainly the case with most shy people. By finding a condition or an emotional problem they shift responsibility to a healer. They need make no effort, nor must they feel guilty about their lack of social competency. It is fate that makes them sick. They can take their pills, make their weekly visits, and wait for a miracle.

We tend to reward sickness in our society. When people are sick, they are excused from work, and their needs are tended to by others. When a shy person decides to be sick, there is an expectation of this kind of behavior from other people. Shy people resent it when they are ignored. What they must learn is that people who are not shy regard shyness as a form of incompetence and would prefer not to deal with it. It is not the responsibility of the nonshy to minister to the needs of the shy, however sick shy people think they are. Skillful speakers regard shy people as boring and uninviting, not sick. They are easy to ignore.

Thus shy people are caught in a vicious circle. The more angry they are because the rest of the world ignores their "sickness," the more they withdraw and the less likely it is that anyone will notice them. To the extent that shy people believe themselves to be "sick," they deny themselves the chance to be competent. Note that we did not say "get well." Since shyness is not a sickness, there is no way to recover from it.

AN EXERCISE:
HOW SHY ARE YOU?

You can estimate how shy you are by examining the following list of statements made by shy people. Each of the statements is found consistently in the written statements about their shyness submitted by persons enrolled in the Reticence Program. For each statement check whether you are willing to admit it to others, or whether you just say it to yourself. Score 2 points for each statement you make to yourself, 1 point for each statement you would be willing to say out loud. A score of 10 or more indicates that you are seeking excuses to justify doing nothing about your shyness.

1. Most social activities are boring.
2. Some people are born popular.
3. Most people I know, know more than I do.
4. I would rather listen and learn.
5. Better to keep your mouth shut and let them think you are stupid than to open it and let them be sure.
6. People don't take to me when they first meet me.
7. There's too much talk in the world, why should I add to the confusion?
8. I don't feel well when I talk. It aggravates my (hypertension, ulcers, asthma, migraine, nervous stomach, other symptoms—fill in your pet ailment).
9. People are always jumping on my ideas.
10. I'm okay when I talk to kids or old people (or pets or plants).
11. On my kind of job you don't talk much, so I'm just out of practice.
12. I have no problem talking. I can do it if I want to, but I just don't want to.
13. I don't know enough about language to speak well. I'd be embarrassed.
14. I wasn't lucky enough to be born into a talking family.
15. Talk is cheap. Actions speak louder than words.
16. Small talk is so boring I just don't bother with it.

17. It's part of my personality to be quiet.
18. I'd talk more but no one seems to want to talk about serious ideas.
19. I don't know how to start a conversation.
20. I guess I'm just a loner.
21. My (wife, husband, boyfriend, girlfriend, etc.) does enough talking for both of us.
22. Most people talk without thinking. By the time I think what I want to say, it's too late.
23. Some people are just naturally poised and self-confident. I'm not.
24. I don't want to learn to talk because that would be manipulative.
25. When I finish this (psychotherapy, TA, est, encounter, meditation course), I'll be okay.
26. They ought to discontinue public speaking courses in schools.
27. I don't like classes where they have discussions. I'm paying good money to hear the professor talk, not people just as stupid as I am.
28. People who talk a lot have empty heads.
29. I'd talk more if people were willing to share their emotions with me.
30. There's no point to talking. People don't listen anyway.

HOW DO SHY PEOPLE FEEL?

Reports from more than three thousand shy people indicate that misery is standard in their lives. The people who have participated in the Reticence Program are not the most shy people. They are the tip of the proverbial iceberg. Whatever they feel, you can bet that there are a great many people who feel worse, so bad that they cannot even come forward to get help when it is offered.

Generally, shy people find their feelings very hard to express. They complain of feeling "awkward," "uncomfortable," "apprehensive," "uneasy," "incompetent," "inferior," or similar kinds of adjectives. They are unable to specify their feelings, describe their symptoms in anything other than general terms, or point to particular times and places where they feel what they feel. They tend to associate their feelings with their experiences with other people. When they are questioned, they agree that they feel worst when they are compelled to talk. They specifically mention experiences of having to stand up in front of others to give a report, being asked questions that they must answer, giving or receiving interviews, or being greeted by strangers at a social gathering.

Some report that they feel bad when they even just think about some situations. These kinds of people are helped by various forms of desensitization, for often they can build up such apprehension that they cannot even approach social situations. Others have vivid memories of some painful experience in the past. Incidentally, most people can remember some incident when they were embarrassed in public or performed ineptly, but it doesn't seem to interfere with their lives. Shy people focus on the giggles and smirks they remember. They do not seem to be able to accept error as normal and ordinary, and thus they find it hard to learn performance behavior. They seek infallible formulas for success.

Shy people appear egocentric in their feelings. They express the belief that no other people feel the way they do, and they understand that their particular misery keeps them out of contact with the world. Many apply some kind of name to themselves and then act as that name impels them to act. Here are some of the names they use.

Timid	Easily frightened	Fearful	Bashful	Retiring
Diffident	Reserved	Quiet	Humble	Afraid
Anxious	Apprehensive	Antisocial	Meek	Cautious
Tight-lipped	Taciturn	Uncommunicative		Silent

None of these words expresses the kind of personality most people seek in the people with whom they associate. In general, examination of a thesaurus indicates that the words associated with shyness have unpleasant connotations. Here are some of the synonyms:

Skittish	Shrinking	Cowardly	Uncourageous
Demure	Wary	Elusive	Crafty	Suspicious
Demurring	Laconic	Cunning	Shifty	Distrustful
Circumspect	Guarded	Stealthy	Prudent
Impenetrable	Reserved	Succinct	Recondite
Secretive	Self-contained		

There is no way shy people can escape the effects of their self-classification. The world gangs up on them literally, to make them earn the epithets that they apply to themselves.

There is no question about the fact that fear is associated with shyness. We "shy away" from situations that threaten us. However, most shy people do not know exactly what they fear. They cannot describe the tangible harm that they think would come to them if they spoke out. They express vague apprehensions about what people might think, but they can offer no evidence that people might think it or what it would look like if people thought it. Thus they have no empirical connection with the reality of communication. Furthermore, they cannot describe what successful social behavior looks like. They are disabled because they cannot change their behavior. They do not know how they behave and they do not know how they would like to behave. It is this paradoxical position that causes them so much pain.

It is dangerous to use the word *fear* to describe so general a condition. *Fear* is a word properly associated with walking across graveyards, through bad neighborhoods late at night, or watching a tornado dance across a prairie. Fear is a process used by the body to get ready to defend itself. Soldiers about to enter combat and athletes ready to meet the opposition know the meaning of fear and they know how to use it to best advantage. Fear is a human experience needed to overcome threats and obstacles. Normally, once a person has acted and overcome the obstacle, the feeling disappears, and the person feels relieved.

If a human being feels afraid but does not act, the tension persists. If the person acts ineptly and still feels threatened, the tension persists. We refer to the result as anxiety. The great psychiatrist Harry Stack Sullivan believed that anxiety was the most horrible feeling a human being could experience.[3] When you are anxious, you are constantly looking over your shoulder for danger that is not there. If you see no tangible danger, you make whatever you see into tangible danger. Anxious people are afraid of what will happen to them in the present; they remember only the agonies of the past; they face the future with great trepidation.

Human beings need tension in order to learn. It is tension that stimulates the organism and moves us ahead. It is tension that gets our minds and bodies to act. However, a permanent state of tension is paralyzing. The problem is how to use the tension to your advantage. The answer is to learn to perform.

Shy people do not perform. They react and sometimes they respond, but they do not act. Their tension turns to fear, which they use to defend themselves against experiencing other fearful situations. Thus they prevent themselves from learning to cope with the situations that menace them. They cannot imagine themselves succeeding because they cannot imagine success. They take refuge in "low self-esteem," which they earn as a result of performing so poorly. Shy people thus build themselves a trap in which they are permanently caught. Once this pattern is etched into a personality, those who do not retreat from social contact seek treatment. Their litany is, "I have a condition that needs a remedy because I am anxious, and I cannot do anything about it until I am no longer anxious, and so I will not do anything at all and I will wait until the healer comes along and heals me." An alternative bleat is, "I am now anxious and cannot act, and when I am no longer anxious, I will not want to act." To support their self-image many of them take on a variety of physical miseries. They flush and blush, feel butterflies in their stomach, their skin tingles, and their heart beats loudly. They think other people can see their miseries and thus ought to feel sorry for them, and they resent it when people ignore them and their miseries. A noted psychiatrist offered the view that mental illness is really a strategy used by some people to gain for themselves the advantages that come from being sick.[4] When people are sick, others have to care for them, and they are absolved from responsibility. That is why shy people want so desperately to be sick. It is their "cop out," their guarantee against the stress of taking action on their own behalf.

These are the misconceptions of shyness. As you read this section, you may have begun to identify with some of the feelings. If this has happened to you, a refresher course in the myths and realities might be useful to you.

MYTH: Shy people like me suffer from a disease that can be cured by the right healer.

REALITY: You yourself are the only healer. You can feel better by acquiring skill.

MYTH: I would be all right if I weren't so anxious.

REALITY: You need tension. You must make your feelings work for you.

MYTH: It is the nature of some people to be shy. Nothing can be done about it.

REALITY: While some people are more talented than others, everyone can learn the basic skills of being with people.

MYTH: Planning and practicing talk is unethical and manipulative. Effective communication is spontaneous and comes only to the few who are well endowed.

REALITY: Considerate talk is always planned with the listener in mind. Effective social action requires careful consideration of others.

MYTH: Shyness is a disease waiting for a cure.

REALITY: Shyness is a label people apply to certain kinds of behavior. The label changes to accommodate changes in behavior.

The most important reality is that you are what you are because of the way other people see you. If you want to become something else, you must do it with other people in mind. If you learn to change, then other people will see you differently. If you can learn to make declarations through your talk and behavior that earn you positive labels, you will have your good feelings about yourself confirmed.

In the following chapters we will discuss where shyness comes from and what you can do about it.

REFERENCES

1. Philip Zimbardo, *Shyness* (Reading, Mass.: Addison-Wesley Publishing Co., Inc., 1977).
2. Richard Rabkin, *Inner and Outer Space* (New York: W. W. Norton & Co., Inc., 1970).
3. A. H. Chapman, *Harry Stack Sullivan: The Man and His Work* (New York: G. P. Putnam's Sons, 1976), p. 78 ff.
4. Thomas Szasz, *The Myth of Mental Illness* (New York: Harper-Hoeber, 1961).

RECOMMENDED READINGS

Robert C. Carson, *Interaction Concepts of Personality* (Chicago: Aldine Publishing Co., 1969).
Kent A. Sokoloff and Gerald M. Phillips, "A Refinement of the Concept 'Reticence,'" *Journal of Communication Disorders* 9 (1976): 331–47.

chapter 3

Where Shyness Comes From

Can shyness be prevented? Of course! In this chapter we will try to help you understand the role your past may have had in building your shyness. We will focus your attention on future possibilities for improvement.

TRY AN EXERCISE

It is now time to get started in your effort to overcome shyness. Do this exercise. Follow the directions very carefully.

1. Select a person with whom you have frequent contact: your spouse, roommate, brother or sister, parent, neighbor, friend.
2. Contact the person face to face or by phone and say, "I have to do an exercise for an antishyness training program I am working on. Can I have ten minutes of your time on   (state a date and time)   at

(name the place) ?" If the other person wants a different time or place, go ahead and accept the change if you possibly can.

3. Once you have agreed on a date and time, make the following statement: "I want to tell you why I think I am shy and how I got that way, and I want you to ask me three questions about it, okay?"

4. If the other person says yes, confirm the date and time. If the other person says no, thank him or her and move on to another person.

5. If the other person asks you, "Why?" make the following statement: "This is an opening exercise in my antishyness training. I need to get used to talking about my shyness with other people, okay?" Be sure to end with the "okay?" question and wait for agreement.

6. When you get together with the other person, say this: "I have been reading a book about shyness and I think I am shy because . . . ." (Fill in three reasons, such as "I don't like parties," "I can't ask a stranger for directions," "I can't handle interviews." Be sure that you do not talk about how you feel—just about what you can't do or can't do well enough.)
"I avoid the following situations: (Name three: cocktail parties, coffee breaks, whatever fits you)."
"This is what I do when I get into a situation I don't handle well: (Describe what you do: "I say "and-uh" a lot,' 'I don't talk at all,' 'I give one-word answers')."

7. When you have finished your statement, say, "Do you have any questions?"

8. If the other person expresses sympathy about your problem, say, "Thank you. It's okay, I'm working on it. Thanks for your help. I may need you again, okay?" (Be sure to end with the question so that you can get the other person to respond to you.)

9. The other person may ask for details. If so, say, "This is all I need to do now. Thanks for your help. I may need your help again, okay?"

10. If the other person tells you that he or she has the same problems, help out by asking him or her to tell you the answers to the same questions. Then say, "Thanks. It helps to know that someone else shares my experience. Maybe you should read the book, too. Maybe we can work on it together. Thanks again for your help. I'll call you, okay?"

You can try this exercise over and over again with as many people as you like. What you will discover is that virtually everyone shares some of your experience, even though he or she reacts to it differently. Some of them will accept your overtures as an excuse to talk about their own shyness. What you must concentrate on is avoiding talk about your feelings. If others want to talk about feelings, let them. You concentrate entirely on how you behave, where, and with whom. And be sure to close each of your sentences with the "okay?" question. This is a technique used by skilled conversationalists to get the other person to respond.

CAN YOU REMEMBER HOW YOU BECAME SHY?

When did it start with you? Can you remember the first time someone told you to "speak up!" or asked, "Cat got your tongue?" Did you ever have problems with an overpowering aunt or rough-and-tough uncle who smothered you and tossed you around but never let you speak? Did you feel that hardly anyone listened to you? Did your parents tell you that children should be seen and not heard? Was your teacher a strict disciplinarian who told you to shut up and whacked you every time you opened your mouth? Did you travel with a gang where the leader clobbered anyone who talked back?

We all learn to talk somehow, though few of us are formally taught. It happens in a very haphazard way. Thus people have developed different skills. The way you talk now is the result of the rewards and punishments your talk earned you when you were younger.

PARENTS

Parents are the most important influence in learning to speak. We get our first words from the people who hugged us, fed us, and changed us. We learned by imitating the sounds they made and we learned to connect those sounds with things we got or things we wanted done. We learned to influence the world by talking to it. We tried to get others to pay attention to us and our needs. When we finally got control of words, we learned to use them to get results, although sometimes the results we got were decidedly unpleasant. Sometimes our words brought us food and comfort, sometimes punishment and abuse.

We don't mean that parents are the only cause of shyness. Often parents who talk little and insist that their children be quiet produce highly verbal and aggressive offspring. It depends on the decisions you made about what got you most in the world. You learned to be silent in some situations and to talk in others.

Sometimes adults who are very shy can be fluent with children. Such parents tend to pressure their children into shyness. Parents are the most important influence children have to respond to. If parents don't exactly make children shy, they establish the conditions in which shyness is possible. Sometimes shy people maintain their silence because they regard the whole world as full of parents waiting to shut them up and disapprove of them. They are afraid to talk back because it would be like "sassing" mother.

SOCIETY

Our society tends to reward verbal people. Some choose shyness because it is a way to escape pressure. Kids feel pressured early, and sometimes they are not ready for pressure because they don't have the skill to do anything well. If you were pushed into situations that demanded that you speak well to impress others, you might have chosen shyness as a way of avoiding the pressure.

We are often called upon to talk in "high stakes" games. At home we had to be careful not to be disrespectful, not to interrupt, not to ramble on or to say bad words. Many of us were punished for talking at the wrong time, but we observed other people getting payoffs when they said something right at the right time. The only thing was, no one ever made it clear what the wrong time was and what the right time was. When we had to argue with Mom and Dad about privileges, allowances, the use of the car, it sometimes got to be such a hassle that it was easier to make other arrangements.

Problems in the world are sometimes heavier than they are at home. In school the way to show how smart you were was to talk properly, to recite, to report, to ask and answer questions, to make small talk with the teacher. If you wanted to get ahead, you had to learn how to do those things. And if you didn't learn to do those things, teacher thought you weren't very smart, and your grades were not so good, and you had to try to explain why you got poor grades to Mom and Dad, who didn't understand anyway. Sometimes you tried to give the impression of being an intense listener, a deep thinker. It all depended on how skillfully you were able to con people. You may also have made the discovery that if you could memorize and show it on a test or if you could put together a good paper, you could avoid talking. The schools let you off the hook in a number of ways. They never tried to teach you to talk.

SCHOOL

If you don't know how to handle social situations, in most cases you can avoid them, except at school and at work. The problem with being shy is that you are often disabled in absolutely critical situations. For example, the first time a child has to perform in Show and Tell, he may freeze simply because no one ever told him how to get his ideas together so that he could talk. No matter, from them on the expectation of failure is set. Once you experience that leaden feeling of disaster that accompanies a poor oral performance, you approach every subsequent act with tension. Teachers don't really know what to do when this happens. They encourage the child; they say, "It's all right, you can try again later"; and that is perhaps the most fearsome thing of all, because later is the same as now if you really don't know what to do. While all this is going on, some glib character is talking about her horsie or some wise guy is talking about his trip to the ball game. Every good presentation makes you look worse. Teachers reward good talkers and justly so. It is important that people learn to speak, because they will need the skill later on. But children who come out of school unable to talk in important situations find their social and vocational advancement stymied. Shy children face a life in which they know the way to get ahead but there is no one around to help them do it.

What is commonly offered as speech training in high schools and colleges does not qualify at all. It is mostly concerned with debating or platform speaking or acting, and it appeals to people who are already skillful. Those schools that have developed programs to meet the needs of shy people can serve only a small proportion of people who need training.

Later on we will demonstrate that shyness can be overcome by learning specific oral performance skills. Some children appear to learn these skills early in life by observing successful people. There is no doubt that children of highly verbal, socializing families acquire skills very quickly, probably by imitation. It is not clear what they are looking at, and if we knew, it would help in the training of shy adults. We do know that an important step in overcoming shyness is learning how to observe what people do that works well.

Schools have the opportunity to affect the way people learn to speak. Those who, as children, attended schools where discipline was heavy tend to avoid speaking. People from very permissive schools also appear shy and diffident, perhaps because their school environment made approval too easy to get. Children who learn to rebel are also inept speakers as adults although it may not be from shyness.

Perhaps the most important influence of the school is entirely social. There is a conspiracy of "misery loves company" among shy people. Sometimes about the only thing they can talk about is their inability to talk. When they form a silent social group, they encourage each other to remain silent. By clinging to companions who are also shy, they lose their chance to influence people in other social groups. Furthermore, legends of the terrors of performance shared by those who have had bad experiences elevate the tension and make performance even more difficult. Thus, without an antidote administered by the teachers, shy people learn skills of shyness rather than those of performance.

It is not really that schools make children shy, although some teachers do more than their share to silence young mouths. It is that the schools, by inaction, do nothing to help people who are disqualified from social interaction. The students who speak up properly are noticed and rewarded; those who speak improperly are punished; those who do not speak at all are consigned to obscurity. Furthermore, it is sometimes pleasant to have a classroom filled with quiet little children, so that for a teacher to encourage talk would be almost self-defeating. Thus there are little rewards bestowed on those children who do not rock the boat.

MARGINALITY

It is very painful for a child to come into a new school and a new neighborhood. Children who move from town to town often become very skillful at meeting new people, though they remain inept at building lasting relationships.

The problem is that every time you move, you become marginal and need to learn a new set of social skills. Moving from city to country or vice versa, or from one geographical region to another contains the potential for considerable social misery. Even moving from suburb to suburb within the same city has its perils. Every move requires the learning of new norms. We must discover what topics are permissible and what must not be talked about. We have to learn who is important and who is not, what activities are valued, what risks ought to be taken in order to win approval. Adults must learn how to express political and religious beliefs, and what the appropriate pattern of socialization is. Newcomers must learn where it is okay to congregate.

But even if adults make some mistakes in the community, they are mobile and have relationships at work as well as in their home neighborhoods, and they are thus not locked into a particular place for their associations. Youngsters, on the other hand, particularly teen-agers, must make it in their school, or else. Members of minority groups find it doubly hard to move into new locations. Old timers tend to be suspicious of them as minorities and as newcomers. Most learn that it is best to stay in the background until they learn the moves.

Adults who move frequently learn to use community organizations as well as how to find people of similar interest and social style. They know how to keep away from associations that might be threatening or hard to manage. If they do not know this, they may eschew socialization altogether. Young people do not have these opportunities either, so many of them become loners.

This same pattern seems to apply to ethnic groups moving from homogeneous communities to heterogeneous ones. Upward-mobility ethnics—blacks, Jews, and nationality Catholics—are often rejected as pushy when they attempt to socialize in new neighborhoods. Some newcomers know the right moves, but they make them awkwardly and are rejected. "Natives" try to keep out newcomers of all kinds and if there is some disqualification potential, such as ethnicity, the long-time residents are quick to use it. Thus ethnics are usually pushed into association with their "own kind," usually through ethnically oriented groups, social and political groups, and the church. Their children, however, often wish to ignore ethnicity and make it with the group they see as socially acceptable. They may keep quiet about their racial or national origins and simply try to be background for the right people, but this rarely works. Even if they are grudgingly permitted to socialize marginally, whenever there is a falling out, they are reminded of the fact that they simply are not the right kind of people. Such treatment impels a number of so-called marginals to choose shyness.

UNFAMILIAR SITUATIONS

People are often shy when they do not know the right moves. Going to high school or college or taking a new job requires learning the right moves. Many people acquire skill at this, and most major institutions have ways and means to integrate newcomers into the mainstream. People who cannot avail themselves of these opportunities remain marginal. Sometimes they appear to remain silent and cool, sometimes silent and sullen, sometimes just silent. Very often once shy people discover that they are not able to adapt, they simply stay where they are, probably under the premise that one place is just as bad as another.

Social experiences like joining a new club, attending a cocktail party, or entering a new country club are also threatening. Your opening moves are evaluated, and decisions are made immediately about your social acceptability. If you are adept at learning the subtle skills, you win acceptance. Old-timers have their ways of testing newcomers. New people are always regarded with suspicion, but skilled relaters know how to overcome suspicion by acting "right." Shy people cannot do this.

Shy people need training in how to appear "unshy," not a "treatment" that focuses on their internal dynamics and deep personal feelings. Such help can only be offered by someone skilled in training techniques, though there is a great deal you can do on your own, if you care to act.

EXERCISE TIME

Take a good look at the world in which you live and try to discover some reasons why other people react to you as they do. Follow these steps in order.

1. Pick a social situation in which you find yourself often, one that has a consistent cast of characters such as the people at the coffee break, PTA meeting, lunch hour, laundromat. Get a piece of paper and make five columns.

Names of people present	adjective that describes his or her behavior	what the person does to earn the label	adjective he or she uses for you	what you do to earn it

Be sure to write behaviors, actions, or specific words said in columns 3 and 5.

2. In column 2 draw a red circle around the adjective you would like to have used on you, and in column 4 draw a blue circle around the adjective you would not like to have used on you.

You now have the beginning of a program of self-improvement. By concentrating on the behaviors associated with the adjectives you can make a list of what you need to stop doing and what you need to learn how to do. Save your list. It will be helpful to you when you begin to set goals for your behavior change.

RECOMMENDED READINGS

Howard Gilkinson, "Social Fears as Reported by Students in College Speech Classes," *Speech Monographs*, Vol. 11, 1942, pp. 141–60.

Larry Steward, "Attitudes Toward Communication" (Ph.D. diss., Pennsylvania State University, 1968).

Lynne Grutzeck, "A Search for Invariant Characteristics of Reticent Elementary School Children" (M.A. thesis, Pennsylvania State University, 1970).

Kathleen Domenig, "An Examination of Self Reports of Reticent and Non-Reticent Students before and after Instruction" (M.A. thesis, Pennsylvania State University, 1978).

Michael Hyde, "The Experience of Anxiety," *Quarterly Journal of Speech* 66 (1980): 140–54.

Carrie Rubinstein, Philip Shaver, and Letitia Anne Peplau, "Loneliness," *Human Nature*, February 1979, pp. 58–65.

chapter 4

What the "Experts" Say

Shy people often seek help from psychiatrists who offer them a variety of treatments: drugs, analysis, conditioning, understanding, and various kinds of training. Generally, it is this latter form that is most effective, but most shy people do not need psychotherapy at all. The evidence is clear that instruction and communication training are generally effective. Some shy people need help with problems other than their shyness and should, of course, seek the proper professional. For those whose shyness is the result of an inability to communicate effectively or a lack of understanding of social strategies, the instructional approach advocated by this book is usually enough.

Originally the problem of generally ineffective performance was called stage fright. Back in the 1800s, students were expected to be able to declaim. They were required to memorize pieces and speak them in

Prepared with Lynne Kelly, supervising instructor of The Pennsylvania State University Reticence Program.

class. They were taught stylized diction and gestures. Many students were not able to learn declamation. They preferred to leave rather than stand and stammer. Unwillingness to perform, accompanied by visible physical symptoms, was associated with a disease called stage fright, which is discussed in most psychiatric textbooks.[1]

By the early 1900s there were dozens of treatments for stage fright, including the old favorites of looking into a mirror and announcing how you are improving or visualizing your listeners as if they were sitting on the john. By and large the old shot of whiskey before performing was the consensus choice. Some enterprises flourished, however. The Dale Carnegie Courses have, for several decades, provided quality instruction for shy people.[2] However, the Carnegie Course is somewhat like Alcoholics Anonymous. You have to be willing to admit that you need help and you have to believe in the system. Academics tend to turn up their noses at the Carnegie system, and to this day there has been little connection between them. However, Carnegie graduates do learn something about performance, and although the charge is leveled that "they all sound alike," their personal accomplishments are considerable. Organizations such as the Toastmasters Clubs are also available for shy people who are willing to grit their teeth and master a discipline. The Toastmasters provide the additional advantage of a social organization as well.[3] Unfortunately, however, there is not much carry-over from public speaking to ordinary social life.

ENTER ANXIETY

Recently many speech communication specialists have become interested in a number of speech-related difficulties referred to as reticence, communication apprehension, unwillingness to communicate, shyness, and unassertiveness.[4] There has been considerable confusion because of lack of agreement on names and meanings. While scholarly authorities struggle for refined taxonomies, most practicing teachers use the terms as if their meanings were interchangeable.

There are three basic points of view that represent the controversy over the nature of these problems. First is the point of view of this book, that shyness is mostly a matter of skills deficiency. A second group of authorities regard the problem as primarily psychological, characterized by anxiety and lack of self-esteem. A third position is that the problem arises from lack of understanding of appropriate ways to use speech.

This book represents the "reticence" point of view. People who are unable to speak effectively in social situations have inadequate skills. They do not understand the situations sufficiently to prepare themselves to deal with them, and they are inept at executing oral maneuvers. The problem arises when people discover their ineptitude and decide that they can gain more by avoiding communication than they can by trying to participate. There may be anxiety or other emotions associated with the skills inadequacy, and sometimes the individual may not understand social processes. Mainly however, the issue is straightforward. Shy people cannot do what they need to do, and therefore they must learn to do it if they are to improve their condition. Anything less does not result in effective improvement.

Those who regard the problem as caused by apprehension do not take into account the role of skill in building confidence. To remove apprehension in a person with no skill would produce an inept communicator who would only become anxious again. Those who seek to make people assertive fail to take into account the fact that others can assert back. As a result, many people who experience assertiveness training are cowed back into silence when they discover that their attempts to assert are greeted by strong retaliations. In general, people with speech communication problems cannot be identified with one cause or treated with one technique. Neither can they be identified by their attitudes alone. Paper and pencil tests are useful in alerting people to potential problems, but in the final analysis a person has to be able to identify times and places where communication is difficult or impossible, and the remedy has to be designed to work where it is needed. It is the purpose of this book to make it clear to you that the way to improve your effectiveness is to identify your specific problems and work on them directly.

CONSEQUENCES OF THE PROBLEM

All authorities agree that the main effect of a communication problem, whatever it is called, is that the person who experiences it either does not participate in much social interaction or participates poorly. Some authorities take note of physiological symptoms, such as blushing, perspiring, trembling, or reports of headaches, palpitations, and loud heartbeat. Another observable behavior is that shy people are often not very expressive in their reactions to others. They tend to show little expression on their faces and they move their bodies very little. Many avoid direct eye contact with people who are speaking to them. Thus they make a very poor audience. Instructors in the Reticence Program have reported their own agony on the first night of a new class when they face a whole classroom full of totally expressionless people.

From descriptions of life histories it is clear that shy people often make major decisions to accommodate themselves to their shyness and to avoid situations with which they cannot cope. Their choice of residence is often dictated by a desire to avoid neighbors; they frequently marry early and cling to an exclusive partner to avoid the necessity of additional socializing. They may seek occupations that do not appear to require interaction on the job. In social gatherings they can be observed on the margins, standing apart from other people even when ostensibly involved in conversation.

As a result, most shy people are passed by in social and vocational life. Because they give the appearance of ignoring others, they are often ignored themselves. In fact, many effective interactors clearly cannot distinguish between shyness and aloofness, and shy people are thus often characterized as snobs. Being pushed aside tends to foster emotional illness. Shy people can sometimes be pushed into alienation or rebellion, though it appears that the most frequent emotional reaction is one of depression and apathy. In cases like this, the problem may be too broad to be managed simply by learning skills. The most effective way to discover how severe your shyness is, however, is to attempt to acquire some skills. If you derive satisfaction from your new accomplishments, then further expert advice is probably not necessary. If, on the other hand, you still feel distressed and physically limp, the services of a psychologist or psychiatrist may be warranted.

THE CAUSES

This book is directed at ways to improve your speech communication skills. It regards shyness as a lack of skill, regardless of the reason for it. Generally, shy people lack one or more of three capabilities: (1) the ability to think up appropriate things to say, (2) the ability to say things effectively, and (3) the ability to assess how well they are doing.

Some shy people fear social situations. Removal of their fear, however, does not automatically make them skilled communicators. Some shy people have been punished for talking or feel uneasy about who they are or how they look. These feelings of inadequacy can be overcome, but it is still necessary to learn skills. Some people became shy because their parents did not train them well or because their schools did not emphasize learning how to talk. They too must acquire skill.

Furthermore, there is no one kind of skill training that works with everyone. Some people may have to learn to be more assertive, others more understanding. Some may need to learn how to size up social situations, others may need some work in tension reduction. Regardless of the cause of shyness, all shy people need to learn how to choose what to say and when to say it, how to say it well, and how to assess the results of their talk. And, this must be tailored to particular situations.

Most of the alternatives to skills training seem to assume that speech is some kind of automatic process. It is not. Our speech mechanism was not designed to produce talk. Lungs that provide the power for speech are used for breathing. The larynx is a valve to keep food out of the lungs. The mouth is used to chew and swallow food. It really takes a great deal of conscious control to learn how to use these parts of our body to produce effective speech.

Shy people can try psychotherapy, assertiveness training, encounter groups, relaxation therapy, or self-esteem building as they feel they need them. In the final analysis, however, they must eventually learn how to talk well. It may be easier for them to choose to be sick for a while, but once they learn they can be effective, they can choose actions designed to make major changes in their lives.

Since your level of self-confidence has grown out of the way people have responded to you in the past, it is reasonable to assume that if you change the way you perform, you will change the way they respond, which in turn will change the way you feel. If you learn to control your behavior to evoke positive responses, you can gain self-confidence. You must, however, learn what a positive response looks like. Many shy people force themselves to reject positive responses from others because to accept them would be to demand change from themselves.

A second important point to remember is that change cannot come about from learning abstract theory. Reading about something doesn't mean that you have learned how to do it.

Third, consideration for others must be the foundation of learning. The problem with both sensitivity training and assertiveness training is that they are both egocentric. They presume that human beings can learn in some kind of social vacuum. The position of the systems theorists seems to be much more accurate, that is, if one component changes, then all components must change. Therefore, the improvements you make in your behavior must be made with the cooperation of other people.

The principles of instruction offered in this book are based on a method called rhetoritherapy. This is a system that provides skills in analyzing situations and people so that behavior can be stylized to accommodate itself to their needs as well as to your own. Everything we offer you has been tested and evaluated as being effective. The people who use it can tell you how it works and why it works. It is considerate of the other person, since social decisions are collective decisions.

Before moving on to the next chapter, try this important exercise.

Following is a description of a person who is effective at human relationships. We will offer you a general description consisting of a series of adjectives. Your task is to try to think of some people who fit the description and then to describe their *behavior* that earns them the adjective. Make a list of the actions and the words associated with them and add them to your list from the previous exercise. This will expand your pool of possible goals.

When you have completed this task, contact the person with whom you have worked before and ask that person to do the same thing. While you read the description, your associate is to list the behaviors he associates with each underlined word. When you are through, talk over your lists to see where you agree and disagree. When you disagree, try to figure out why. Try to eliminate all of the words and references on your lists that do not refer to behavior.

THE EFFECTIVE RELATER

Effective relaters are **goal-centered** and **businesslike**, even when **having fun**. They do not permit **unnecessary distractions**. They complete **conversational tasks**. When they **explain**, they do so in a fashion that helps everyone **understand**, and they offer **careful answers** to questions. When they want others to **believe** them, they are **persuasive**. They offer **reasons other people can understand**. When they want to be **friendly** or **entertaining**, they are able to do so.

Effective relaters **adapt** themselves and do what is **appropriate** both to the situation and to the people around them. They seem to be able to avoid **insulting** others, **talking down to them**, or **talking over their heads**. They make people feel that they **belong**, though they remain at the **center of the situation**.

They are **clear** and **organized**. They are **fluent**, able to make **transitions** smoothly, and they are **concise**. They **adapt** to their listeners. They are almost always **interesting** and sometimes **witty**. People enjoy being with **them**, and they **pay attention**. Effective relaters are not **boring**. They are **informed** and they avoid **clichés**. They **respect** others, and they do not **attack** or **demand** from their listeners.

You will never find anyone who measures up to all these qualities. But each quality is made up of behaviors that can be learned. It is up to you to set a priority list for yourself, but you cannot do this until you have identified precisely what behaviors you want to change. Some of the key words are **goal-centered**, **adaptable**, **appropriate**, **clear**, **interesting**, and **respectful**. Pay particular attention to your meanings for these words.

Once you have a list of behaviors from which to choose, you are ready to proceed to the next chapter.

REFERENCES

1. James C. McCroskey, "Oral Communication Apprehension: Summary of Recent Theory and Research," *Human Communication Research*. Vol. 4, No. 1, Fall 1977, pp. 70–95.
2. J. Berg Esenwein and Dale Carnagey, *The Art of Public Speaking* (Springfield, Ma., Home Correspondence School, 1915); also Ralph Keyes, "Meanwhile Back at Dale Carnegie . . ." *Human Behavior*, Vol. 6, No. 11, Nov. 1977, pp. 57–60.
3. Toastmasters International, *Communication and Leadership Program* (Santa Ana, Ca., Toastmasters International, 1977).

4. Gerald M. Phillips and Kent A. Sokoloff, "An End to Anxiety," *Journal of Communication Disorders*, Vol. 12, 1979, pp. 385–97.

RECOMMENDED READINGS

For an overview of various positions on how to overcome shyness see *Communication Education*, August 1980, where nine authorities make specific recommendations for the treatment of shyness and reticence. For specific statements on major points of view, see the following.

Assertiveness: Ron Adler, *Confidence in Communication* (New York: Holt, Rinehart & Winston, 1977).

Cognitive Restructuring: William Fremouw and Michael D. Scott, "Cognitive Restructuring: An Alternative Method for Treating Communication Apprehension," *Communication Education* 28 (May 1979): 128–33.

Systematic Desensitization: Gordon L. Paul, *Insight vs. Desensitization in Psychotherapy* (Palo Alto, Calif.: Stanford University Press, 1975).

Rhetoritherapy: Gerald M. Phillips, "Rhetoritherapy versus the Medical Model," *Communication Education* 26:1 (January 1977): 34–43.

Psychological: Philip Zimbardo, *Shyness* (Reading, Mass.: Addison-Wesley Publishing Co., Inc., 1977).

chapter 5

Starting to Change

The one thing shy people have in common is that *they do not communicate well in one or more social situations*. They have exercised their right to silence because they think it is helpful to them. In any social situation there are people who wish they could talk more and feel bad about their limited participation.

Shyness is an adjective imposed by others as a reaction to the behavior they see. We never call ourselves shy until someone else offers us the label. This is very much like the explanation offered for stuttering that says that people begin to stutter once they have been identified as stutterers and that those cultures that don't have a word for stuttering have no stutterers.[1] We have already ruled out the "disease" explanation for shyness. The term *reticent* is a more useful way to talk about shyness because it does not have the implication that there is any need to diagnose and treat it medically. You can learn not to be reticent!

The Reticence Program at Pennsylvania State University was founded in order to teach people how to become more effective at accomplishing social goals, such as meeting new people, making social conversation, asking and answering questions in the classroom and on the job, participating in groups, and interviewing, and speaking in public. The problems it can deal with are always stated specifically so that people participating will not have the opportunity to talk about their feelings and emotions.

People have the right to be quiet, if they choose. We are concerned only about people who are involuntarily quiet.

It is important for quiet people to discover that the world is not divided into talkers and nontalkers and that virtually everyone feels shy and reticent in some places and with some people. A format for handling new situations is the most important thing that shy people can learn.

Our first effort was made with twenty students selected because they were ready to drop out of school rather than take a required speech course. We had five instructors to work with them, so it was not astonishing that eighteen of them made it through and graduated. We thought that all of them looked and sounded a little better, but we clearly did not know how to proceed with instruction. The original group had problems with everything. They could not talk to merchants or to their landlords. They were afraid of their academic advisors, they could not go to interviews, they could not give oral reports or work in groups, and they were all friendless because they did not know how to meet people. It was clearly an exceptional group, of a kind we never saw again. Because we had the worst cases all together, we were distracted from the problems ordinary people have. We thought we were dealing with some kind of sickness and we talked about "pathology" and "therapy."[2] Later we discovered that what was important about that original group was the list of situations in which they had trouble. When we learned to concentrate on the situations, we discovered that we had a program of instruction with wide appeal.

The way we identified reticent people was through their own reports. Every student at the university was required to take a public speaking course. We offered the program as an alternative. People who qualified could enter the Reticence Program and work on their own particular problem. We tried paper-and-pencil screening tests, but we discovered that such tests identified some very competent speakers, and furthermore, many people who obviously needed instruction refused it. We could only work with willing students, and so even when we identified a problem speaker, we still had to conduct an interview. We finally used the simple device of advertising the course with a list of the problems with which we could deal together with an invitation to come in and be interviewed to those who felt they had the problem.

Subsequently we offered the program to adults in the community and discovered that reticence was something that affected all ages. Adults reported the same difficulties. Although all of them had "agonies" when talking about their feelings and emotions, when we could get them to give us specific details, they identified the same list of situations:

- Dealing with service personnel, merchants, cab drivers, etc.
- Asking and answering questions
- Undergoing interviews
- Talking to authority figures (supervisors, parents, etc.)
- Participating in group discussions and problem-solving sessions
- Speaking up at meetings
- Public performances of all sorts
- Meeting new people
- Conducting social conversations

It appeared that this list represented the basic arenas for socializing in our society.

A major grant from the federal government helped the program grow. We were able to set up demonstration programs in the public schools for children of all ages. Once again we discovered that reticence or shyness affected all age groups and that the situations in which it was reflected were common to all. Of the forty thousand schoolchildren we contacted, we discovered that nearly 25 percent were so shy that it interfered with both their schoolwork and their social lives. A recent book on shyness reported that 50 percent of the population are unable to function well because of shyness.[3] Clearly our efforts to provide training for shy, or reticent, people had a potential audience.

We tried a number of methods and rejected them simply because they did not work. We consulted a variety of authorities and used only the advice that seemed to produce results. The results we were looking for were a demonstration by our students that they could do the things they had not been able to do when they came in. We wanted to see them speak in public, meet new people at social gatherings, survive interviews.

We wanted them to be able to take what they had learned in the class-room and apply it in their own way to their own lives. If we could not do this, then the enterprise was pointless.

Our experiments with sensitivity training showed us that while it sometimes made people feel a little better when they were in the group, once they went back to their own lives, the methods did not work. We discovered that sensitivity training assumed the existence of a particular kind of environment and life-style. Our efforts to use desensitization showed that it had no effect at all on speaking skill. An intense study showed that the group without desensitization that was allowed to talk about their problems showed greater gain than those who had been desensitized.[4] Efforts with cognitive restructuring were a little more promising. We discovered that a number of our students needed to change their ideas about the nature of speaking and socializing. However, they still had to learn and practice skills. Our conclusion was that skills training was our only effective alternative.

ENTER RHETORIC

Our search for an effective learning system led to the rediscovery of a two-thousand-year-old art, rhetoric. The ancient Greeks used to study rhetoric, "the art of persuasion."[5] Rhetoric was a formal system in which speakers used logic, emotion, and their own personality to per-suade others to a point of view. It consisted of learning to discover ideas, organize them, phrase them, and deliver them in particular cases. In fact, the essence of the rhetorical system was that every case must be considered on its own merits.

Rhetoritherapy is a system of instruction designed to train people to improve their communication skills in the particular situations they face in their lives. It is heuristic, that is, it consists of a series of practical principles that can be applied to situations one at a time. It is not a universal technique. Basically rhetoric is a method of planning and executing communication. It is nonspontaneous and is entirely consid-erate of the other person. Its basic propositions can be summed up as follows:

1. In order to influence others, you must know yourself.

2. There are three ways you can influence others: through your personal reputation and authority, through logic and organization, and through the emotions.
3. Every case involving human beings is different in some way from all other cases. We can have general rules for examining each case and deciding what to do, but we cannot have a universal system to apply to all cases.
4. We must proceed through Aristotle's dictum "The fool tells me his reasons, the wise man persuades me with my own." When we seek to influence others, we must be considerate of their needs and wants.
5. The art of rhetoric can be learned.

Communication is seen as both a process and a relationship between people. It cannot proceed through hard-and-fast rules, but it must transcend the emotionality of human relationships. It is based on both a hopeful and a practical philosophy. In order to gain skill at the art of rhetoric, you must understand the following major ideas:

1. You must select a goal to accomplish every time you speak. You must not permit your speaking to be guided by unconscious goals over which you have no control.
2. Your goal must be adapted to the goal seeking of others. If you can learn to address other people in ways that will help them accomplish their goals, they will be more favorably disposed to helping you achieve your goals.
3. People can understand each other best if their ideas are clearly organized according to commonly accepted organizational patterns, then adapted to the particular case and individual.
4. People have the right to refuse any request made of them. Rhetoric does not always work, because we cannot always know what the other person is after, and even if we do, sometimes we cannot or will not adapt to it. However, you have the right to refuse the other person's requests if you wish.
5. Everyone can improve relationships by thinking through goals.

Aristotle's notion that the best ideas will win if given an equal hearing is an important basis of the notion that rhetorical skill is an equalizer in human relationships. So long as we have a democratic society, those who are most skillful at persuasion will achieve the most. But acquiring skill at persuasion is a reciprocal process. As you become skillful, you help others to become skillful. Think of those rare occasions when you met other people so skillful that they could bring you out of yourself and pull you into participation even though you felt a bit uneasy. Those people were not "using" or "manipulating" you. They merely understood that to be skillful at relationships required them to be sensible, considerate, and coherent.

The process of applying rhetoric is simple in conception, although usually difficult in execution. You must

1. Decide what you need to learn and discover what it is possible for you to learn. Sometimes we distract and frustrate ourselves by trying to learn or do the impossible. Rhetoric demands practicality from its practitioners.
2. Decide on the people with whom you are going to try out your new learning. Carefully select and arrange your experiences so that you begin with people who are less vital or threatening.
3. Develop a plan for execution. Select behaviors that will indicate to you that you have accomplished the goal. Plan your own behaviors and provide yourself with a good reason for doing what you do.
4. Think through and revise your plan. Develop alternate plans to accommodate yourself to possible responses from the other person. Schedule when you will try to put your plan into operation.
5. Do it!!
6. Examine the response from the other person and decide on what to do next.

The first point is the most difficult to accomplish. As the old saying goes, "If you don't know where you are going, any road will get you there." Most of us have a general idea of what we want from others. We know that we are pursuing happiness, looking for security, seeking love. We normally do not think though the intermediate steps, nor do we figure out what it would take to convince us that we found what we were after. The procedure called goalsetting[6] seems most appropriate to accomplish this objective. Robert Mager has devised a system for classroom teachers to use in preparing their teaching objectives. Mager advocates that goals be specified as behaviors. There is a difference, he believes, between goals and outcomes. An individual can seek goals for his or her own behavior. Goals cannot be sought for the behavior of the other, but desirable outcomes can be specified. Planning would consist of trying to fit the goals you have for your behavior to the outcome you anticipate. The idea is to make a close connection between what you do and what you expect so that what you do is adjusted to your listener in such a way that it will evoke desirable behavior because that other person wants to do it. Everything must be phrased in terms of behavior, however—your behavior and the behavior of the other. It is not legitimate to seek behavior from the other that will make you "feel good." "Feeling good" is a luxury you can have after you see the desired behavior.

Effective communicators are quite clear about what they seek. They have specific goals for themselves to achieve specific outcomes with the other person. They can select appropriate things to say, since they know what *appropriate* means. They adjust "appropriately" to the requirements of situations and persons, and they have a pool of successful experience from which to draw possible behaviors. They also understand that they may not get what they want with the first try, so they have alternative plans to plug in. Finally they know that they can't win them all, so they know when to quit and move on to someone else.

BASIC PRINCIPLES OF RHETORICAL ACTION

First and foremost, you must remember that *communication must be adapted to others*. The concept of "audience" is terribly important. Even if you are talking to just one other person in an intimate setting, you have an audience. Thus you cannot just say what comes off the top of your head. If someone is giving you the benefit of his or her time, you must consider that person's needs and wants in what you have to say. That means that you have to understand your audience if you want to be responsible and responsive. You must understand that the people in your audience have their goals, and they hope that you are about to offer them something that they can use. When you both understand that there is mutual gain through your association—I will do something you want and you will do something I want—then you have a *rhetorical exchange*.

The second point you must remember is that *effective communication consists of a series of statements organized in such a way that your audience can understand them*. The way we organize our thoughts will depend on what we are trying to get the other person to understand or do, as well as upon that person's level of sophistication and intelligence. There is no *one* organizational pattern. In fact, part of the reason we want to analyze audiences is so that we can select the kind of organization that is best suited to them.

The third point is that *communication is effective when it is interesting*. Top speakers have repertoires of things to say. They are able to select from their memory statements that appeal to others. They have gone through their ideas and have gotten the "bugs" out of them. They can give coherent directions and provide reasons for their beliefs that others will find important in their lives. They can give reasons why you would benefit from the requests they make. They are not egocentric and they concentrate on interesting and amusing you.

Fourth is the notion that *improvement comes from analysis of the effect you have on others*. Speaking with others is not an automatic process. People are not robots that can be managed by pressing the proper button. There is no one way to accomplish any goal. Everything you do must be specifically adapted to the person to whom you direct it. The other person will respond to you out of personal and private motivations. If you do not succeed in getting the response you want, you can only analyze your part in the process. You can decide whether the content of your talk was appropriate and effective and whether or not you executed it well. You cannot blame the other person for what he or she does.

The fifth important point is that *behavior will not change unless you decide to change it*. Furthermore, feelings will not change at all unless there is some reason for them to change. You cannot will your feelings out of existence, but you can change the effect they have on you by the way you name them. The same feeling can be called uneasiness, tension, fear. *Uneasiness* gives no information; it is unspecific and cannot be dealt with. *Fear* suggests a condition that is paralyzing; it keeps you from acting. *Tension* however, is a positive term in that it represents something that can be constructive, since you can then ask what the tension is about and begin to prepare yourself to use it.

The important thing about changing behavior is to determine whether or not you are physically capable of doing what you want to do. You might not be capable of playing the guitar like Chet Atkins if you have never had a lesson. You might not be able to run fifteen miles if you have a heart condition or lift fifty pounds if you have a hernia. But you can probably learn to specify goals, think up main lines of talk, organize them, and say them. If you have lived this long, you have demonstrated that you are physically capable of doing it; if you have read this far, you have demonstrated that you are intellectually capable.

You will not be able to change your communication behavior unless you are with people. This may take a real act of courage and commitment on your part, but the information in this book will be of no use to you unless you try it out.

Learning to talk effectively is a matter of controlling your own behavior. You cannot control the behavior of other people, nor can they control yours unless you let them. When you plan what you are going to say and do, you are not manipulating the other person, you are manipulating yourself. You have developed a hypothesis about behavior. You have made your best educated guess that if you talk in a particular way, it will evoke a particular behavior. You could be wrong, but this is the important point: You can act and you can control your actions. The simple process of exerting this control will make you feel a good deal better about yourself, even if you do not get a single, solitary expected response from other people. Effectiveness comes with practice, but practice begins with self-control.

Finally you must remember that *change comes slowly and in small steps*. There is no magical way to change yourself immediately. The old legend about buying new clothes is not quite accurate, although new clothes are the start of a new image. If you want to lose weight, you must control your food intake for a long time. If you want to learn to drive a car, you must practice patiently under all kinds of conditions. This book is organized so that you can start to change right away. By changing in small ways in situations that are not critical, you can learn how it feels to change. By succeeding in small steps you can encourage yourself about your own competency. In the Reticence Program we take care with our students to encourage them to move slowly and consolidate their learning before they attempt truly important situations.

START WORKING NOW

The following are a series of exercises and tasks that will get you started in overcoming shyness. Please work through them carefully. You can read on into the next chapter, for it will provide you with important background material, but you should complete all of this work before starting Chapter Seven.

SKILL SCALE

By now you have accumulated information about behaviors that you would like to learn. The following list of skills was contributed by students in the Reticence Program. They represent legitimate and attainable goals. Check those items that represent a situation and skill that would be important for you to master.

1. When I talk to my supervisor on the job, I sometimes think that I don't say enough, or I leave important ideas out. I want to plan a statement and then say it to her without leaving anything out.

2. I do not answer questions asked of me as fully as I would like, even when I know the information. The next time I am asked a question, I want to give a complete answer, and if I do not have a complete answer, then I want to ask my questioner to come back in fifteen minutes so that I can have a chance to prepare an answer.

3. I often refrain from asking questions because I don't seem to be able to phrase something sensible in time. I want to prepare three questions to ask my boss or teacher and ask them before 3 P.M. tomorrow. If necessary I will write them out on cards.

4. I don't seem to carry my share of the conversation. I want to prepare a two-minute statement on the Pittsburgh Steelers or the *Empire Strikes Back* and say it completely to the next stranger I meet at a cocktail party.

5. I don't seem to be able to open conversations or meet new people properly. When I get introduced to someone, I say nothing, and they move on. I want to prepare four questions I can ask the next new person I meet.

Notice how precise each of these statements is. They are the result of careful consideration and goalsetting directed toward behavior. The remaining statements have blurry language in them. Take the italicized statements and restate them as behaviors exactly as the first five have been stated.

6. I don't make social engagements because I don't seem to be able to ask people out and I feel rejected if they refuse me. *I want to be able to make dates with people.*

7. Tradespeople and service people intimidate me. I don't get proper service because I don't know what to say to them. *I want sales clerks to give me the treatment I am entitled to.*

8. I don't speak up at committee meetings even when I have something worthwhile to say. *I want to be able to say what's on my mind.*

9. Other people borrow my ideas because I can talk about them in private but not in public. *I want to get full credit for my ideas.*

10. I hear a lot of ideas that I think are foolish and dangerous and I'd like to argue with them, but I don't seem to get my ideas together in time or I can't talk back strongly enough. *I want to be able to fight back.*

11. When I do get to talking, I forget large blocks of what I wanted to say. *I want to be able to express myself completely.*

12. After I leave a group of people, I think up some really fine things I could have said. *I want to say smart things on time.*

13. There is more I want to say to the people I love, but it doesn't seem to come out. *I want to be able to express my feelings to the people I care about.*

14. I don't seem to be able to represent myself well when I apply for a job or when I try to show my boss how good I am. *I want people to know how competent I am.*

15. I am known as a follower. *I'd like to be a leader.*

16. My social or vocational future depends on my ability to talk in situations where I just simply cannot talk well. *I want to be skillful in those situations.*

17. People seem to forget about me when they issue invitations. *I want to be popular.*

18. I am generally awkward in my relationships with the opposite sex. *I want to be more successful.*

19. I often feel as though other people push me around and don't take my wishes into account when decisions are being made. *I want to exert my share of influence.*

Notice how difficult it is to "operationalize" these goals. Did you find that some of the later ones were virtually impossible to rephrase? That was because they were too global. In number 18, for example, you might have been better off to rephrase it, "Sally does not pay attention to me and Joe ignores me, and I would like to get their attention." You could then specify the behaviors you think you would use in order to get the attention you desire.

In the following exercise you will take one simple goal and work it through the steps of analysis so that you get familiar with the questions you must ask about your own behavior.

SITUATION ANALYSIS

Think of a situation involving other people in which you are not satisfied with your behavior (Thanksgiving dinner with the family, the coffee break, the new-product meeting, the block party, exchanging merchandise at a store, etc.). Try to describe it by answering the following questions:

- Where is this place? Describe the scene.
- Who is there with you?
- What do you want to accomplish? (What do you want the other people to say or do?)
- What do the other people want to accomplish there?
- What, if anything, do they want you to say or do?
- How do you know all this?
- What would you normally say in this situation?
- What would the other people say back?
- Now think of that ideal communicator you worked on awhile ago; what would that person want to accomplish in the situation?
- What would that person say to the other people present?
- What would they say back?
- Why do you think you answered the way you did?
- What is better about the response the ideal communicator got?
- What would you have to change about your behavior to act more like that ideal communicator?

You can do this exercise with as many situations as you like. It might be a good idea to get four or five worked out so that you will have a supply to choose from when you get started experimenting with your new behavior.

It is important for you to identify the situations in which you want to work. The more specific you can be about the situations, the more effective your rhetoric will be. *The process of preparing for a rhetorical situation is one of applying the answers you get to general questions in the specific case.* Notice in the exercise you just did how you could take the questions "who will be there?" or "what would they want?" and apply them to virtually every social situation in which you find yourself.

In the following chapter you will learn some basic principles of communication. You can then proceed to master the five basic steps of rhetoritherapy.

1. Set a goal in actions and words.
2. Analyze the situation and the persons in it to discover what their motives are.
3. Plan your talk by selecting the ideas you want to express, putting them in order, and selecting words in which to say them.
4. Talk!
5. Examine the result and set the next goal.

REFERENCES

1. Wendell Johnson, *People in Quandaries* (New York: Harper & Row, Publishers, Inc., 1946), especially the last chapter, "The Indians Have No Word for It."
2. Gerald M. Phillips, "A New Direction for the Speech Profession," in Johnnye Akin, ed., *Language Behavior* (The Hague: Montan Co., 1970).
3. Philip Zimbardo, *Shyness* (Reading, Mass.: Addison-Wesley, 1977). See Chapter 1.
4. Dennis Kleinsasser, "The Reduction of Performance Anxiety as a Function of Desensitization, Pre-Therapy Vicarious Learning and Vicarious Learning Alone," (Ph.D. diss., The Pennsylvania State University, 1969).
5. For an overview of the history of rhetoric see Lester Thonssen and A. Craig Baird, *Speech Criticism* (New York: Ronald Press, 1948); see also any edition of Aristotle's *Rhetoric*.
6. Robert Mager, *Goal Analysis* (Belmont, Calif.: Fearon-Pitman Publishers, Inc., 1972).

RECOMMENDED READINGS

Karen Horney, *Self Analysis* (New York: W. W. Norton & Co., Inc., 1942).
Lloyd Bitzer, "The Rhetorical Situation," *Philosophy and Rhetoric*, 1 (1968).

Roderick Hart and Don Burks, "Rhetorical Sensitivity and Social Interaction," *Speech Monographs*, 39, 2, June 1972, pp. 75–91.

Robert Mager, *Good Analysis* (Belmont, Calif.: Fearon-Pitman Publishers, Inc., 1972), pp. 1–14.

chapter 6

Communication and Human Relationship

Talking is a very complicated process that requires careful coordination of mind and vocal apparatus. It also requires careful learning of words and the rules by which they are connected. Talk is never an accident. It must be thought out and directed at some object, and it must be coherent. When we do not talk according to social expectation, we are classified as deviant. We are regarded as strange, stupid, or disturbed. In fact, talk serves as the basis of most diagnostic systems for mental illness. Thus if we do not impose careful conscious control over our talk, personal feelings may take control and carry us into difficulty. Sometimes our emotions get the best of us, and we feel the urge to shout or scream or speak emotionally. When we do this, we violate basic social expectations and we run the risk of annoying or boring the people who hear us. In general, talk that is not carefully managed is wasted at best and dangerous at worst. Thus we advocate following a rule of *negative spontaneity*, that is, we monitor our talk so that we can inhibit the kind of talk that will cause difficulty and speak consistently in ways that will evoke the most positive responses from those around us.

Human relationships are formed and maintained through talk. We make friends through our talk and we do business through our talk. We make friends and do business with people we trust. We trust them because their talk and behavior are rewarding. In general, we want to be with the people who give us more of what we want and we avoid the people who thwart us or do not respond to our needs. Thus the nature of any relationship between people can be identified and described by listening to their talk.

Sometimes we fail because we try to talk our way into the impossible. We also fail when we are not clear about what we are trying to obtain with our talk. The story of the Tower of Babel is quite instructive. If we read it correctly, it means that God understood that if humans achieved perfect communication, they might, indeed, reach up to Heaven. God "confounded" the speech of humans. He gave us different languages, according to the biblical legend, so that we would not overreach ourselves. We could argue the theology, but the important point is that it appears that humans can become very powerful if they learn to talk effectively.

REASONABLE PURPOSES

There are only a limited number of responses we can obtain through talk. We might not be able to obtain "trust," but we can get people to believe that our words match our actions. We can't get affection, but we can offer words that might persuade another person to offer us kind words and positive sentiments back. Talk cannot accomplish much directly, but it can provide information on which other people can base their decisions about us. If other people decide to do what our words direct them to do, then talk is effective. We should also note that talk can be used to entertain, as in literature, poetry, and theater. Sometimes we are impressed by people because of their ability to entertain us with their talk.

We can use talk to express feelings and emotions. Unless this is stylized and used for entertainment purposes, it is an uneconomical use of talk. Our urgency to display our feelings is entirely egocentric. People do not really want to share either our pain or our joy. As a matter of fact, they want us to share their pain or their joy. We tend to compromise, to respect the rights of others to be spared from our emotional outbursts. Expressive talk is essentially purposeless and usually nonproductive.

We can use talk to ask for or to give information. Most of our talk is little more than an exchange of information. Information can be accurate or false, simple or complex. When you consistently offer accurate information that can be checked against reality, people learn to trust you. That is, they tend to act on the information you give them as though it represented reality. When you mislead people, whether accidentally or by design, they may become suspicious. When we need information, we usually seek out a person we can count on. Usually we are sufficiently grateful for accurate information to be willing to offer something in return if asked. Sometimes the something is respect and the willingness to do something later on. Giving accurate information generally buys you coupons you can cash in subsequently for behavior you want.

Information is not useful unless we can be persuaded to accept it. If someone gives us information in a flat tone of voice or does not look at us while giving the information, we tend not to believe him or her. Furthermore, when offered information for which we have no use, we do not listen. If I want your interest, I must either talk about what you are willing to listen to or I must give you a reason to listen to what I want to talk about.

We can talk to present, defend, and argue beliefs. Sometimes arguing is wasteful, but most of the time it is the constructive way we have to decide on what we are all going to do together. Arguing does not mean fighting and yelling. When we argue, we express our ideas and give what we think are good reasons for them. Other people may disagree and offer their opinions and their reasons. We do not try to convince each other. We argue in front of people who have the authority to make decisions, a judge and jury, the boss, parents, teachers, a committee, the electorate.

Intelligent and effective argument is customarily based on evidence. Those skilled in argument know how to evaluate information and present it so that it is fair to their premise as well as to their listeners. Argument is not a science, although scientists often argue. Argument is a skill that can be learned, and it is an important skill for the continued existence of a democratic society. When people do not argue, minority opinions often prevail. Thus it is important for shy people to learn to argue.

We use talk to entertain or impress. Sometimes it is a pleasure to talk about nothing at all of great consequence. Talk is used as a social lubricant for people to get to know one another. People make small talk in order to impress each other, to advertise themselves as good and interesting people. When we engage in talk with others, they make decisions about us, and we evaluate them in order to discover whether there is potential for further association. Thus our pleasure has a practical purpose as well. Initial decisions about our associates are generally based on physical appearance and talk. Talking is a way of getting close to another person psychologically.

IMPORTANT EXERCISES

We will now try to get you started with a series of exercises designed to get you moving toward your goal of more effective communication. You will be using the results of your earlier efforts to help you.

First you must understand the nature of "personality." One great psychiatrist said that personality is the relatively enduring interpersonal arrangements you make in your life.[1] To be more explicit, personality is the way people *see you*; it is not a part of you. There is no intrinsic personality. You are made up of the impact you have on others. Thus when other people see you behave, they assign a classification to you based on what they see. They do not know what is going on inside you. They do not know your "real self." They take you as you appear to them.

Following are some words commonly used to describe personality. Which are used on you? Check the words that have been applied to you (or that you would apply to yourself) and assign some behaviors to it. Check your work in previous exercises for help on this one. You can also call on the person who has been working with you to help out with this exercise. You can share your observations to see where you agree or disagree. Note that some of the words evoke positive feelings, and others evoke negative feelings. By thinking about your work on this exercise in conjunction with previous exercises, you will have an even more clear idea of the behaviors you are seeking to accomplish.

Sociable	*Popular*	*Warm*	*Genial*	*Facetious*
Gracious	*Ingratiating*		*Unctuous*	*Cordial*
Humorous	*Caustic*		*Friendly*	*Trenchant*
Persuasive	*Cogent*	*Sarcastic*	*Cynical*	*Forceful*
Credible	*Fatuous*	*Dependable*		*Sycophantic*
Reasonable	*Sententious*	*Self-righteous*		*Incisive*
Sophisticated	*Pompous*	*Erudite*	*Seductive*	*Tactful*
Loquacious	*Discreet*	*Effusive*	*Circumspect*	

Your task is to find ways to talk that will lead others to use your chosen adjective on you. The principle is one of "handsome is as handsome does," and by extension "sociable is as sociable does." If you want to be seen as sociable, you must act like a sociable person.

Your task in the future will be to convince others to use adjectives about you that you would choose. Sometimes we have little control over their judgments; some people will see us the way they want us to be, and if they want to dislike us, they may do so. Most of the time, however, we can persuade people to see us in constructive and positive ways. Thus we have a great deal to gain or lose when we talk with others. Most of us have regarded our talk as so natural that we have never thought about managing it. Thus when we do not get the result we want, we have not been able to explain it. But remember:

- Your reputation is based on the way others *connect your talk and your actions*
- Your ability to manage your emotions and those of others depends on *what you say and how you say it.*
- Your ability to have an impact on events depends on your ability to *select ideas and say them well.*
- Your ability to make and keep friends *depends on the way you talk*, and your talk will get you a few enemies.
- The influence you exert on decisions that affect you depends on *what you say, to whom, and how well.*

Remember—you can learn to talk well. Talk is the currency of social contacts.

- It always has an effect on the people who hear it.
- It shapes the attitude other people have toward us.
- It guides the decisions people make that involve us.
- It influences the way we respond to others.

Now think of a person you "trust."

- Write down three pieces of accurate information you received from that person.
- How did you know it was accurate information?
- Think of a person you "agree with."
- What do you agree about?
- What reasons did that person offer that led you to agree?
- How did those reasons apply to your life?
- Think of a person you "like to be with."
- Write down what you enjoy doing with that person.

Now think of a person you would like to have trust you, agree with you, and like to be with you. Write down the name.

- Think up three bits of useful, interesting, and reliable information you could offer that person.
- Think up some imporant issue you like to get agreement about and write down three reasons why that person should agree.
- Think of something that person enjoys doing and write down what you would say when you invite the person to do it with you.

Now prepare about three to five minutes worth of conversation to offer to this person. Don't be afraid to write yourself a script. Study it. Practice it with the person who is working with you. Then act! Invite the person in question for a cup of coffee and say your lines. If you feel the least bit uneasy, don't hesitate to say you are working on an exercise prescribed by this book. You will find that statement very effective.

Caution! You may make mistakes! It is only human to make a mistake or two.

EXCHANGE

Every relationship is an exchange, and talk is the process used to negotiate it. If you want a laugh and the other person wants to tell a story, there is an exchange. If you want an answer and the other person is flattered by questions, there is an exchange. People exchange goods and services through arrangements they make through talk. They may exchange feelings and emotions about each other, advice and information, precautions and predictions. It is not necessary to trade one for one. You may offer information, and the other person may offer advice. You may offer support, and the other person entertainment. When an exchange becomes regular, when you discover what you can do for each other, the result is "friendship." Sometimes people are required to make exchanges on the job or in the professional world. The teacher gives information, the student gives attention. The employee gives work, the boss gives money. Exchanges can be evaluated as either satisfactory or unsatisfactory. To the extent that you can talk accurately about what you have to give and what you would like to receive, you can build strong and lasting friendships. If you do not talk enough to give the other person a good idea of what you are seeking, you will not get your fair share in relationships.

AN EXCHANGE EXERCISE

You can assess your own needs for exchanges by examining the items on the following list. For each item ask yourself, "Is it something I need?" Then see if you can name someone who is presently providing it to you. If you cannot, name someone who could provide it. Once you have named someone, figure out what you are giving or what you could give in order to get it. Find at least ten items you need.

- Who is providing it now?
- What do you provide in return?
- Who could provide it?
- What would you have to provide to get it?

1. I want someone to enjoy movies (concerts, sports, etc.) with.
2. I want someone to eat out with.
3. I want someone to invite over who will invite me back.
4. I want someone whom I can bunk with when the going gets rough.
5. I want someone to drink with from time to time.
6. I want someone who can give me advice on how to deal with my boss.
7. I want someone who can give me advice on how to deal with my mate (lover, mother, father, brother, sister, etc.).
8. I want someone who can loan me clothes (records, a car, money, etc.).
9. I want someone to travel with.

10. I want someone who can explain to me how to do some complicated task.
11. I want someone to talk with about my hobby.
12. I want someone to cheer me up when I am miserable.
13. I want someone to bring me chicken soup when I am sick.
14. I want someone to share good news with.
15. I want someone who would stand by my side at a funeral.
16. I want someone to talk with about plays (music, art, philosophy, etc.).
17. I want someone to argue politics with.
18. I want someone who has already experienced what I am experiencing and can tell me what it is going to be like.
19. I want someone I can tell my personal feelings to, in order to find out if anyone else ever felt that way.
20. I want someone to convince me I am not crazy.
21. I want someone to tell me I am a nice person.
22. I want someone who will call me up on my birthday.
23. I want someone to give me advice on where to buy things or what dentist to go to.
24. I want someone I can sit in silence with.
25. I want someone who will help me test my ideas to see if they hold together.
26. I want someone who will tell me how to become better at what I do.
27. I want someone to help me lift heavy objects or unscrew jar lids.
28. I want someone to walk down memory lane with.
29. I want someone I can call up at 3 A.M. if I need to.
30. I want someone to cuddle with.

Once you have struggled through the list, you will discover a lot of specific "I needs." If you need them, so does someone else. What can you deliver? All of this should convince you of the possibilities for exchange that exist in virtually every relationship. Remember, however, that some people have a number of relationships going and they do not have the time or energy to take on more. Your best chance to develop an exchange is with someone like yourself, someone seeking new friends and relationships. Remember also that there are dark and hidden forces operating in all of us. Sometimes you meet someone and simply do not like his or her looks. The Freudians refer to this as transference.[2] The person may unconsciously remind you of someone with whom you have had an unpleasant experience. Once you know this, you can overcome the effects of transference in yourself, but if you are the object of someone else's transference, you may simply get rejected, through no fault of your own. You need not feel bad about this, so long as it has nothing to do with anything you have done. Shy people are notoriously eager to take the blame for anything that goes wrong. You needn't. The chances are about equal that it was the other person's fault.

No relationships, public or private, can be formed and sustained without talk. Relationships are between people whose identities are formed by the relationship. It sounds circular, and it is. As the relationship gets stronger, you become what the other person is seeking and vice versa. When disappointments set in, the relationship breaks down. Lasting relationships are composed of people who continue to struggle to be what the other is seeking in order that the other will continue to respond to them.

Because the best relationships are between people who exchange effectively, it is important that you learn to plan your talk. Until recently most people thought such planning was unethical. But we have made it clear that it is impossible to manipulate other people. People do not do what they do not want to do. What they do is to seek what they think they want from other people, and when they think they are getting that, they accommodate the person who is giving it by acting in the ways directed. In order to overcome shyness and make strong relationships you must take the interests and concerns of others into account whenever you deal with them. Once they discover you are attentive to their needs, they will attend to yours, *but* if they do not offer something in return, you are entirely justified in breaking off relationships. You cannot control other people, but you can control yourself, and part of that control is knowing when a relationship is not going to be productive. There are options on both sides. Shy people have trouble because they do not know how to talk in order to exercise their options effectively. Consequently they give the appearance of being satisfied when they are really not, because they are afraid that if they act dissatisfied, they will lose the relationship and not be able to make another.

CRITERIA FOR EFFECTIVE TALK

People cannot read what is inside your head. The only way you can show what kind of a human being you are is by what you say and how you say it. Thus if you restrain your talk and cannot make it clear to others how your mind works, *you are voluntarily handicapping yourself*.

- You must understand what the stakes are in communicating, what you can gain or lose.
- You must understand what you are seeking so that you know when you are satisfied.
- You must be able to find something to offer to the other person, otherwise there is no hope of any sort of relationship.
- You must be able to analyze situations to discover opportunities.
- You must be able to organize your ideas and be able to say them so that others can understand you.
- You must be able to perform your talk in such a way that it is interesting enough to hold the attention of the other person.
- You must know how to assess the responses of the other person so that you can know how well you are doing and what to do next.

If you concentrate on these objectives, you can use your tensions to help you become an effective talker. Most people do not regard themselves as effective talkers. In fact, they do not think much about it. They ascribe their successes and failures to luck, fate, or the machinations of others. Thus when they attempt to improve themselves, they often focus on the wrong skills. The skills just listed are what are required of an expert talker. Notice that nothing is mentioned there about feelings or attitudes, or about luck or fate.

Shy people are tense in virtually every social situation. They worry before, after, and during their experience. They rarely get relief from a "job well done" because they do not know what a job well done looks like. They exist in a state of pervasive anxiety, which they use as an excuse for not making an effort to improve. Their fears force them to focus on past failures and thus prevent future successes.

It would seem reasonable to remove these fears and expect improvement to result, but merely removing anxiety does nothing to improve it. If you are already a good speaker and have become excessively tense, of course removing anxiety would have a positive effect. On the other hand, if you are not yet an effective speaker, you will need some tension to get yourself to perform well. If you are too relaxed when speaking to others, you may respond emotionally or without thinking of the possible consequences of what you say.

Shy people must come out from behind their screens. Some reticent people play Walter Mitty roles. They live rich fantasy lives, and because of their fantasies they convince themselves that they *can* do it. Sometimes they go further and convince themselves that they *have done* it. Sometimes they get carried away by a fantasy and act as if their fantasized relationship really existed. The person they want to relate to is, of course, surprised by their presumptuous behavior. That person, after all, did not participate in the fantasy and therefore has no idea why the shy person is behaving in that fashion. Most shy people, however, wallow in self-pity and seek cures for their disability.

What reticent people forget (or never learned) is that everyone is tense when something is at stake. The athlete and the actor know the meaning of tension and would be lost without it. Most of us have so much to gain in our daily contacts with others that our tension is entirely natural. Relationships with other human beings can never be taken for granted. Therefore tension is neither to be avoided nor is to be feared. Some shy people get themselves into a locked-in state because they are not only tense about talking to others, they are tense about being tense. The first thing to understand is that tension is all right. It is constructive and can be used productively. Removal of tension does not make us effective, it makes us apathetic. Not caring means that we will not make an effort to get what we want, and thus we will not deal with others appropriately. Tension keeps us alert to the possibilities of success or failure in every social situation.

EXERCISE TIME

Television commercials constantly appeal to shy people to get some magic into their lives by shining their teeth, smelling nice, or dressing right. In fact one of the most insidious messages offered by the media is that dress that emphasizes sex will make you popular. This appeal is beamed to both sexes and is dangerous because of the latent suggestion that sex is the only reason for relationships between people. Your logical sense should tell you that changing your shaving lotion or your brand of undergarments won't do much to change the way people think of you. In fact, you might add to your notebook of knowledge the notion that after seven seconds the nose is not even aware of an odor, pleasant or unpleasant.

Shy people are very much like Willy Loman in *Death of a Salesman*. They want to be well thought of. Willy's problem was that he attended to his shoeshine more than to the needs of others. Shy and reticent people often have that problem. They get concerned with details and decide that they are not well thought of because of some trivial error in grooming they have made. They are looking for magic. You can discover the extent to which you are counting on magic by answering the following questions with the answers "frequently," "sometimes," "hardly ever," "never." You are entitled to five "frequently" answers or ten "sometimes" answers. If all your answers are "never," you might be thoroughly insensitive. Notice that none of these items has anything to do with the real content of what you say to people. Have you ever worried about:

1. People staring at you because you might be unzipped or unbuttoned?
2. People seeing blemishes on your face?
3. People thinking your clothing is unkempt or unsuitable?
4. People concentrating on your secondary sex characteristics?
5. People thinking you look "freaky"?
6. People thinking you are too fat, too thin, too old, or too young?
7. People thinking you are stupid?
8. Hurting someone's feelings because you blurted out some insult?
9. Disagreeing with someone because you might get into an argument?
10. Asking someone for a date for fear you will be refused?
11. People abruptly ending conversations with you and walking away for no good reason?
12. People you are talking to looking around for someone else to talk to?
13. Talking while you are holding food or drink for fear you will spill or slobber?
14. Burping or passing wind while you are talking?
15. People noticing stains on your clothing?
16. People going out of their way to insult you?
17. People giving you lectures for your own good?
18. Not being able to shake hands properly?
19. Using bad grammar when you talk?
20. People being annoyed by the way your voice sounds?
21. How you would handle it if someone accused you of lying?
22. Being unable to defend your own opinions?

23. People laughing at you behind your back?
24. Your hair not being combed or having dandruff?
25. Having body odor or bad breath?
26. Your makeup being smeared or your needing a shave?
27. Your underclothing showing?
28. Too much of your body showing (when wearing shorts or bermudas)?
29. Not being invited back?
30. Not being able to tell jokes?
31. People being concerned about your race, religion, or nationality?
32. Not remembering someone's name when you see them?
33. Not being built properly?
34. Not being able to smile because your teeth are not white enough?

Have you done anything about any of these concerns? Have you bought products or avoided situations because of them? Do you notice these problems in other people? Are you aware of their odors or teeth? How avidly do you watch the commercials? Do you ever say, "I have to buy that," because of a message similar to the ones above?

If you think you have some of these problems, there are constructive actions you can take. You can do something immediate about clothing styles and the way you look more easily than you can about your talk. The reason people cling so tenaciously to magical notions about how to improve is because it is encouraging to believe that your life would change completely if you could just find the right outfit or toothpaste. However, only attention to your behavior will help you make genuine progress. You might notice that people who do really well socially are often quite unconcerned about the way they look.

A good communication personality is characterized by the ability to respond well to what is going on around you, so that you haven't time for petty details. In his book entitled *The Culture of Narcissism* (New York: W.W. Norton, 1978), Christopher Lasch has pointed out that narcissism is characteristic of life in America today. Some shy people become narcissistic because they have never learned how to care about others. Because they cannot relate well, they devote all of their thoughts to themselves. If you worry about a great many of the items on the foregoing list, it may mean that you are not paying attention to other people sufficiently to help you understand how to relate to them effectively.

EFFECTIVE COMMUNICATION
TAKES EFFORT

Communication requires two or more people, each of whom is trying to accomplish some goal.

Each of the steps in the process requires thought. By paying attention to what is happening, you can be informed about what you are going to do and say next. Talk sometimes seems automatic because we are not conscious of controlling it. We can't avoid communicating while we are in the presence of another person. Even our silence is interpreted by the other. So the basic principle of effective speaking is to try to control as much as possible what comes out of your mouth.

A recent article about tranquilizers and alcohol pointed out that chemicals can help us quell our fears, but habitual use of chemicals makes us less able to adapt to changing conditions.[3] Rather than improving our lives, removal of tension makes us less effective people. You need a tense, sharp mind to help your body perform. Tension alerts your hormone system, pumping adrenaline into your body so that you have the energy to act. Some hypertense people become compulsive talkers, but tension can also help you to focus on what the other person is saying and doing so that you can really understand and respond properly. Talk is reciprocal. There must be as much energy devoted to listening as to talking. Sometimes a nod or a facial expression will signal to the other person that you really care and are tuned in to what is being said. Attention to what the other person is saying will help us phrase good questions.

BARRIERS TO EFFECTIVENESS

There are a number of barriers to effective communication besides our tension. Often our attitudes and beliefs interfere with our ability to choose effective responses. The following is not an exercise, although you might find it helpful to check which of the attitudes you have. If one of the following paragraphs fits you, be sure to read carefully to discover how to overcome it.

Do you believe it is unethical to plan for social situations? Planning of even the most casual contacts is very important. You must concentrate on the proper clichés of talk. You have to know the rules in order to be effective and you have to listen to what the other person says to you in order to reply properly. You can take nothing for granted, even when doing basic conversational routines. If planning is important at these preliminary stages, it is even more important when you get to know people. You have to plan in order to talk to them in terms they can understand and offer them reasons and ideas that motivate them, as well as to avoid hurting or insulting them.

Do you believe that friendships "just happen?" Making friends takes effort. There is usually a good reason why people become friends. A recent study showed that most people who have been friends for a long time are consciously aware of what they have been giving and receiving from the relationship.[4]

Do you believe that people get together because of "vibes?" There is no such thing as a "vibe." People often choose people for initial contacts because they remind them of someone with whom they had a favorable connection in the past, and they avoid people who remind them of unpleasant people in the past. These are not vibes, these are transferences, and they can be understood and overcome.

Do you believe that it is unethical to try to get someone to like you? It may be unethical if you really don't care about the person, but if you care, it is certainly appropriate to call attention to your good qualities. The conscious effort to make your interest known to another person is a keystone of friendship formation.

Do you believe you ought to do things for others even when it is inconvenient or difficult for you? To do so without an understanding is bribery. On the other hand, if you have a caring relationship with another person, it is sometimes necessary to inconvenience yourself to meet his or her needs. Nobody loves a martyr, however. When something is inconvenient or difficult, you ought to be able to talk about it and make some kind of mutual decision.

Do you believe that people ought to understand the "real you"? There is no "real you." What you see is what you get. There is no way to understand your inner self, because what you are has been created by agreement with the other person. It is, of course, possible to change or to call attention to other aspects, but this means a conscious effort on your part to persuade the other person to see you differently.

Do you believe it is unethical to conceal your real feelings about other people? It certainly gives you a feeling of relief to tell other people what you really think of them—until they either talk back, punch you out, or sue you. It really accomplishes little to "tell someone off." Furthermore, premature disclosure of affection can be quite embarrassing unless there is a genuine reason to believe that it is acceptable to the other person. To avoid hurting or embarrassing others, it is important not to show your hand too early.

Do you believe conversation is boring if it is trivial? "Heavy" conversations properly take place between people who are close to each other. Painful and laborious conversations about world affairs, philosophy, or religion can be conducted by agreement only, and it is unreasonable to expect casual acquaintances or people you just met to engage in such talk with you. As a matter of fact, the small talk characteristic of people who do not know each other very well is terribly important because it gives people some leeway to make decisions and it protects everyone against insult and injury. It is wise to stay within the social game plan and give people a chance to size you up through your small talk.

Do you believe it is phony and affected to try to change the way you talk? Learning of any kind demands change in the way you talk. Doctors learn doctor talk, lawyers learn lawyer talk. When you take on a career, you learn both a new vocabulary and a new delivery style similar to those people who are already doing the job. Without it you cannot communicate. When you move into a new social group, you must understand the way they carry on talk and try to accommodate yourself to it. Therefore, it is not reasonable to try to improve the way you talk in general, only to learn ways to accommodate yourself quickly to the talk requirements of any group you encounter.

Do you believe that people ought to be more considerate of the feelings of quiet people like you? To most people, your silence is a signal that you want to be left alone. If they do not solicit your ideas or invite you into the interaction, it is because you are giving them the message that you would not welcome their intrusions. People who want to be considerate must demonstrate it through their participation. Consider your own behavior. Are you attracted to silent people who appear to be paying little attention to you?

Do you believe that there are some rules for success at talking that you do not know and other people do? There is no secret formula for success. What effective socializers know is how to analyze and adapt. They learn this from experience. The only way you can get enough skill to handle most experiences is to handle experiences. There are no "ten ways to be interesting," and "five ways to be convincing." We can equip you with some techniques for analyzing the process, but you must provide the effort and the attempt to make things work.

Do you believe that you are not succeeding because of your personality? It may be true that some people have a genetic tendency to be very active and others to be relatively quiet. However, your personality is not a part of you the way your gizzard or your spleen is. Personality is the way others see you, and you can develop it through your own actions.

Do you believe that if you could only overcome your anxiety, you could do better socially? We have already dealt with this point. If you were to lose all of your tension, you would become an apathetic lump. What you need is to learn to manage your tension.

Do you believe that you cannot change? But you have changed. You changed when you learned to read and when you learned to drive a car. You can learn to change even more by changing the way you speak.

Do you believe that you need therapy if you are unable to socialize effectively? It this were the case, we could never produce enough therapists. Everyone has been anxious about some relationship at one time or another. All of us have goofed and ruined a good potential relationship at one time or another. Everyone can learn to be more skillful. However, this does not mean you don't need a therapist, only that your shyness is not necessarily a therapeutic problem.

Do you believe that if you like someone, he or she should like you back? No one has any such obligation. You have the right to approach the other person, but you have no right to pester. All of us are rejected at one time or another; we are probably rejected more often than we are accepted. The person who wants attention must make an effort to get it and must go away when it is clear that the attention is not going to come. Liking each other is the result of a mutual effort over a period of time.

Do you believe it is rude to break into conversations? Look around you! That is the way it is done. We take turns in conversation. When one person stops talking, the other person must break in. Otherwise the first person will regard it as a signal to keep on talking. What you need to learn is timing, so that you break in at logical places.

Do you believe that social conversation and public speaking are different? One of the foremost authorities on public speaking pointed out that speech is nothing more than enlarged conversation.[5] We can reverse the epigram and say that conversation is nothing more than scaled-down public speaking. Learn one and you can apply what you have learned to the other.

What this all adds up to is that we human beings have a choice about what we want to accomplish with others and how we go about accomplishing it. We can continue blundering and hurting others as well as ourselves, or we can make an effort to learn systematically the skills we need to know. We can't always win, but we can certainly improve our chances.

If we choose, we can see ourselves as weak and impotent. We can avoid responsibility for our ideas simply by keeping quiet. We can retreat to a small area and console ourselves with the thought that we aren't doing much damage in the world. On the other hand we can learn to represent ourselves as competent, considerate, and cooperative and thus win the approval of the people whose affection we seek. We can learn to give useful and accurate information, supporting our arguments and opinions with proofs that appeal to others. We can make ourselves interesting and entertaining. In short we can control how much influence we have.

BEING AN EFFECTIVE SPEAKER

If you can keep your own interests in mind and take into account other people's interests, you will have rewarding relationships. If you can respond to directions and orders and demonstrate your skill and competency, you will have success on the job. If you demand or bribe or wheedle or whine or cry, you may get temporary results but you will soon be rejected. If you do nothing at all, you will get no response.

Recently there have been a number of books published on how important it is to be selfish. These books are foolish and misleading. It is not wrong to think about what you want and need, but it is unwise to believe that you are going to get it just because you are you, without giving something up. Any success you have is going to be the result of a bargain, an exchange you make with another human being with whom you have developed a harmony of interests. We can only become effective when we discover that *our success depends on making others successful as well*.

Effective talk results when you can identify what you need from whom, followed by sensible decisions on your part about what to request. It is based on planning how to provide what others need in exchange for what you are seeking. Effective talk results from careful thought and action and has little to do with feelings, but communication economy demands that you call your shots and do not waste time trying for what you cannot get.

People often have prior commitments that interfere with them giving you what you want. You can do nothing about this. People are sometimes vicious, uncivil, inconsiderate, and exploitive. You can do nothing about this. Well, not quite—actually, what you can do about both sets of circumstances is to walk away. The man who seeks attention from a woman committed deeply to a career and the woman who attempts to attract a man totally dedicated to his mother each face eventual disappointment. Sometimes there is simply nothing you can do about the other person's priorities. It is imperative that you observe the facts and the substance of what is going on and pay no attention to your emotions.

Progress and success (in moderation) come to effective communicators. Effective communicators possess the following ten skills:

1. They can decide which of their needs to seek now and which to defer. They know what is impossible and they do not aim for it.
2. They can analyze situations and people and select the people most likely to respond.
3. They can get information about people to discover what to expect from them and what is necessary to do to get it.
4. They can analyze themselves for resources to exchange.
5. They can spot taboos and mandates in social situations.
6. They can set goals for their own behavior and separate them from feelings.
7. They profit from their own experience and that of others so that they can learn new skills and expand their repertoires of possible behaviors.
8. They are able to put words together so that they make sense to others.
9. They can respond to others, and they are not disappointed if they get less than they sought.
10. They are able to respect the rights of others, and they operate successfully and respectably.

When people cannot perform effectively, it is a deficiency of skill. In the following chapters we will offer you ways of acquiring the ten skills we have listed. Once you have acquired them, things will not be perfect for you. You will have to continue to be attentive to what is going on with other people and their needs. But you will no longer be shy. You will be a full participant in life, winning not all of them, but at least winning your share.

REFERENCES

1. Robert C. Carson, *Interaction Concepts of Personality* (Chicago: Aldine Press, 1969).
2. Sigmund Freud, "Papers on Techniques, the Dynamics of Transference," ed. James Strechey, standard ed., vol. 12 (London: Hogarth Press, 1953–74), pp. 97–108.
3. Stanton Peele, "Addiction: The Analgesic Experience," *Human Nature* 1: 9 (September 1978): 61–67.
4. See survey reported in Gerald M. Phillips and Nancy J. Metzger, *Intimate Communication*((Boston: Allyn and Bacon, 1976).
5. James Winans, *Speech Making* (New York: D. Appleton Century Co., 1938).

RECOMMENDED READINGS

Phillips and Metzger, *Intimate Communication*.
John Wilson and Carroll Arnold, *Public Speaking as a Liberal Art*. (Boston: Allyn & Bacon, Inc., 1977).
Mark Knapp, *Social Intercourse: From Greeting to Goodbye* (Boston: Allyn & Bacon, Inc., 1978).
Paul Watzlawick, Janet Beavin, and Don Jackson, *Pragmatics of Human Communication* (New York: W.W. Norton & Co., Inc., 1967).

chapter 7

How to Set Goals

The first step toward change is to decide when, where, and with whom you would like to make an effort. Experts set goals for themselves in particular situations so that they can show proper care in selection of things to say. They are so skilled that they do it rapidly, so that it appears to be effortless. To start, you must select one of the situations you discovered in your exercises in which you would like to show more skill. Select a simple situation at first, one that is not critical to you. It is helpful to list several situations and then rank them from least important to most important so that you have an idea of the stakes you are playing for in any given case.

Your best bet is to start with situations with which you are familiar and which do not involve you with total strangers. A great many books on overcoming shyness advise you to take risks with strangers. We caution you that you cannot count on the goodwill of others. It is our intent to help you acquire skill but we advocate doing so in small doses, a little at a time, until you are skilled enough to tackle major situations.

THE PRINCIPLES
OF GOALSETTING

Like most important tasks, goalsetting sounds simple at first. You will find it fairly easy to specify your goals, somewhat harder to plan strategies, and even more difficult to carry them out.

1. Select a person or persons with whom you want to accomplish something.
2. Select the situation (time and place) in which you plan to accomplish it.
3. Describe how things would be if you accomplished your goal. For example:
   a. I want to accomplish my goal with the teller at window 3 at the bank.
   b. I want to do it next Friday when I deposit my check.
   c. I want her to follow my instructions to the letter.

   or

   a. I want to accomplish my goal with Alice Barton.
   b. I want to do it on the phone Wednesday night between 8 and 9 P.M.
   c. I want her to say yes when I phone her and ask her out for Sunday.

   or

   a. I want to accomplish my goal at the supervisors' meeting next Tuesday.
   b. I want to do it with all of the supervisors.
   c. I want them to sit and listen to my three-minute statement about a new in-basket routine.

The end product is the most important step because it tells you what you want from the other people. You must define exactly what you want to have happen, described in terms of behaviors and talk. Alice says yes, the teller does the task, the supervisors sit silently for three minutes. Statements such as "The clerk will cooperate," "Alice will be affectionate," or "My colleagues will respect me" are not useful because you have no way of knowing whether or not you accomplished them. The only guide you have to your success is your observation of what the other person does.

GOALSETTING EXERCISE

Here is an example of what we want you to do in this exercise:

Bill says, "I want to feel welcome at the party." We want to help Bill set goals properly, so we correct his goal statement to read: "I want to shake hands with at least three people within five minutes after I enter the room. I want to be standing in a conversational group right after I get my drink. I want the hostess to take me by the arm and introduce me to at least one person." Each of the three statements could now be coordinated with Bill's behavior. To accomplish the first, he could direct himself to move to three people. To accomplish the second, he needs to get his drink and move to a particular location. To accomplish the third, he needs to go to the hostess and ask her to introduce him to someone.

Take each of the following statements and help the person who made it by rewriting it into behaviors that can be observed. Don't worry for now about what the person would have to do to accomplish the goal. Just make sure the goal for the other person is a behavior, either action or talk.

- Sally says, "I want Gus to be more courteous when we are on a date."
- Elaine says, "I want the boss to pay attention when I talk."
- Ernie says, "I wish I had more self-confidence."
- Denise says, "I want to be an expert public speaker."
- Kurt says, "I want to be popular."

Produce three behavior statements to indicate accomplishment of each of the goals. Check them carefully to make sure you could see or hear the result from the person who is the target for the goal. For example, you can't hear "poise," but you can hear someone taking turns in a conversation by talking every three minutes.

Now take five of the goals from your own list and specify them in the form of three behaviors just like you did for the goals above.

THE DOABLE AND THE DESIRABLE

Once you have identified person, situation, and end behavior, you will be able to decide whether or not your goal is possible. Any goal that is not phrased in terms of behavior is not possible. You can't "be witty," but you can tell funny stories. You can't "be warm," but you can issue various greetings. You must evaluate the end behavior desired in order to decide whether or not you have a chance to succeed.

There are rules for buying and selling in a department store, and even though they are not written down in a manual, virtually everyone involved knows them. There are things that you can say, services that you can request, and protections against being cheated that you can use. But people who do not know how to ask for service usually do not receive it and end up empty-handed or with merchandise they do not really want.

Even a process as simple as walking down a public street is rule-bound. If you try to push against the crowd on the wrong side of the street, you risk a collision and someone's anger. People at parties have a common commitment to sharing time pleasantly, and if you spread gloom, other people will avoid you. So, in any situation it is important for you to know the common agreement on what is to be done and what you can expect from the other people present.

Some situations appear very complicated because the people in them have a great many options in the way they act. Options are fairly limited in the department store. However, at a party they are virtually unlimited, within whatever bounds of decency prevail in that social group. It is important at the outset to know what is unacceptable, what is undesirable, and what gets approval from others.

In a crowded department store you cannot stand in the middle of the floor and read a newspaper without risking anger from the other people there. You cannot just grab merchandise and leave without risking intervention by the law. You cannot take up a clerk's time with a discussion of the political situation. If you do not act in socially acceptable ways, you are either removed from the scene or you forfeit your chance to get what you want. At a social gathering if you cannot at least do the minimum of what everyone else is doing, you are ignored, you meet no one, and you have a miserable time.

Consider, for example, a business meeting at a company. Such a meeting brings colleagues together for the purpose of solving problems. It is important to appear competent at meetings like this, otherwise you may forfeit possible rewards, such as a raise in pay or a promotion. There are frequent breaks in the continuity of business, and during these breaks it is possible to make yourself socially desirable to your associates. Normally you do not try to socialize during business times, but it is generally all right to talk business during social times.

At business meetings it is also wise to discover who is in charge and what kinds of behavior are preferred. It is useful to know the punishments for inept behavior and what the boss sees as inept. If the boss likes "cool, analytical" people, then it is wise to do things that the boss will classify as "cool and analytical." If the boss enjoys a good argument, then raising arguments is productive, but if the boss likes unanimity, then you cannot regard it as profitable to rock the boat. We all have choices to make, within limits, about where we work and how we do our work, but we must know the consequences of our actions.

You need not go along with practices you do not approve. On the other hand, if you choose to attack the "establishment" at a company meeting, you may win applause from your fellow workers but you may also earn a "pink slip." If temporary approval from your colleagues is more important than economic security (or if you are independently wealthy), then your actions are warranted, but you must remember that applause is fickle, and once you leave the company, you sacrifice your opportunity to win rewards both from the establishment and from your fellow employees.

The distinguished sociologist David Riesman commented that Americans seem to have an "internal radar" that enables them to sense how others behave in public so that they can accommodate themselves to it.[1] Reticent people often lack this radar. Ernest Becker claimed that people are able to run "inner newsreels," in which they play out their own actions against those of others and anticipate responses.[2] If you are not accustomed to such controlled daydreaming, it may be necessary for you to learn to observe more effectively so that you can do realistic planning through some form of internal rehearsal. If you are able to imagine consequences realistically, your ability to set precise goals will improve.

AN EXERCISE

Think through your experiences in the following situations and list the kinds of behaviors that got rewarded and those that got punished. Describe the reward and the punishment (in terms of behaviors or tangible benefits, i.e., a kind word, an epithet, a bonus, etc.). For the moment do not concentrate on your own behavior. Think instead of the people whom you have seen act in ways you have classified as successful or unsuccessful. You can think of the behaviors *you* must see in order to attach those labels.

For example, at a cocktail party where most of the people are strangers to one another the reward is having people talk to you and the punishment is standing alone. The behavior that gets rewarded is going to people, greeting them, and shaking hands. The behavior that gets punished is silence. Perform the same kind of analysis with the following situations:

- A blind date where neither party knows the other
- The first day on a new job
- Presenting merchandise to be returned to the adjustment department of a store
- A public meeting devoted to discussion and debate of a controversial issue

Add some situations of your own that you are likely to experience. Be sure you describe both successful and unsuccessful behavior.

PRELIMINARY ANALYSIS

If you could identify rules about what successful and unsuccessful behavior looks like and what happens as a result, you would be able to decide what you can accomplish in some simple social situations. In trying to figure out the regularities, keep your eyes and ears on the action. Once you have decided what the rewards and punishments are, don't evaluate them. Concentrate on items such as Bill speaks loudly, Susan walks away, Charlie speaks softly, Tom stays close by, Karen shakes hands, Tom offers food to others, and so on. It will not take you long to find out what the "norms" are. From these generalizations you can develop rules.

- Susan responds in a quiet voice, and the host continues talking to her. (How would my voice be classified? What request could I make?)

- Sarah does not speak when the others are talking about sports. (If I want Sarah to talk to me, should I avoid the topic of sports?)
- My husband seems to change the subject when I try to discuss finances when the kids are in the room. (Should I bring up financial business after the kids go to bed?)

Public situations such as work, shopping, or cocktail parties are relatively easy to figure out because there are, at least, some limits on the possibilities of public behavior. Private and intimate situations are a good deal more difficult to understand.

Friends and couples work out their own rules and roles. If you fail to participate in the process, then you must act according to the rules the other person made if you want to maintain the relationship. Once you give in and concede to the other person the right to make the rules, you sacrifice the opportunity to participate in future decision making. Many divorces have their start when the quiet member of the couple suddenly insists on rights in the decision making.

In order to begin the process of goalsetting, follow the example of a preliminary goal analysis:

- I want "speedy and efficient" service at the store!
- By "speedy and efficient," I mean   (describe the behavior you seek)
- To get this, I must do the following   (describe your actions)
- And I must not do the following   (state what you will avoid doing).

For example, "speedy and efficient" means that the clerk will greet me in turn, give me undivided attention when it is my turn, and do what I specify.

The "I must do" could include the following:

- I will position myself where the clerk can see me.
- I will greet the clerk with a nod.
- When it is my turn, I will begin to speak by stating my request.
- My request will be explicit. "I would like to see the shirt there in the case." I will point to it.
- I will ask what sizes it comes in.
  And so on.

The "I must not do" could include the following:

- I will make no personal comments to the clerk.
- I will not demand special privilege by asking for service before it is my turn.

See what you can do to clarify the following goals:

- I want to expand the number of activities my friend and I engage in.
  I want to demonstrate my skill at the process to my boss.
  I want to talk at the next neighborhood improvement group meeting.
- I want to meet three new people at the party I am attending Friday.

In each case specify what the desired behavior looks like, provide at least two behaviors the person seeking the goal could do, and list at least two forbidden behaviors.

Here are some questions about goals commonly offered by reticent people. See what kind of answer you could give to each.

1. How do you get your doctor to spend five more minutes listening to you talk about your symptoms?
2. How do you get a waiter to speed up the service at a restaurant?
3. How do you get a colleague on the job to listen to your advice?
4. How do you get your colleagues to listen to you tell a joke at a coffee break?
5. How do you meet at least two eligible people of the opposite sex at a cocktail party?
6. How do you talk your way out of going to your mother-in-law's for Thanksgiving dinner (without alienating your spouse and kids)?
7. How do you explain your ideas to someone who liked a movie that you hated?

You can add some of your own goals to the list.

Now here are some sample answers: To get more efficient service from a waiter in a restaurant, I will ask the waiter for his advice about two items on the menu; I would ask what a particular dish was made of and I would ask how often it was ordered; I would ask which dish the chef enjoyed making; I would ask the waiter what he would order. To suggest a new activity to a friend, I would ask on the phone if he or she had any ideas about something different to do Saturday; I would be prepared to agree if any suggestions were made; I would offer two good reasons for liking the idea; if no suggestion was made, I would suggest (list what you would suggest). To show the boss how well I am doing on the job, I would prepare a two-minute statement describing three things I had done to perform the job more efficiently and I would ask if he wanted me to suggest these to other workers as well.

To modify the way you talk it is important that while working out behavior changes you keep your emotions under control. You may show emotion that appears to respond to the other person. You may smile, nod, or in other ways suit your facial expression to the attitude you wish to express about what you just heard. Concentrate on offering responsive emotions. Keep in mind that emotions are undifferentiated and have no particular meaning until you assign meaning to them. Thus if you demand that your emotion be a response to the other person, your tensions will support you and make you more effective. You may use this premise to understand how the other person is responding to you. You cannot really tell what a particular facial expression means until you have known the person for some time, but there are polite conventions that will tell whether or not you are receiving attention. You should be able to see the other person's eyes; he or she should not yawn; there should be some flicker of upward motion of the lips if you say something that could be construed as humorous, and so on. But you must also keep in mind that it is characteristic of shy people not to respond, so in any given case if you think you are receiving no response, it may well be that your respondent is shy and would like to respond but cannot. By attending carefully to the facial expressions and physical responses of other people, you will, as you get to know them, be able to find a barometer of your own effectiveness. By the same token, if you understand that people need this kind of support and reinforcement from others, you will make a conscious effort to suit your responses to your attitudes about what the other person is saying in order to encourage communication.

Remember that we are operating from a rhetorical model, which emphasizes the uniqueness of the individual case. For this reason, you must be careful about the generalizations you make, both about your success and about your failure. Cases that look alike may not require the same action on your part. As you build your repertoire of behaviors, you will have more options from which to choose, which in turn will improve your chances of success, but there will never be *one way* that will work in all cases. For this reason, when you succeed, you know that success is possible, and when you fail, you know that failure is not inevitable. One authority advises shooting for about a 51 percent success ratio.[3] Anything beyond that is gravy, anything below it is not hopeless.

TESTING GOAL STATEMENTS

The test of a goal statement is whether or not it is phrased entirely in behaviors. You need to describe what you will do and what you consider an acceptable response. You cannot set goals for the other person, nor can you do anything about his or her attitudes and feelings. Each person has the right to decide how he or she will respond. The best you can do is to discover what it is reasonable to expect and try to get that response.

Everyone gets refused from time to time, and it happens to the best speaker more than you would expect. If the other person does not respond the way you want, it is not the end of the world. It means that you must rethink the situation and revise your own behavior accordingly. If you do not get a desirable response, check to discover whether your expectations were reasonable, whether you had a satisfactory plan, and whether you carried it out well. If you expected too much, you can alter your goals. If your plan did not work, your failure will provide more data, which will lead to a more effective plan. Remember that there are a good many reasons why other people may not behave the way you desire:

- They may not want to because they have something else on their mind.
- They may not be able to because they are encumbered with other relationships.
- They may not understand what it is you want.
- They may be so involved with their own goalseeking that they are not paying attention.

Whatever the reason, you *can* control your own behavior, and so you should be able to respond in a way that is satisfactory to yourself, whatever response you get. You are the one judging your behavior.

When you think about the behavior you want from yourself, ask how you would know the behavior if someone else did it well. Sometimes we lose sight of the fact that individual human experience is the source of first-rate generalizations. If you have observed other people act and you can describe your actions, you can use the actions you approve of as guides to your own behavior. Remember, you can't "be charming," but you can smile throughout someone's comments to you. There are really only a limited number of ways people can behave in social situations. Those who violate norms usually suffer the consequences.

When you describe what other people do, attend also to what their audience does. For example, "they ask the storyteller questions while she is talking." But don't go too far beyond the description. It is all right to think, "Because they ask her questions, it helps her tell the story. Could it be that the way she tells the story persuades them to ask her questions? I will look further." As you observe her behavior, you notice that she pauses slightly at particular places in the story and looks directly at individuals who are listening. Her glance seems to impel them to ask her what happened next. By getting her listeners to ask the questions, she persuades them that she is telling the story because they want it.

Goalsetting becomes excessively complicated if you think about too many options. Most situations, however complicated they may appear, may be divided into several simple scenes. Take one scene at a time and work on your behavior. You will only frustrate yourself if you seek global changes. Stay within the limits of what is possible in a given scene. For example, if your eventual goal is to become "more effective" at casual social gatherings, you may have to divide "more effective" into "meeting strangers," "carrying on conversations," "excusing myself," "asking for further contact." By dividing one goal into four components you can gradually introduce yourself to overall effectiveness by building on individually effective acts. Keep in mind that your aduience will never have *your* interests uppermost in their minds.

Of course, there are always people with whom you can never succeed. You must prepare yourself to accept this fact of life. People who succeed have the ability to fail. They have the courage to face the prospect of things not going well. Social rejections are not intrinsically wrong.

They are opportunities, in one sense to try harder, in another sense to learn something about the range of human behaviors.

TARGETING YOUR GOAL

In phrasing goal statements you must be sure you are addressing the correct person. This is particularly important when you are making requests of people who are in socially defined roles. For example, if you want a refund for defective merchandise, the clerk who sold it to you may not be the proper person to address.

I will approach the clerk and ask if he has the authority to deal with complaints. If he says he does not, I will ask who does. If he says he does not know, I will ask for the manager. If the clerk will not provide the information, I will ask another employee. If I get no satisfaction, I will approach the Better Business Bureau of the Chamber of Commerce. If this does not work, I will seek help from the law.

Notice how many alternatives have been considered in this statement. Goalsetting involves the construction of simple but careful scenarios that account for major possibilities and prepare you to respond to whatever happens.

If you have to speak to a group, your alternatives may be expressed like this:

In preparing my report I will emphasize the ideas that Smedley and Hopkins have endorsed, although I will not mention them by name. I will be careful not to attack any of the ideas that Hoople and Dinwiddie have supported. I know the kinds of questions Greenstone and Whipple are likely to ask, and I will try to offer the information in the presentation so that I reduce the risk of interruption. Clark is a new man, and I haven't the vaguest notion of what he might do, but I guess I will find out.

This kind of statement presupposes a fairly sophisticated knowledge of the situation and the people in it but one that is not unreasonable to expect if you have been working with these people for a while. If you are new in a company, you may have to wait to accumulate some data about what you can expect before you make your move. But you can't afford to wait too long. You must have a schedule for action and go ahead with the data you have. Your shyness may have paralyzed you before simply because you did not want to act with what you considered insufficient information. The truth is that there is no other way to act, since it is never possible to get all the information.

As you observe the behavior of others and figure out how they respond to what, you must take care to avoid the risk of "getting along by going along." When we advise you to analyze the situation and the people in it when setting your goals, we do not mean that you should revise your goals so that they will bring instant approval from others. If you do this, you will find yourself representing points of view that are repugnant to you. The important thing is that you adapt what you say to accommodate yourself to others *so that you can maximize the chance that they will agree with you.* You cannot let your urgency to get approval corrupt your ethical standards, nor can you back off from saying what you believe because it might offend someone, even someone you like. It is this kind of courage that must be developed if you are to overcome your shyness, but it is not so difficult to do if you concentrate on facts and behaviors, not on interpersonal dynamics. Sometimes people are amazed to discover that they win considerable respect by standing up for what they believe, much more than they win simply by agreeing in order to get approval.

Furthermore, you do not need to cope with every situation. No one does and no one can. You must understand your limits. You may have to struggle to master techniques in particular situations that you must experience, such as those on the job or with the people you care most about, but if this kind of socializing or that annoys you and there is no obvious benefit in it for you, you are within your rights as a human being simply to say, "I don't enjoy that sort of thing and I needn't worry about it." By making the admission honestly to yourself, you are able to help yourself do without whatever minor but seductive benefit may be lurking in the situation.

It is useful to contemplate both the best and the worst that can come in a situation. You may discover that the best is not worth going after and the worst is not so hard to bear. You may discover that the best is quite desirable, worthy of your best efforts, or that the worst is so dreadful that it isn't worth the risk. You make your own choices. The point is, once you have some skill, your choices of success are sufficiently improved so that you will discover that you have more of an advantage from participating in more situations.

GOALS AND OBJECTIVES

It is all right to have general goals. If you have ever written a federal grant application, you know that they call for both "goals" and "objectives." They define a goal as an overall statement of what is to be accomplished, and objectives as specific accomplishments on the way to the grand goal. For our purposes it makes more sense to talk about general and specific goals or long- and short-range goals. To have a general or long-range goal means that you must have associated short-term or specific goals. For example, the following would be an effective long-range goal:

I am new in this town. By this time next year I want to be in a social group.

The general goal might be phrased as follows:

I want to develop relationships with at least three people whom I see at least once a week for recreation or whom I can call up frequently for social conversation.

These statements can be adjusted to fit developments. For example, you might meet two people who are all that you can manage, or you may suddenly find yourself in a group of six or seven people. Broad, long-term goals can be reduced to specific and immediate statements like

I am going to a cocktail party Saturday afternoon and I want to find at least one person of either sex who is willing to talk to me for ten minutes about anything at all. If this happens, I will try to arrange a dinner date with him or her during the week.

Immediate choices can be made once you are at the party. For example, the hostess identifies someone to you as a friend of hers and asks if you want to meet him. You are willing to accept the hostess's references, so you agree. The short-term goal would look like this:

I will talk to the guy in the blue suit, after the hostess introduces me to him, for ten minutes. I will introduce two topics: What can a new gal in town do for recreation after work? And where can I find a good dentist? I will be able to make conversation about most recreation suggestions (because I go to movies and plays and am familiar with football and baseball) and I really do need a dentist. I will try to figure out whether there is potential for a future relationship, and if there is, I will suggest getting together for dinner, dutch treat.

Notice how the goalsetter is protecting herself. She has control over what will be an acceptable contact with the new man. She has provided a variety of escape hatches for herself and she is making her approach to someone who is known to the hostess, under the presumption that the hostess is not likely to know rapists and molesters. Self-protection is important in goalsetting. You must anticipate and be prepared for possible dangerous or "sticky" situations, and you must allow yourself ways to escape from a contact that you find unpleasant. It is better to do this early in the relationship, before you are pulled into a regular socializing routine. In the next chapter we will deal with assessment of situations to understand their potential.

Your overall goal need not mention specific behaviors, but it should specify an end state. "I want some friends" is not specific enough. You should provide a number and should specify the type—"same sex," "potential lovers," or whatever. People can set a goal to graduate from college but they cannot set a goal to "be educated." They can decide to invite five people to a party, but they cannot decide to "enjoy" themselves. To avoid these kinds of paradox, at some point you must deal with "empirical" data, that is, data you can see, count, and describe physically.

We have already noted that it is helpful not to name your feelings until you have some reason to give them a positive name. Before the fact you must concentrate on action. After the fact you may say to yourself, "I was nervous, but I did it anyway, wow!" or "I think I really did sound warm and encouraging when I talked to Gus." When you use "warm and encouraging" in this fashion, you are using these words properly, as adjectives describing and evaluating your behavior, and you are in no danger of misinterpreting them as things to be sought.

If you tell yourself you are nervous before you act, you have provided yourself with an excuse not to act. If you set out to be warm and courteous, you set yourself up for failure. Furthermore, if you do not have empirical directions for yourself, you may not say what you want to say, you may forget, you may do any number of things precisely as you have already been doing them.

Adjectives are customarily used after the fact to display critical judgment. If someone tells you something and you believe it, you may call the person "credible." By using the adjective you are expressing your opinion, and you know it. When you change *credible* to *credibility* and start looking for it for yourself, you will never know when you have found it. If you want to appear "credible" to others, then you must practice behavior that you think will earn you the evaluation if other people see it.

The basic principle of goalsetting is to start with small goals and raise your chances of success by actually succeeding. By building on success you will be able to take on increasingly more complicated situations. The more you try, the more you will accomplish. The more you accomplish, the more alternative behaviors you will have at your disposal and the more likely will be your chances of success at major goals.

GOALSETTING EXERCISES

Now try your hand at setting some specific goals. Following are some stated goals taken from initial interviews with shy people in the Reticence Program. Take each of the italicized words and phrases and describe the end-state behavior of the "audience" that would lead them to use the phrase on you. Then identify five situations in which *you* might try to accomplish the goal.

- Getting *satisfaction* when dealing with store clerks and waiters.
- Making new friends *to enjoy time* with.
- Getting the boss *to see you as a productive* employee.
- Being *more effective* in arguments with your loved ones.
- Getting *to know* some of your neighbors.
- Getting *cooperation* from your fellow workers.
- Making yourself *clear* to a professional person (doctor or lawyer).

Following is a list of words taken from those same interviews. They are words that might describe the kind of person who could accomplish the goals above. For each word, describe precisely how a person would have to behave in order to persuade you to apply that word to his or her behavior.

Poised   Friendly   Spontaneous   Warm   Considerate
Helpful   Encouraging   Confident   Witty   Competent
Creative   Incisive   Affectionate   Interesting   Exciting
Cooperative

It reads like the objectives for the Boy Scouts or Girl Scouts. Struggling through them will be a final check on you before you complete your own goalsetting. There follows a master format for goalsetting. Answer all of the questions for each goal you want to accomplish. Take up to ten goals from the lists you have worked up for previous exercises and fill out a format sheet for each of them. Then put them in order from least to most important. You will start with the least important goal.

Be sure to give precise answers to each of the questions. The following two chapters will deal with ways and means to carry out goals in general. The remainder of the book will be devoted to a discussion of goalsetting in particular types of settings by specific kinds of individuals. Take your time with this exercise because it will be your guide to overcoming shyness. You will keep these forms around throughout your efforts to change. When you learn to use this form effectively, you can apply it to the new situations you encounter in your life. Remember that it is not a guarantee of success, but rather a way of preventing failure. When you have had a good deal of experience, the format will be almost automatic for you in most situations.

SETTING A GOAL

(When you answer these questions, use as much space as you need to be specific.)

1. Write your goal in a single, simple declarative sentence, for example, "I want to go in to see my boss and ask him three questions."

---

2. Success is measured by the response of the other. State how you would know success when you try to accomplish your goal, for example, "The boss will answer two of the three questions."

---

3. To accomplish a goal, you must understand your listener. You can do this by answering the following questions:
   Who will be listening? (name) _____
   (position) _____
   Why is this person important to you? _____
   What reason will you give this person for listening to you? _____
   Why is this reason important to him or her? _____
   What will you gain if this person listens to you? _____
   Why is this important to you? _____
   Where will you be when you try to realize your goal? _____
   Anything special you must do because you are there? _____
   Anything special you should avoid doing because you are there?
   _____

4. You should be prepared with the ideas you want to say. List the topics you intend to cover when you talk to this person. List them in order.

   _____

   _____

   What will you say to start? _____
   What will you say when you are done? _____

5. You should be prepared for responses from your listener. You can do this by answering the following questions:
   What questions might the person to whom you are speaking ask you? How would you answer them? _____

   _____

   What is the best thing that could happen? What would you do if it happened?

   _____

   What is the worst thing that could happen? What would you do if it happened?

   _____

   What is most likely to happen? What will you do if it happens?

   _____

   You can regard yourself as a success, regardless of what the other person does, if you respond to his or her response as planned. Remember that you can never take more than 50 percent of the blame if talk with others does not work out.

6. Now list the steps you will take in planning and executing your action to reach your goal.

    1. _____

    2. _____

    3. _____

    4. _____

7. NAME YOUR DEADLINE!!! I will carry out this plan on _____
   at approximately _____ o'clock.

You may have to wait until you read the next two chapters before you can handle all of the details of this form well, but try to fill it out now anyway and keep your sheets so that you can edit them later on. You may even want to type out this form and have it duplicated so that you can use it whenever you face a new situation.

REFERENCES

1. David Riesman, *The Lonely Crowd* (Garden City, N.Y.: Doubleday & Co., Inc., 1950).
2. Ernest Becker, *The Birth and Death of Meaning* (New York: The Free Press, 1962).
3. Philip Slater, *The Pursuit of Loneliness* (Boston: The Beacon Press, 1970).

RECOMMENDED READINGS

Robert Mager, *Goal Analysis* (Belmont, Calif.: Fearon-Pitman Publishers, Inc., 1972).

Robert Mager and Peter Pipe, *Analysis of Performance Problems* (Belmont, Calif.: Fearon-Pitman Publishers, Inc., 1970).

Robert Mager, *Developing Attitudes toward Learning* (Belmont, Calif.: Fearon-Pitman Publishers, Inc., 1968).

chapter 8

Analyzing Situations

There are no rules that govern all social interactions. Each person must adapt his or her behavior to that of the other person. The most important thing to remember is that no relationship succeeds unless each party considers the needs of the other. The contemporary trend to look out for Number One must be changed to consider Number Two. When a relationship works, it is because two people are doing it together. Here's what we can gain in a good working relationship.

- We can spend time pleasantly.
- We can ask for information or provide it.
- We can request amusement or provide it.
- We can offer advice or ask for some.
- We can offer comfort or ask for some.
- We can exchange opinions and evaluations.
- We can argue.
- We can feel good because the other person is around.

- We can, in certain cases, do some touching and stroking.
- We can, in certain cases, be sexually involved (as opposed to sexually active).

Successful relationships are built on exchange.[1] We assume that if people stay in a relationship, they are getting more out of it than they think they will get from an alternative one. This, however, is not always the case. There are some people who cling to relationships even though they are intimidated, exploited, harassed, and hurt emotionally and physically. They may not know how to get out of the relationship.

Thus successful relationships occur when both parties agree to be together because they can gain something by being together. We can be together in a variety of ways and on different levels, depending on our needs. We choose our associates and they choose us because of the "pleasure" we can provide. Even on the job, where we have no apparent choice in the selection of the people who work next to us, we can decide on how close the contact should be and the extent to which we want to go beyond what is absolutely required by the nature of the job. By understanding that choices are possible, we can think about the situations in which we find ourselves and want to find ourselves.

- We have some people with whom it is pleasant to pass time. We tell stories and check out our attitudes on recreations and cultural matters, restaurants and stores, and we tell jokes.
- We have some people with whom we can carry on serious conversations about important issues, such as politics, religion, social justice, personal ethics, and other matters that transcend recreation.
- We have some people with whom we can exchange confidences. We can discuss our frustrations, sorrows, and defeats as well as our triumphs and our joys.
- We have some people whom we can count on for help in time of trouble.
- We have some people with whom we share a common vocational commitment.
- There are people with whom we are acquainted sufficiently so that when we are together, it is not painful. These represent a pool of potential friends.
- There are people with whom we must compete. Some of them may be unethical about their strategies. From this pool comes potential enemies.
- Finally there are those with whom we have formed "twos"—our

mates and lovers, our parents and children, our siblings, various relatives, and those few good friends for whom our affection is very deep.

Recently a group of sociologists have taken a hard-headed look at human relationships. They have come up with an idea called equity theory.[2] It is a very simple notion. It says that people are satisfied with their relationships to the extent that they believe they are getting out about as much as they are putting in. It doesn't matter what level the relationship operates on. If your agreement is to share time pleasantly and one person becomes too somber or depressing, the relationship is broken.

There are some people, mostly shy people, who do not fit this rule. For them the fact of relationship is more important than the empirical details connected with it. This is part of the "battered wife" syndrome. It is why people cling to relationships that to outside observers hold no possibility of reward. Shy people form these relationships on all levels. They will often socialize with a clique whose members insult and ignore them. They will stay with a mate long after the mate has given every sign that the relationship has been terminated. People who get into this situation can easily become alienated and often become depressed.

Shyness or reticence comes about when you feel that you cannot seek equity in your relationships. To overcome shyness you must learn to manage each relationship so that you get your fair share.

GETTING ACQUAINTED

When people first meet, they have two goals in common. The first is to make the time together as comfortable as possible. The second is to discover what "use" might be made of the other person. The word *use* is perfectly appropriate. People are not obligated to relate to each other except on a basic social level of courtesy and politeness. One person need not get into a relationship just because the other person wants to relate. Before people decide to relate to each other on any level, they ought to try to figure out what the possibilities are in a relationship. That is why people make small talk. It fills time decently while such an assessment is being made.

Most people start relationships without thinking very much about them. They react to requests from the other person. Sometimes we are flattered because someone is seeking our attention. Sometimes we are so much in need of a relationship that we accept anything that comes along. If someone smiles, we regard it as an invitation to come close. An initial kind word is seen as a promise of more kind words to come. When someone frowns, we are rejected, wounded, ready to crawl back into the hutch. There are two dangerous possibilities here. The first is that by reacting to initial kindness or come-on we risk relating to someone who may injure us. The second danger is that if we react too strongly to a serious face, we run the risk of not having a relationship with a very desirable person. The point is that initial manner and facial expressions cannot be construed as promises of what is to come. Shy people, for example, really are not able to provide the kind of encouragement to others that more outgoing people can. As a result, very decent shy people are often passed over in favor of superficial relaters who have skill in welcoming newcomers. Furthermore, any person you meet may be reacting to more than just you as a person. A sour stomach, a headache, or a bad day can wipe the smile off a person's face without impairing essential decency. We also suggested earlier that your initial reactions are very likely to be the result of transference.

The intricate pattern of meeting and greeting that is characteristic of American middle-class society is designed to give people an opportunity to make mutual choices. It is perhaps the most important step you can take toward overcoming shyness to begin to participate in the selection process that goes on at social gatherings when you meet people for the first time.

Formal socializing is a safe way to meet and greet people. Proportionately there are not that many dangerous people around, but the opportunity to meet in a public place first is important, for meeting in private carries a presumption that may not be warranted. Cocktail parties and similar gatherings give you an opportunity to make a brief contact, exchange a few words, separate, think it over, try again, explore, decide to do or not to do. They also spare you the pain of rejection, since it is the norm to meet briefly and then move on.

The idea of getting people to give information about themselves in a limited way is intrinsic in social training systems. The Dale Carnegie method, for example, advises you to ask questions about the other person, not intimate questions about personal feelings, sorrows, miseries, and woes, but simple questions about occupation, hometown, marital status, recreational choices. This provides you with the kind of information that might help you decide whether or not the relationship is worth moving up to the next level of attempting light recreation together. It gives you some information with which to start. It is also an experiment: If you give the other person a chance to talk about himself or herself, will that person give you the same courtesy?

Some of us are so eager to talk about ourselves that we forget how boring it is to listen to others talk about themselves. We come on to the other person as though he or she owes us an audience. When the other person makes a polite excuse and moves away, we are hurt. None of this needs to happen if you understand the basic rule for first meetings: *If you can't take turns talking about yourselves, then there may be no point in continuing to talk.* The corollary to that rule is never to take anything that happens at a first meeting too seriously. If someone seems unpleasant, step back and consider the possibility that the person is not reacting to you. Try again later. If the other person is highly complimentary, consider the possibility that this is a style of relations. Step back and watch that person's performance with others. If it looks like you got a warmer welcome than others did, then you can go back again. If someone says, "We ought to get together sometime," don't whip out your date book, for it is merely a polite closing line. And if someone offers a time and place, don't feel you must accept or accept on the terms offered if you don't want to.

LEARN TO USE CLICHÉS

A great deal of what gets said at initial meetings is cliché. Much of the conduct of our daily lives depends on cliché. While the stakes and personnel of each situation are unique, the circumstances and possibilities are not. Thus we can perfect a few socially acceptable statements that we can use wherever and whenever other people are using them. We don't have to concentrate on what we are saying, and we can attend to being polite and to reacting to the other. In a sense our actual words do not matter here, but the way we say them does. We all understand, for example, that the question "How are you?" asked anywhere but in the doctor's office does not mean that you are entitled to recite your symptoms but rather you are to answer in kind. Even if your doctor meets you at a social gathering and asks how you are, you may not respond with literal details. If you do, he or she may send you a bill. The question "What's new?" does not call for a detailed explanation of the duties of your new job, although it might warrant a very terse "I started my new job last week." If the other person wants to draw you out, you may be asked for more information. You have the same prerogative. Any cliché lines can be used either to keep the socializing casual or to extend it a bit. And if things don't seem to be working out, you can excuse yourself for another cookie or another drink (that's why they have refreshments).

If it should happen that you meet someone with whom you want to exchange more than small talk and that person seems to want to do the same, you can adjourn to a corner of the room. You can stand face to face and concentrate on each other so that no one else joins your group, or you can go down to the coffee shop or the soda fountain where you can be alone (but in public) and continue the discussion. Until you are sure of your moves, it is probably not a good idea to adjourn to a private place at first meeting. This is true not only of opposite-sex relationships but of same-sex relationships. If you are in a public place drinking a cup of coffee or eating a dish of ice cream, you have something to do if things do not work out. Just because you left together does not mean you are obligated to stay together. You can finish your refreshment and go back if the conversation wears thin. If, however, you elect to go to a private place, you are stuck with each other's company until one party can figure out how to end the thing graciously. And, of course, if you are with someone of the opposite sex, being alone is commonly seen as an invitation to physical intimacy. If this is not your intent, it is wise to avoid the suggestion.

Thus the first step in the analysis of any situation is to discover the appropriate clichés. Once you have mastered the cliché, you can concentrate on the second component of analysis: Is there anyone here with whom I would want to work out a more defined relationship? The third step is to discover whether that person is willing and able. The fourth step is to figure out how to proceed. Once you have decided to go beyond small talk, you are involved in a purposive relationship.

UNDERSTANDING PURPOSEFUL SITUATIONS

Once you have decided that it might be pleasant or useful to have a relationship with another person (or you have accepted the other person's invitation), you need to take a serious look at what is possible. In the first place you must remember that each of you may have a different stake. If there is a disparity in the amount of value assigned to the relationship, there is the possibility for considerable unpleasantness. You may be seeking a companion for enjoyable events. The other person may want a more serious relationship. An important element of your analysis is to try to discover what goals the other person has for the relationship. If you simply go along, you may find yourself exploited, participating on a level that you did not choose simply because you did not question the moves.

The most important consideration is what you stand to gain or lose. You can discover what you can gain by examining your present relationships to see what you need and what you have time and energy for. Next you can figure out to what degree you want what the other person is offering and, more important, what you have to offer back in order to get it. Your data will be primarily inferential, since it is gauche and unproductive to ask explicitly. You need to study behavior and draw conclusions. If, for example, someone you met goes to lunch with you and then proceeds to call you every night trying to arrange more social contacts, you may decide that he or she needs more than you are able to provide. If the other person accepts an invitation from you but does not extend one back, you might conclude that you were not providing what the other person was looking for. You need not be afraid to examine relationships this way. Before you did this kind of analysis, you may have felt rejected as a person when the other did not want to do what you had suggested. If, on the other hand, you see both parties in terms of a cost-benefit analysis, you can understand that the other person may have decided not to continue with you for reasons that are very good, that is, inability to provide what you are seeking. If you are looking for a best friend and the other person already has one, there is no reason to continue. If, on the other hand, it appears that both of you, at least at the moment, are seeking casual socializing, it may be worthwhile to continue. You can decide whether you want to go on to another level later on. Most of us have a few friends with whom we socialize from time to time and with whom we do no other serious business.

Every decision you make about what to do or say with another person is based on a hypothesis. You cannot know for sure what the other person is after. It may well be that the other person is not sure either. You are learning a system of personal analysis that the other person may not know. Most people go through the early stages of relationship by trial and error. They do not think about possibilities until, very often, it is too late. It is precisely that situation you are trying to avoid by doing this analysis.

As you observe and listen to the other person, you can make some guesses about the effect of your behavior. In this way you are acting very much like a scientist doing an experiment. If the scientist knew exactly how the experiment would come out, she might not need to do it. On the other hand, she has a reasonably good idea of the possibilities, otherwise she would not take the risk. In essence, you must operate from the same premise.

If you get into a discussion with someone at a cocktail party about where the two of you can go together, it is safe to hypothesize that the other person is looking for a companion of some sort. If you suggest a date and the other person proposes an alternative date, then you may conclude that the only thing that separates you is convenience. If the other person seems to back away from concrete suggestions, it is very likely that he or she was merely being polite in the first place. Willingness to negotiate for future contact is a sign of interest. Phrasing invitations in general terms is a sign of lack of interest. When this happens, your best hypothesis is that you would enjoy a drink and a chat with someone else.

Initially you act on limited information, and there is always a reasonable chance that you will be incorrect. Shy people generally cannot accommodate themselves to being incorrect. They are either frustrated by the ambiguity in situations or they distort situations to fit their idea of what ought to be happening. If they are in a "success oriented" mood, they may interpret rejection as acceptance and make foolish commitments. If they are in a "failure oriented" mood, they may completely ignore positive signs in order to confirm their prophecy of disaster. Consider the vast number of people who pass through your life with whom you form no relationship at all and you will get an idea of how complicated and unpredictable relationship building is. Reticent people often try to classify themselves as failures when they try once and it doesn't work out. But there is no way to know what moves will work at the inception of a relationship. Attempts at prediction are foolish until you have more information. And you acquire information by using clichés within the accepted social framework until you have some data you can work with.

It is most important to discover whether the other person is available for contact. Sometimes we forget that other people have been living lives without us for a long time. We assume that everyone is free to pursue a relationship with every interesting person who comes along. This is not so. If people have obligations and commitments, they might not even notice our overtures, or even worse, they might misinterpret them as unfortunate boldness or presumption. Discreet inquiry during the preliminary stages of a conversation will usually elicit the important information you want. Prior commitments may not always entail other relationships. Someone who is heavily involved with a job, with political commitments, with heavy social obligations, or most important, someone who has no particular urgency to acquire a friend does not make a good risk for a relationship, and there is no point in being anything more than polite and grateful for whatever enjoyment you may have had with the brief contact.

You must also inquire into the moves other people make toward you. If they offer opinions, are you required to discuss or agree or merely to listen? What would agreement cost you? Do they want information? Do you have it to give? Do they give any cues at all that they might be interested in future contact? What are those cues? Is there some kind of service implied, such as a request to be driven home? If there is no move at all in your direction, it might be a waste of time to continue to try to make contact. It is always possible, of course, that they may be shy also.

Once you have decided to try to further the relationship, you need to figure out some possible places where it could continue. It is relatively simple with business contacts. Once you discover a common economic interest, you can negotiate an appointment during working hours. That can be done quite directly. Developing a social relationship is somewhat more difficult, since there is no necessary common connection. In business the desire to succeed leads people to inquire about the possibility of mutual benefit through collaboration, which, in turn, leads to contact. The situation is not at all as clear in purely social contacts.

A premature move could jeopardize the relationship at the beginning. If you invite the other person to some kind of event, it should be an event that the other person approves of. If you invite a relative stranger to your home, there is some suspicion of prematurity. If you invite the other person to a restaurant, there is the small problem of financial contingencies, for there is often considerable awkwardness in figuring out who pays the check. If you say, "Join me for dinner" you might mean, "Be my guest for dinner" or "Let's go to dinner separately together." Your invitation should be specific. "I have two tickets. Would you like to come with me." "May I take you to dinner?" "How about a dutch-treat lunch on Tuesday?" are examples of explicit invitations.

Disclosure is another issue to consider in the early stages of a relationship. It is important to display caution in the information you give out. It is all right to tell someone where you work and what you do, but you needn't spill all the details of the tenuous relationship you are having with your colleague at the next desk. You may tell someone that you are legally separated from your mate, but you needn't describe the whole sordid affair. This kind of information is important to the other person, who has to make a decision about whether or not you are eligible for contact. But if it goes beyond that at an initial meeting, it may mean that the person is seeking greater intimacy than you are able to give. If you give too much information, you may suggest that you want intimacy and you may find yourself rejected or worse, accepted by someone who regards your invitation as meaning much more than you intended.

There are some basic assumptions about the nature of socializing human beings that you can use to guide you on whether or not to go on with a relationship with someone you have just met and are having a conversation with.

- You can assume that people enjoy smiles and kind words so long as they do not appear effusive, patronizing, or sycophantic.
- You can assume that people want a chance to say something about themselves.
- You can assume that everyone could use at least one more casual friend with whom he or she could chat or socialize from time to time.
- You can assume that virtually all people enjoy hearing something they never heard before that appeals to their interests or needs.

It is safe to make these assumptions because, generally speaking, this is what we want from others. On the negative side, we can also assume that

- Most people would prefer not to be criticized, even when it is for their own good.
- No one likes to be embarrassed, laughed at, or have his or her secrets exposed to the public.
- No one likes threats, physical or psychological (although there are some people who delight in head-on arguments about issues).
- No one enjoys bickering over details, such as how to split the check, what street to take, or what time to leave. No one likes to be nagged.
- And the reason people come together in the first place is to dispel loneliness and boredom. If a person is as bored with someone as he or she is alone, then there will probably not be a second chance.

Keep these ideas in mind in the early stages. People like to be respected and feel that they have some influence over what is going on. By avoiding risky situations and by appealing to common needs and wants, it is possible to make most initial contacts pleasant and interesting, whether they lead to anything else or not. If the relationship is to escalate to other levels of association, it depends on how important each party sees it. It jeopardizes a relationship to try to advance it faster than the other person wants to go. A distinguished sociologist believes that admission to intimacy should be a reward for successful behavior on the previous level.[3]

There are some cautions about social relationships with the people with whom you work. On the job, most people like to be respected for what they can do and credited for their accomplishments. They would also like to avoid having their mistakes made public. Attention to these simple requirements is sufficient to make yourself socially acceptable with your fellow workers. On the other hand, as we will point out in detail later on, it is sometimes very chancy to put a great deal of energy into social relationships with fellow workers. There is too much at stake on the job that might jeopardize a social relationship.

ANALYZING PRIVATE SITUATIONS

Shy people tend to be insecure about their intense private relationships. Studies show that shy people have a tendency to lock themselves into exclusive relationships much earlier than people who are not shy.[4] They invest a great deal in these relationships and they are devastated when they come apart. It is obvious that shy people lock onto a few close relationships in order to convince themselves that they do not need to make the effort with other people.

There are very few relationships conducted entirely in private. Virtually all relationships have a public component. Most shy people feel very awkward during private time, even with people they care about very much. They tend to worry about offending the other, and they are commonly clinging and dependent. The dominant member of the relationship makes the decisions, the shy person is apparently glad just to be along.

The key to satisfactory private time is *equity*. Each person must get a fair share, and this is commonly arranged by a careful negotiation over time. In intimate relationships each party has an opportunity to participate in generating the rules for the relationship. The best way to handle private relationships is to think of them as little governments.

A private relationship is a two-person society. When two people decide to relate in private, they must organize themselves and establish rules of behavior. Despite what the popular magazines say, this must include more than sexual behavior. Sex is only a small part of a genuine two-person relationship. It is not, in itself, the relationship. Sex is valuable if both parties agree on its meaning. It is possible to get sexual enjoyment without any real social contact. But if the sexually relating parties have different ideas about what the relationship means and what constitutes success and satisfaction at it, it is doomed to disappointment. The same admonition can be offered about every aspect of a relationship.

Intimate relationships are based on intimacy and exchange, and the goals of each party must be compatible with common agreements, but individually satisfying as well. While behaviors in public are generally specified and easy to learn, in private everything must be worked out. Each person has a right to contribute to the agreements, and if you do not protect this right at the outset, it is easy to be victimized. It is not that the other person wishes to exploit you, it is only that if you do not express your preferences, it is easy for the other person to assume that you agree. Over time, what you do habitually becomes your constitution, and if you have locked yourself into a submissive position, it is very difficult to alter your role. The other person may well be relating to you simply because you are submissive and that person may be entirely convinced that you like it. This means that if you start to change your behavior, you are violating the rules of the relationship. It may mean that the relationship will end, because what you require may not be within the capacity of the other person to provide.

When you consider the private relationships you have with family and friends, you must consider the following questions:

1. Who is in charge? Who says how we do things? Does one person make all the decisions, or is decision making divided? What is the nature of the decision making? Does one person act and the other comply, or is there discussion? How is the discussion carried on, and who decides it is over?

2. Whose job is it to carry out decisions? Does the decision maker also do the detail work, or does one person make the decisions and then order the other to do the work? If there is a division in this authority, how are decisions about the division made?

3. What happens when someone breaks the rules? Is there an argument? Does one person sulk or pout? Is there intimidation and pressure? When the issue has been identified, how is it resolved? How do you make up?

4. What are the topics of conversation? What must you talk about and what must you avoid? What are the sensitivities of each party and how are they respected? What happens when new issues are introduced?

5. How is privacy handled? What parts of your life are reserved? What does your partner keep reserved? What happens when one party is suspicious of the other concerning what goes on in the reserved parts of life? What happens when one party infringes on the privacy of the other?

6. What do you get out of the relationship? What do you think the other person is getting? Is this a permanent exchange, or has it been modified in the past? If it has been modified, how were the decisions made?

7. What is your policy toward outsiders? How are mutual friends selected and developed? How are public activities selected? How are individual friends dealt with? What happens when you disagree about some outside party?

One reason for feeling queasy in intimate relationships is not understanding what is going on. While they do seem to take the magic and romance out of intimacy, these questions must be raised from time to time. It doesn't mean that the couple has to talk about them as if they were negotiating for a settlement of a lawsuit. But if one party discovers that equity is being reduced, then it is necessary to introduce the subject and make some alterations before the other party gets used to the situation. This kind of analysis can lead to selection of important goals for conversation with an intimate partner. Furthermore, we can use these questions to analyze any friendship regardless of how intimate it is. It is not possible to relate to a person on any level for any period of time without developing regularities that can be examined through the use of the preceding seven questions.

EXECUTIVE FUNCTION

Many relationships contain one bossy person and one milquetoast. Such relationships can be satisfying to both parties. In some cases, however, the subservient partner feels resentment and looks forward to the time when the tables are turned. The anticipation of revenge on the partner is not a good reason for sustaining a relationship. Shy people despair of ever taking charge, and more often than not they will decide to "take their lumps" in relationships, since the alternative is facing life without any relationships at all. One of the most important reasons to overcome shyness is to improve your private relationships.

Even though we can regard relationships as little governments, one person does not have to be in charge all the time. In democratic societies leadership often changes hands. Any decision can be carried out by the person most competent, and pairs of friends can make a whole series of agreements about who is in charge of what. The person who has the time and the interest usually is the best one to implement a particular aspect of the relationship. In a marriage, for example, one partner can be in charge of landscaping the house and one in charge of housekeeping, and the assignments need not necessarily be sex-related. By understanding that *you* have the right to participate in the executive function of your relationship, you have the possibility to set a whole series of goals designed to strengthen your interpersonal position.

Many people have been raised in traditional families, where age or sex determines who controls things. This kind of arrangement seems to work for people who come out of cultures where this is the norm. They are not necessarily models for contemporary relationships, however. More and more people coming from one-parent families are trained in the possibilities of shared management without reference to the traditional agencies of power. Thus females can handle traditionally male interests and vice versa. Even child rearing does not have time to be a sexually defined process. But whatever the definition of responsibility, it must be a shared decision. The person who is in an unwilling role is subversive to the relationship.

Many shy people have come from authoritarian homes, where reasonable discussion was not possible. They have learned to put up with it until they can take it no longer. But intimate relationships need safety valves. Problems need to be handled on an ongoing basis. Shy people often hang back even when their partner urges them to take control, then later lash back at the excessive control assumed by the partner. It is not fair to trap an intimate partner in such paradoxes.

Check your own executive position by asking the following questions about each of your intimate relationships:

1. When did you last give orders to your partner? Did your partner seem to resent the order?
2. When were you last given an order? Did you resent it?
3. What is the relative proportion of orders you give to orders you receive? Are you satisfied with this proportion? Is your partner satisfied? How do you know?
4. Have you ever talked about order giving and directing?
5. Does your partner seem to pick at small details about you? Do you notice small details about your partner?
6. Have you ever thought about alternative ways of getting things done in your relationship?

LEGISLATIVE FUNCTION

Two people in a close relationship must have a way to talk things over. Often communication in private relationships is one-way. One person talks, the other either listens or tunes out. Often individuals try to talk their partners into some course of action (or intimidate them, bribe them, or involve them out of sympathy). Matters such as sexual activity, how to spend money, which friends to choose, and how to raise the kids are matters of great importance in relationships, and without participation of both parties the decisions made could be unfair and lead to later disruption.

Really strong relationships seem to make decisions by consensus. Each party seems to be sensitive to what is truly important to the other. They developed this sensitivity, no doubt, by talking about it over a long period of time, during which the couple struggled with ways to deal with important issues. Some couples seem to be complementary. That is, in each particular area of the relationship one is leader, the other follower. Some couples seem to play a mutual role in decision making. Such couples give no overt evidence of who is in charge of what. Their friends admire the way they seem to share leadership. It is important to understand that that symmetry in relationships can only come about when each person is willing to assume a fair share of responsibility and accord that right to the other party as well. Many shy people believe they are not qualified to take control of anything and push responsibility off onto anyone who is willing to take it. The danger of this process should be obvious. The shy person has no recourse when decisions are made that are dangerous or unpleasant.

HOPING FOR TOO MUCH

One of the most dangerous ideas you can have is that you will always be happy. If you seek perfection you will fail constantly. Wendell Johnson created the idea of IFD Disease (idealization, frustration, demoralization), which, he alleged, was the most common disease of people who are not doing well with others.[5] By setting unclear and unattainable goals, people guarantee themselves catastrophe.

In more recent times, the idea of *actualization* has dominated the literature.[6] According to advocates of this idea, people had to struggle to meet needs on various levels: first survival, then coping, then actualization, which meant they had achieved a position of almost complete independence from others and were in full control of their "powers." Once again the potential for frustration was available. Very often, people seeking actualization were placed in a position from which it was necessary for them to exploit others in order to attain their goals.

This doesn't mean you have to put up with your lot in life. It does mean that it is terribly important to first set clear goals so that you have a good idea of what you have to do to attain them and so that you recognize them when you do attain them. Second, it means that you must take the needs of other people into account as you struggle to attain your goals. By helping them attain their objectives, you enlist their aid in helping you to attain yours. Cooperative striving for clear and attainable goals is the most effective prescription for human relationships.

SETTLING DISPUTES

Every relationship has its bad moments. Changes in external conditions, the influence of new people, simple boredom, and many other events over which a couple has no control are capable of stirring up discontent. The more rules there are in a relationship, the more infractions there are likely to be. The longer and more intense a relationship and the more binding the rules are, the more painful it is when they are broken. Once an infraction is called, then it is necessary to talk about it, complain about it, argue about it, wheedle your way out of it, or otherwise dispose of it. It doesn't matter whether the infraction is putting out a cigarette in a saucer or a flagrant case of adultery—getting the issue resolved can be just as difficult.

Sometimes shy people in relationships are quite aware that a serious infraction is going on, but they do not call their partner on it for fear that they will destroy the relationship. This theme repeats itself over and over again. In a recent survey more than 50 percent of the people polled reported that they would rather stay with an unsatisfactory relationship than run the risk of being without a relationship at all.[7]

People in relationships are often called upon to defend themselves against accusations of infractions or complaints by the other partner. There are all kinds of defenses, ranging from topping the accusation with a greater one to abject apology and throwing oneself on the mercy of the court. Shy people have very little tolerance for ambiguous situations, and thus they try to get themselves into a position where very little can happen to them. In their primary relationships they are generally subservient and highly attentive to the needs of their partner—and abject in their misery. On the job they look for safe positions where they can perform orderly routines that are easily measured so that they and their supervisors can be sure they are performing. They fear competency in themselves because they believe it might get them into a position where they will be asked to assume too much responsibility or have too much contact with other humans.

Even when there is little at stake, such as in a casual contact, shy people recoil at the thought of something going wrong. They are very sensitive to real and imagined slights, but they are not at all sensitive to the needs of the people they meet. A person excusing himself or herself to get a cocktail can mean the end of their happiness at a party. If someone does give them a kind word, they are usually ready to go along with anything, and sometimes they push others into the position of exploiting them because they never make clear when they are being imposed on.

When shy people finally form a close relationship, they cling very tightly to it. They have a great deal to lose if the relationship breaks down. This does not mean that they are satisfied with their relationships. They often feel great pain about them, which they can do nothing about because of their fear of losing the person to whom they are relating. Many unexpected divorces come about when a shy person finally breaks out of his or her frustration and begins to stand up to the partner. Sometimes the antagonism and resentment have gone so far that the relationship cannot be mended, although if grievances had been handled earlier, things might have worked out.

In order to avoid traumatic experiences, partners in a close relationship must pay attention to equity. Neither partner can make demands without considering their effect on the other. Shy people need to take more responsibility for claiming their share, and their partners have an equal obligation to assist the quiet partner to express important ideas.

The usual techniques of handling relationship problems are perilous. Some couples fight it out head to head and seem to enjoy it. This is all right so long as the partners are of relatively equal strength (including loudness of voice) and know how to get an argument finished. Procedures designed to teach couples how to fight fair have been advocated and hold some promise as long as the two partners are willing to make an equal commitment to maintain the relationship.[8] Sometimes, however, fights are generated to end the relationship, and there is nothing that can be done about it. Divorce lawyers have encountered shy partners who are bewildered by the unfair accusations made by their mates, unable to justify what is happening to them, and not willing to admit that their partner is unilaterally casting them out. Sometimes fear of the unknown world of new relationships is so great that people cannot realistically examine what other people are doing to them. That is, of course, why we have consistently advocated close attention to reality.

Sometimes partners try to deal with infractions by denying something like money, privileges, sex, or love. Sometimes they try to win the favor of the partner by acting like a medieval courtier obsequiously seeking favors from a noble. Fighting and denial of affection have a cumulative effect. The partner who loses feels pain, and the result is the development of quiet resentment, passive resistance, or, worse, the partner develops a slave mentality and is of no use at all as a human being. Stronger partners have been known to express dismay at the subservience of a mate whom they carefully broke to be obedient. When this happens, the weaker partner is usually cast off, and the stronger looks for another person to work over.

There are, of course, successful intimate relationships, and not all shy people suffer the pain of being browbeaten by a dominant partner. Pairs of shy people can live perfectly satisfactory lives, and sometimes a partner's shyness is a virtue to be prized by someone who lives part of his or her life in a competitive and vigorous world. But if there is something amiss, it is necessary to set goals to deal with it once you have gained skill at managing your own social behavior.

Every relationship has normal and nonthreatening content, and it is here that you can make your first efforts. Your awakening involvement in the relationship should be a signal to your partner about the possibilities in other aspects of your partnership. It is the mundane and regular that makes up the bulk of a relationship, and when things go reasonably well in everyday areas, the couple can usually manage the stresses and emergencies that come to them.

But sometimes couples begin to get a little tired of the regularity of their everyday life together, and their pattern of behavior begins to bore the people around them. It is here that the shy person can make a first intervention by suggesting ways and means to improve the relationship before trouble starts. Familiarity may be important, but changing things around a bit—trying a different kind of movie or a new restaurant—can do a good deal to rejuvenate a sagging and dull relationship. Furthermore, when you begin to make suggestions and take the initiative in planning, you begin to become a more exciting person. If you can assume your share in pushing for new ideas and new events, you will be on the way to assuming full partnership in the more tense areas of your relationship.

EXCHANGE AND EQUITY

Every relationship, whether public or private, contains an element of exchange. People do not remain together unless they are convinced they are getting something out of it. Sometimes what you get is very clear and tangible, and sometimes it takes great effort to convince yourself that a particular relationship is valuable. If you do not see any profit to yourself in a relationship, you either terminate it or live in a state of despair. A great many shy people seem to prefer the despair. That is, perhaps, the major casualty of shyness.

Exchanges are often small and are not necessarily in kind. One person tells funny stories, the other provides analysis of events. One partner drives, the other buys the drinks. As relationships become more and more intimate and as space is shared, agreements have to be made about who does what. He handles cleaning the bathroom, she the kitchen. He decides about what to do for recreation, she decides on who to enjoy it with. She performs one set of services for the children, he another. Many of these decisions are not formally made, but they are very clear and must be maintained with regularity because they become part of the constitution of the relationship.

Relationships are usually unstable at first because the currency of exchange has not been worked out. People need attention, and in a relationship exchange of time and attention is what gets things started. Exchanges of goods and services—records, books, driving, small gifts— sometimes engender enough trust that exchanges of a more subtle kind—affection and goodwill, for example—can grow. Learning to talk about possible futures is an important goal for shy people, for looking forward to shared experience provides an opportunity to decide how to divide up responsibilities. By exchanging talk about preferences, people can work out mutually satisfying activities. What to do to make us both satisfied can provide a very constructive agenda for every relationship. Questions such as what can we do together? what must we avoid? what should we talk atout? and what can we do to make life a little better? all provide agendas that make relationships closer and more satisfying. If you can figure out what it is possible to get from a relationship, you can figure out how to give to it. Mutual getting and giving is what binds relationships and thus should be a major matter of conversation and concern.

FOREIGN POLICY

Hardly anyone relates to only one person. Everyone lives in a world of complicated social connections and linkages. Sometimes the demands made by outside parties can place intolerable strain on relationships. People often lose sight of the fact that their friends and lovers have other people in their lives and obligations that might distract them temporarily from their partners. Family ties, old friends, or payment of old social debts can all be distracting. Many people who are married to divorcés are disappointed by their partner's attention to old aspects of his or her life, such as children or even the previous mate. Newly formed couples face continual agitation until the proper amount of attention to parents, relatives, and old friends is worked out.

Work associates and professional colleagues are also a potential distraction. Many a mate has discovered that the partner's occupation is a harsh overseer demanding time and attention away from the relationship. Jealousies can grow about the time spent on the job and the people associated with. Social contacts with people from work can be very boring to the other partner, particularly when there is a great deal of shop talk.

Couples need to talk about the other people in their lives. Shy people often refrain from mentioning their frustration over the time their partner is spending with others, and consequently their partners take their silence for acquiescence. Jealousy is a strong emotion, and if your partner seems to be doing something else on "your time," it is easy to act on jealous urges. Shy people are often victimized by such behavior because they either can't or won't talk about their relationships, either with their partners or with anyone else who could give them good advice. A legitimate goal for a shy person to accomplish is to talk about external relationships.

RELATIONSHIP CHECKLIST

Here are some questions you can ask about any relationship you have, however casual. There is no way to get a number score, but if you can get the information, you will be able to find empirical confirmation for your discontents and provide yourself with an agenda for discussion. If you can prevail upon your friend or mate to go through the checklist with you, you can accomplish a great many goals in your relationship. Shy people attempting this exercise with a partner might want to ask the other partner to read this section of the book so that he or she has the same background before starting through the checklist. Do not be surprised if your partner objects to the contents of this chapter. The standard objective is that it is "too intellectual," "too calculating," "too manipulative." You may find that you will have a very interesting discussion about these issues. You can ask, "How does one bring about changes in an unsatisfactory situation unless one knows the nature of the situation and is specific about the desired changes?" If you try this exercise with someone very close to you, he or she may well feel threatened by the prospect of changes in your behavior. You might reassure your partner that you are giving him or her a chance to participate in the changes by talking about them with you.

Once you have gone through all this, you may not find it necessary to deal explicitly with the questions. If you have not discussed these issues before, you might find that your answers to the questions represent a pool of goals for you to try once you are moderately sure of your ability to manage the process.

1. What kind of conflict results from suggestion giving in your relationship?
2. How are decisions made in your relationship? Do you feel you have enough say in the decisions? How would you know how much is "enough"?
3. How are disappointments handled in your relationship? How are they called to the attention of the other party?
4. What do you do to make up for injuring your partner? What does your partner do for you? Is this enough?
5. What are the exchanges in the relationship? What do you really

count on your partner for? What does your partner count on you for? What could be eliminated? What would you like to get that you are not presently getting?

6. What are your standard topics of conversation? Are you bored? What would you like to talk about that you are not now talking about? What would you like to hear from your partner that you are not hearing?

7. What do you do for fun? Is it fun? Why or why not? What would be more fun? Why aren't you doing that? What do you mean by "fun" anyway?

8. Of the other people you see regularly, which of them must you see regularly? Which do you want to see regularly? Which could you dispense with? Why don't you? Is there anyone you want to meet? Why don't you?

REFERENCES

1. George Homans, *Social Behavior: Its Elementary Forms* (New York: Harcourt Jovanovich Brace, Inc., 1979), see also Ellen Berscheid and Elaine Walster, *Interpersonal Attraction* (Reading, Mass.: Addison-Wesley Publishing Co., Inc., 1969).

2. Elaine Walster, G. William Walster, and Ellen Berscheid, *Equity: Theory and Research* (Boston: Allyn & Bacon, Inc., 1978).

3. Philip Slater, *The Pursuit of Loneliness* (Boston: The Beacon Press, 1970.)

4. James C. McCroskey, "Communication Apprehension and Marital Relationships" (paper presented to the Eastern Communication Association, New York, 1977).

5. Wendell Johnson, *People in Quandaries* (New York: Harper & Row, 1946).

6. Abraham Maslow, *Motivation and Personality* (New York: Harper & Row, 1954).

7. Gerald M. Phillips and Nancy J. Metzger, *Intimate Communication* (Boston: Allyn & Bacon, Inc., 1976).

8. George R. Bach and Peter Wyden, *The Intimate Enemy: How to Fight Fair in Love and Marriage* (New York: Avon Books, 1968).

RECOMMENDED READINGS

Christopher Lasch, *The Culture of Narcissism* (New York: W.W. Norton & Co., Inc., 1978).

Edward O. Wilson, *On Human Nature* (Cambridge, Mass.: Harvard University Press, 1978).

Stanley Milgram, *The Individual in a Social World* (Reading, Mass.: Addison-Wesley Publishing Co., Inc., 1977).

Neil Postman, *Crazy Talk, Stupid Talk* (New York: Delacorte Press, 1976).

chapter 9

Making Sense

There are very few people who can get the attention of others and hold it. Most social conversations seem to ramble, to make no sense at all. Professional secretaries report that when they try to transcribe casual conversations at meetings, they have a terrible time reconstructing the sentences and find it virtually impossible to pick out the central ideas of the messages exchanged. Indeed, the good leader is the person who can make sense out of the chaos that takes place at public gatherings.

A good way to overcome shyness is to train yourself to do something other people cannot do that they find valuable. In this case we are talking about making sense. People who can talk so that ideas hang together and so that other people can respond sensibly are generally regarded as being very valuable to have around. This skill can be applied to any situation in which you find yourself. It is not all that difficult to make sense. Everyone has to think about talking, but most people do not know how to think about it in an orderly way. They think about what *they* want to say rather than about what it would be *effective* to say. People who say what they want to say are disappointed when people respond the way they want to respond, and it does not normally occur to speakers to offer their listeners a good reason for responding the way they want them to.

When we talk to people, we seek to change them in some way. We can seek to change what they know, what they believe, and what they do. Talk directed at others should seek a specific change, which represents your goal. Your talk should be directed at accomplishing your objectives by making sure that everything you say provides the other person with a very good reason for helping you achieve them. Follow this pattern:

GOAL: HOW ARE OTHER PEOPLE TO BE CHANGED?
What new information will they have after I talk?
What different beliefs will they have?
What action will they carry out?
How will I know the change has happened?

JUSTIFICATION: WHY IS THE CHANGE GOOD FOR THEM?
Why do they need the information?
Why should their attitudes change?
What good will they get out of doing what I want them to do?

ANTICIPATION: WHAT WILL I DO IN RESPONSE TO THEIR RESPONSE?
What is the best possible response I could get and what will I do if I get it?
What is the worst possible response I could get and what will I do if I get it?
What is most likely to happen and what will I do if it does?

PAYOFF: WHAT'S IN IT FOR ME?
Why am I asking for it in the first place?
Is it sufficient to pay me off for what I have to do to get it?
What possible inconvenience will it cause me?

PLANNING WHAT MUST I SAY AND IN WHAT ORDER SO THAT IT IS
THE MOVES: MOST EFFECTIVE WITH THE PERSON I ADDRESS?

Let's apply this analysis to some common situations:

GOAL: I want the clerk in the store to show me at least five items.

JUSTIFICATION: This is good for the clerk because it might result in a sale. Also, if the boss is watching, the clerk will give the appearance of trying hard.

ANTICIPATION: If I get the attention I want, I might buy. If I do not get the attention I want, I might complain. If I get normal attention, I will behave like a normal customer. I will be courteous, I might buy, and I won't complain.

PAYOFF: If I am successful, I will get the service I think I need. It will make me feel important.

PLANNING: I will say, "I often find it hard to make a choice unless I can compare the merchandise. I need to see at least five items, maybe more, before I can make up my mind." (This will acquaint the clerk with my rule system so that he will not think me a pest.) The clerk then knows the minimum he must do to get the sale, so it is adjusted to his needs, since it makes it easier for him to do his work.

Now let's apply this to a social engagement:

GOAL: I want to get Ed to go someplace other than that bar with me Tuesday night. I would prefer the opera, but I will respond to his alternate suggestion if he makes one. Anything is better than sitting and sagging in that bar.

JUSTIFICATION: He may lose a good woman if he is not willing to do something else. We only go to that bar out of habit and because neither of us has initiated a change. If I get him to make a change, our relationship will be better, and that will be good for him, too.

ANTICIPATION: The best that could happen is that Ed agrees to take me to the opera, although I might get stuck for the tickets. The worst is he gets mad enough to cancel our Tuesday together. I can handle that. I can stay home and do the laundry. The most likely thing is that he will want to go instead to see wrestling. I can handle that, one time anyway, and it won't become a habit because he couldn't tolerate paying for the tickets. The next time maybe I can convince him to try basketball or a good movie.

PAYOFF: I can't take the present situation, so any alteration would be an improvement. I actually can't lose. The question is, how much can I gain? And there is nothing Ed can lose either. I can't believe he really likes that bar so much.

PLAN: I won't wait until we meet. I will call him and tell him I have two tickets. If he argues for something else, I'll say, Let's do my thing, and next Tuesday you can pick anything but the bar. That will be an advantage because that will get him away from the bar two times in succession. If he insists on going to the bar, I'll tell him to go without me because I don't want to waste the tickets. Then I'll find someone else to go with me. Total cost, forty-five dollars for the tickets. I can handle it.

On the job, the process might sound like this:

GOAL: I want the supervisors to listen to me for five minutes at next week's meeting so that I can present my plan for improving shipping procedures.

JUSTIFICATION: There are some real problems in shipping, and I think I have an idea that will make a difference. It is not unusual for supervisors to suggest changes like this, but it is unusual for me. I have never done it before and I have always had difficulty getting and holding the floor. I think my plan is good enough so that if I can talk it through, it would help both me and the company.

ANTICIPATION: The best thing that could happen is that I make my report clearly and everyone is interested and votes yes. The most likely thing to happen is that they listen and refer the idea to the planning group. That's okay, that's normal. The worst thing that could happen is that I freeze and never get the proposal out. I suppose it would be bad if they started heckling me, but they don't do that often, and I think they like me. It would be rough if Sam Miller argued with me, but at least if I got the whole idea out, that would be okay. I think I will prepare written copies of the idea to hand out in case the worst happens.

PAYOFF: If I succeed, it will make me feel effective, and I will look better to the brass. If I fail, I will be sick and I will look like a fool. This is a very high risk for me.

PLAN: I'd better have an insurance policy and I will do this by writing out my idea. I read somewhere that it takes two minutes to read one typewritten sheet, so I will prepare two and a half pages on which I outline my whole plan. If things go badly, I will hand it out and ask them to read it, or if I can blurt it out, I'll ask tough old Sam Miller to read it for me. (Maybe I will ask Sam in advance to bail me out just in case—no, that would be too easy; if I knew he was going to do it, I'd cop out for sure.) I could do this by memo of course, but I need to learn how to speak up at the meetings. I'll prepare a one-line introduction and conclusion to my talk and I'll memorize them, and if I can't remember what goes in between, I'll read it.

(At this point the decision has been made to give a speech. Instructions about how to prepare a speech will be found in Chapter Thirteen, "Communicating on the Job.")

Finally, we can look at a plan for a conversation a woman wants to have with her husband.

GOAL: I want to tell Herb that with both of us working, some of the pressure must be taken off my back. I want him to do some of the work around the house, particularly some of the heavy cleaning. I am making as much money as he is, and it is time to equalize some of the labor.

JUSTIFICATION: If he doesn't hear me out and make some changes, we might be on the rocks, and I don't think Herb will do well without me, so it is to his best interest to listen to me and do something about what I think is the biggest problem in our marriage.

ANTICIPATION: The worst thing that can happen is that we have another one of our screaming and yelling fights and nothing changes. Herb takes me seriously enough so that I don't think there's danger of a breakup over this, unless *I* lose my cool and walk out. Frankly, I may do that, so I'd better be ready for the possibility before I start this one. The best thing that can happen is that Herb agrees and makes some changes, and the most likely thing is that Herb will agree but won't do anything about it. He'll keep postponing it like he's always done. He'll say something like, "We'll start the new system after the Super Bowl," or "Let's wait till I finish the midwinter report before we start." If this happens, I'll tell him, "I'm starting how," and that he should be prepared to have me stop doing some of the things he counts on, like packing his lunch or doing the dishes. If I'm not prepared to do this much, there's no point to starting the fight.

PAYOFF: If it works, we'll have a better marriage. If it doesn't, we may have no marriage at all. Seems like a silly thing to break up a marriage for, but if I keep giving in, it will only get worse.

PLAN: Maybe I should start with the payoff line and get all the chips on the table. If I can make it clear to Herb that I mean business, maybe he'll do something. Maybe I should start by stopping the dishes right now. Maybe I can get the conversation going by not making his lunch tomorrow, and when he asks me why, I can pitch him the first line. It's hard for Herb to get out to eat, whereas I can have a sandwich sent up, so I have the advantage here. If he asks why there is no lunch in his briefcase, I can tell him what's on my mind. I'd better have a steady stream of talk ready, so that I can get it all out before he starts yelling.

In each case the person who initiated the action prepared a plan based on knowledge of the situation and the audience. There is, of course, a good deal more at stake in trying to save a marriage than there is in trying to get service in a department store, but the idea of strategic action is basic to both situations. Every social activity has a degree of both payoff potential and risk. The more intimate the activity, the higher the risk and the greater the potential payoff. What both important and trivial goals have in common is the need for a plan. Not letting things get out of control is one of the most important elements in overcoming shyness. If you can anticipate the possibilities of what might happen and what you can do if it does, you can discover that the worst is not so bad and that you can handle almost everything if you are reasonably ready for it. At least if the worst happens, you will not have to respond to it "spontaneously" and emotionally; rather you will have a rational plan directed at the other person. As long as you can keep your mind on your goal and respond coherently, you will appear to be the master of the situation. The idea is *not* to take control of the other person, which is impossible anyway. Rather you must maintain control over yourself in order to represent yourself and your ideas effectively. You are not seeking the "whole pot" for Number One. Your prepared discourse is directed at the advantage potential to Number Two.

AN EXERCISE

This exercise is a refinement of the goal-analysis procedure that you tried in the last chapter. In this analysis you are asked to be even more specific. Answer the following questions, concentrating on behaviors and talk in all of your answers:

1. What is the behavior I seek from the other person? Describe it. What will the other person do and say?
2. What justification will I give for that behavior? Write out a line or two of dialogue.
3. What will I offer in exchange? How will the person know I am offering it? Write out your exchange request.
4. What would the other person say that I would classify as a "best response"? What would I say back?

5. What would the other person say that I would classify as a "worst response"? What would I say back?
6. What is the other person most likely to say? What would I say back?

At this point, you should have something that looks like a playscript with three alternate scenes. You can analyze this script by asking the following questions:

7. What's at stake here? What's the best I can get? What do I have to give to get it?
8. Is it worth the effort?

If you decide it is worth the effort, set a *time* and *place* to put your plan into operation. Call your friend with whom you worked before and try it out in role play. Rehearse it. Memorize your opening and closing lines. For this exercise stay with relatively simple situations. It is still relatively early to work on major problems.

PLANNING

Be sure to consider the other person in your planning. Concentrate on reasons you can give other people to convince them that what you ask would benefit them. Make sure that you make it clear that what you are offering is a reward. People like to get rewards; they don't like to be bullied. By associating your goal with a mutual benefit, that is, offering other people a chance to accomplish their goals, you can overcome shyness *and* make yourself appear a civilized and considerate human being at the same time. *When you succeed, it is because you have solved a problem, not because you have won a battle.*

Your planning should produce a script, though it need not be written. Once you have cultivated skill at this sort of planning, you will be able to write scripts in your head. Remember those "inner newsreels" we discussed earlier? The more formal the situation, the more formal the script can be. The person trying to speak at the supervisor's meeting could use a complete script because the situation is tightly organized and the responses almost predictable. The woman trying to alter her marriage is better off with a loose script in which she has three or four alternate tracks to take. One of the best ways to overcome reticence in any situation is to feel confident about your preparation to handle whatever might happen. Please notice the construction of the preceding sentence. We did *not* say "confident about being able to handle whatever might happen." We said *confident about your preparation*. Preparation is something you can do in advance. Once you have done it, you can be confident in it because you have done it. There is a close association between careful preparation and positive outcomes, but you cannot predict the future, and therefore it is foolish to try to control it. You always need to leave a loophole for the unexpected.

Getting the script into your head is your best method of preparation. Skilled communicators have learned through successful experience how to be extemporaneous. Extemporaneous speech does not look memorized. It looks spontaneous but it is really very carefully prepared. It looks spontaneous because it appears to come easily. It comes easily because it is carefully prepared. Speech that is not carefully prepared has the quality of sounding blurted out. After you have extemporized for a while, you will find yourself able to pull from repertoires of rehearsed possibilities precisely the lines you need to handle a particular situation. You will sound fluent.

You can prepare for social conversation in much the same way as for a public speech. Public speaking is actually the easiest form of communication, because the speaker has the luxury of being able to prepare carefully in advance. The audience does not. The speaker can analyze the audience, select the most appropriate things to say, organize them carefully, criticize and revise, rehearse, make notes, prepare introductions and conclusions, and deliver the speech without interruption. Social conversation comes in spurts, it is often disorderly, and there is no way to avoid interruption. Consequently, if you know what you are after, you have an edge on people who only have a vague sense of what they want. If you take them and their possible concerns into account in your planning, you can help them crystallize goals and accomplish them even while you accomplish your own. By thinking out what you want to say, you will guarantee yourself an advantage in any social conversation. This will make you appear to be a better and more effective human being, which in fact you will be because you are considerate of other people and their concerns. The whole process is one of working together so that everyone can be a little better off.

GETTING READY

There are a number of ways to prepare for talk with others. Once you reject the possibility of spontaneity, you discover that much interaction really is rehearsed because it is the cut-and-dried exchange of clichés that everyone knows. We learn formulas for conversation. We use the same opening lines on people wherever we meet them and under whatever circumstances. In fact, if you don't use the proper opening lines, people will be suspicious of you and probably will not react well to you. When people are seeking illegitimate goals, unpredictable conversational events take place, and rejection occurs. You need to analyze each situation to see what is allowable and what is not and then prepare some opening lines to carry you into conversation.

It is much like rehearsing for a play. When you first try your lines "on stage," they may seem a little stilted and unreal. But once you discover that they work, you will develop and expand a repertoire, playing for applause. We have been trained to be suspicious of people with a good line for the very reason that lines work.

Getting ready is not a matter of innate talent or a special state of mind. You can prepare if you can sit for a while in a comfortable chair and think about what you want to do. In formal programs that teach communication skills, students often role-play scenes with each other to get ready to try new social situations. If you have no one to role-play with, you can take both parts. If you are alone, you can say the lines out loud. It is useful to actually say the lines so that the words feel comfortable in your mouth. The more you run through them, the less awkward they will seem when you actually say them.

Alternate scripts will prepare you to be interesting and effective but still able to adapt to what the other person does and says. This is the way you can assure yourself that you will treat others respectfully and decently. Planned consideration of the other person is the best way to accomplish your goals.

A WORD ABOUT ROLE PLAYING

If you have someone you trust to work with, role playing your scenes will be helpful. If you can get someone who is also attempting to overcome shyness, both of you can benefit by exchanging scenes.

In order to role play effectively, the person who is helping you must be thoroughly briefed in all the possibilities. Discuss your situation thoroughly so that he or she will know some of the alternatives for response. Explaining the situation to another person will help you talk through possibilities. By explaining the situation to another person you will consider your audience once more and be able to anticipate the best, worst, and most likely outcomes. Let your partner think up the exact words, however, so that you can try to respond to the unexpected. Your partner will probably not use the kinds of words your real audience will use, but the experience will familiarize you with the feeling of using prepared material in a responsive way.

If the role play does not work well, you can figure out why and try it again. The only cost is in time, and by going through it a few times you will be able to prepare statements for virtually any eventuality.

There is one very important point about role playing. It will teach you the importance of small strategic moves, how vital the proper vocal inflection or facial expression is in supporting your point. A carefully trained actor knows that overcoming stage fright is really not helpful. What is helpful is learning the moves, and once you learn the moves, the stage fright disappears.

Role playing is a potentially powerful learning tool. There are some psychologists and psychiatrists who make it a cornerstone of their therapy. This is *not* the reason we recommend it to you. We are not concerned with modifying your feelings. We only want to provide you with skills. We have not advised you to consider your feelings after the role plays. No doubt, some of the time you will be satisfied and some of the time you will be frustrated, disappointed, or angry. No matter, you *must* concentrate on what really happened, what you did, and what the other person did. We want you to role play because it is impossible to learn to speak in public alone. Role playing is a low-risk way to get the skill and confidence you need to accomplish your goals.

GETTING THE DUCKS IN A ROW

Most people don't know how to organize ideas so that they make sense to others. Remember the difficulties you had in school when you were asked to write an outline for a composition or essay? Most of the time you probably wrote the composition first and then wrote the outline. You couldn't figure out why the teacher put you through that busywork, because you never understood how preparation in the form of an outline could improve your writing skill. Most poor grades on both written and oral compositions are the result of disorganization, a function of poor outlining. The human mind needs to organize the information it gets. If information comes in a disorderly way, the mind will impose order on it and understand it the way it has ordered it. But the order imposed may not be the order you want. That is why it is so easy for people to misunderstand each other. Therefore, if you want your audience to understand you, you must organize your talk very carefully.

Effective talkers are well organized. Because they know what they want to accomplish, they can be sure that virtually everything they say is directed toward accomplishing their goal. Thus they make sense. It is impossible to influence others when your talk is disjointed, choppy, and incoherent, although it is possible to confuse the daylights out of them.

The reason people tend to get disorganized is because they allow themselves to respond to emotional needs rather than to what is going on around them. They do not understand that managing themselves so that they can have an influence is the best way to feel good. Furthermore, confusion is an escalating process. We feel uneasy about what people might think about what we say, and since we do not know how to discover how our talk affects other people, each time we say something, we have a harder time connecting what the other person does with what we say, so that we get more and more uneasy until we release our feelings with some kind of personal expression, which further confuses the issue. The following outline may make this easier to grasp:

1. If we are not prepared, we feel uneasy about how we will affect people.
2. If we are uneasy about how we will affect people, we concentrate on our uneasiness.
3. If we concentrate on our uneasiness, we are not aware of what the other person is doing and saying.
4. If we are not aware of what the other person is doing and saying, we choose what we say based on our feelings.
5. If we choose what we say based on our feelings, we are likely to say

something that may offend or bewilder the other person and confuse the situation even more.

By having some form of organization in mind, you have a corrective to apply when things seem to be going wrong. You can review the steps in your plan to find out where the conversation strayed and you can think up ways to get back to where you want to be. In fact, once you figure out where you want to be, it is very easy to get back. You can simply say, "Wait a minute, I don't think I said that right, and I may have misled you. Let me try again." Then say it again. There is nothing ignominious about admitting error. In fact, so few people do it that it will make you very intriguing to the people around you.

Personality exists in terms of other people. It is the regularities of your behavior that make up your personality, not your outbursts. The only thing outbursts can do for you is to give you the reputation of being an unpredictable outburster. What you blurt out is not your real personality. It is not authentic and spontaneous to say what comes off the top of your head, for that might not represent your intent at all. At best it represents your frustration at not being able to control your own behavior well. Thus planned social behavior can provide you with the personality you want. People can learn to be confident by speaking confidently, they can learn to be competent by speaking competently if and only if there are specific lines and behaviors associated with the words *confident* and *competent*.

One of the major goals in speaking with others is to *avoid inflicting unnecessary hurt*. Even when you want to hurt someone for some reason, careful analysis will show you that it is neither productive nor appropriate. It is not that you have to give total approval to everything other people say and do or give in to what they want. It means you have to figure out what is important and effective to say. If you disagree, you want to address the reasons for your disagreement to someone who can do something about it. If you do not wish to do what the other person wants, you want to make your refusal clear and provide proper reasons so that the matter does not come up again. There are very few people you will encounter in your whole lifetime with whom you can afford to be completely open and allow your emotions to take control. Most of the time you will have to use your emotions to guide you toward a goal and then conceal and control them in order to say the most effective things to accomplish that goal. The price you pay for being free and open with another person is that person being free and open with you. This is hard to handle, takes time, and there simply is not room for much of it in anyone's life. If we do it with too many people, we have more emotion than we can handle.

With the few persons with whom you share complete intimacy there will be moments of incalculable beauty. It is worth working for, but it doesn't happen early and it doesn't happen often, and if you presume it exists and act like it does when it does not, you destroy a relationship. Building intimacy is a process of careful planning and experimenting characterized by mutual concern for personal feelings and sensitivities. This does not deny what we told you earlier about feelings. Feelings are indeed important, but *they are important to you.*

Many shy people have been hurt by others in relationships. Much of the hurt came when the other person decided that because the shy person did not answer back, he or she was a legitimate dumping ground for random emotions. Assertive people, firm in their egocentrism, tend to blunder ahead, pushing others into shyness. It is not that assertive people are malicious or consciously seeking to control others. They have been trained to demand rather than negotiate, and as a result manage to achieve temporary sovereignty over others. Shy people tend to build walls against these depradations and, unless they voluntarily submit to such control, use their experience to justify avoiding human contact. Shy people can protect themselves partly by understanding the human incompetence of the people who assert themselves and partly through competent performance in return. But one need not become assertive oneself to meet the charge of assertive others. When shy people can meet such attacks with planned and controlled moves in their own behalf, they are able to take their fair share of control in relationships. In fact, it is far better to demonstrate how much more effective a relationship can be when two people participate equitably.

THE BASIC QUESTIONS

You can compel yourself to focus on important elements in interpersonal communication by repeating the basic questions you have already learned:

What do I want to accomplish? What is the other person to know, to believe, or to do as a result of what I say? "I want him to listen!" "I want her to laugh!" "I want him to learn!" "I want her to lend me something!" These statements are to be as specific as possible.

Why should the person do it? Once again, a specific answer is necessary. "Because if he doesn't listen, he will make an error!" "If she doesn't laugh, she will have an unpleasant evening." "I want him to learn, because if he doesn't, he will be fired." "I want her to lend it, because if she doesn't, I may not lend things to her again."

Notice, in each case, that the goal is not a demand. There is nothing egocentric about asking for something you want *because* it will help the other person as well.

ORGANIZING

Once you have your goal clearly in mind and you are sure of your justification, you can start lining up your ideas. The idea is to get the other person *to understand you and to believe that he or she will benefit*. To do the former you have to explain, and to do the latter you have to persuade. Every unit of talk is a blend of information and persuasion.

Fortunately, the human mind, used properly, is a very orderly and efficient machine. Most minds can only receive information when it is organized to make sense. There are only a limited number of ways in which ideas can be organized. If you can find the form of organization that is most appropriate to your goal, you have the best chance of getting the other person to understand.

Ideas can be organized in order of OCCURRENCE. You do this when you want to tell a story, give directions, or explain a sequence of events.

Ideas can be arranged in terms of DESCRIPTION. You do this when you want to describe something or explain how something is made.

Ideas can be arranged by COMPONENTS. You use this when you want to explain the construction of something or when you want to point out its main features.

Ideas can be related by COMPARISON. You do this when you want to make an unfamiliar object familiar by showing how it is like something your audience already knows about. You can also use it to show how two items that are apparently alike differ.

Ideas can be compared against STANDARDS. You do this when you want to explain why something was good or bad or better than something else or when you want to give reasons why you made the choices you did.

Ideas can be ASSOCIATED. You do this when you want to explain what caused something or how one thing changes as another thing changes or when you want to predict the future or guess the outcome.

Ideas can be ARGUED. You do this when you want to convince people that something should or should not be done.

Here are some examples:

OCCURRENCE. "Let me tell you about my day. . . ." "Let me show you how to work that camera. . . ." "Let me explain how this assembly line operates. . . ."

DESCRIPTION. "This is how you can recognize one. . . ." "This is the way the engine is put together. . . ." "This is where the restaurant is located. . . ."

COMPONENTS. "This is what the problem consists of. . . ." "These are the different kinds of skis. . . ." "These are the choices at the theater tonight. . . ."

COMPARISON. "Bill and I certainly had different experiences on the trip. . . ." "You may not believe it, but the greenhouse and the solar home are very similar in design. . . ."

STANDARDS. "This is why Smith is the best choice for governor. . . ." "I think the Brown proposal is the best of the three. . . ." "This symphony is real art. . . ."

ASSOCIATION. "If we raise oil prices, the cost of living will go up. . . ." "They probably got that way because of their upbringing. . . ." "If we don't boost sales by 10 percent, we will have to lay off part of the work force. . . ." "Every time we add unskilled laborers, the number of accidents increases. . . ."

ARGUMENT. "Let's go to that movie because. . . ." "Vote for Smith because. . . ." "This plan is no good because. . . ."

If you know that you want to introduce a topic, but you are not sure how to put it together, you can try out each of the seven possibilities. For example:

OCCURRENCE. "Here's how contact lenses are made." "Here's how you insert contact lenses."

DESCRIPTION. "This is what the lenses look like."

COMPONENTS. "There are two basic kinds of contact lenses." "Contact lenses can be used for four kinds of eye difficulty."

COMPARISON. "Soft lenses are similar to hard lenses in these respects, but different from glasses in these respects."

STANDARDS. "Soft lenses are easiest on the eyes." "Hard lenses are best for. . . ."

ASSOCIATION. "These are the problems contact lenses will solve." "These are the problems contact lenses will cause."

ARGUMENT. "You ought to change to contact lenses."

EXERCISE

As silly as it may sound, you can do this with any topic. Once you have the list, you can select the direction you want to go with the topic. You may also find that some topics may not fit into a particular possibility. Try to make a statement in each category about each of the following topics:

Fruit juices	*Bulgarians*	*Potato chips*	*The stock market*
Socks	*Backgammon*	*High school*	*78 rpm records*
Children's books	*Mustard*	*Square dancing*	*The president*

As one final illustration, here is a set of statements about the mythical grevitz.

OCCURRENCE. "Here is how grevitzes are manufactured." "Here is how you install a grevitz in your ear." "Here is how the grevitz is used to fight forest fires."

DESCRIPTION. "Here is how the blue grevitz looks." "This is the way the eggshell grevitz is constructed."

COMPONENTS. "There are nineteen kinds of grevitzes." "These are the ways you can use a grevitz." "Here is how the grevitz has contributed to the Zekkle economy."

COMPARISON. "The blue grevitz is very different from the peanut butter grevitz in the following ways. . . ." "The orodescent grevitz has a number of features in common with a volley ball."

STANDARDS. "In order to be useful, a grevitz must. . . ." "To select a grevitz, keep in mind these essential features. . . ." "The Silesian grevitz is much more useful than the burned-out grevitz."

ASSOCIATION. "If you want to recover properly from spavins, here's how a grevitz will help." "An overdose of grevitz has been known to cause zelp disease." "Future conditions will demand increased grevitz production."

ARGUMENT. "We should adopt the grevitz as our national bird." "The proposal to buy 14,000 grevitzes should be defeated because. . . ."

The categories of organization direct you to things to say. As long as you don't mix up your categories, you will make sense to others. You can see how even nonsense can appear sensible if you structure it well. Most people hop from category to category when they talk. The mind, however, tries to connect up what it hears. If the speaker is not orderly, the listener must impose order, and often the listener does not impose the order the speaker had in mind. You can help the speaker get it straight by asking questions. Once again, the categories suggest the questions. For example, the speaker is talking about heraldry. You can ask

OCCURRENCE. "What is the history of coats of arms?"
DESCRIPTION. "What does a coat of arms look like?"
COMPONENTS. "What are the requirements of a coat of arms?" "What are the types?"
COMPARISON. "Is there a difference between traditional and contemporary coats of arms?" "What is the difference between a coat of arms and a crest?"
STANDARDS. "In order to qualify as official, what must a coat of arms have?"
ASSOCIATION. "How do people qualify to get a coat of arms?"
ARGUMENT. "Do you think that we should stop giving out coats of arms?"

For each of the following (or as many as possible) topics, try writing one statement and one question in each category.

The National Football League	The local hospital	Pets
Men's and women's fashions	Sanitation	Zoning in our town
	Our governor	The next holiday
	The last book	The weather

My vacation	I read	The movie last
My kids/your kids	Teen-age music	night
Interior decoration	Inflation	Taxes

When you finish with this list, write down some topics that you are likely to talk about at social gatherings and prepare one statement and one question in each category so that you are prepared to handle anything that happens the next time you are out.

ADAPTING

We have been discussing simple conversation as if it were public speech in a courtroom or legislature. A person who makes sense talking with others can make sense on the public platform. A person skilled on the public platform can adapt his or her skill to social conversation. Both public and private talk require time and thought in order to be coherent.

Effective talkers are both well organized and responsive to their audiences. People who seem to get what they want from social situations know how to present their ideas in ways that provide others with reasons to listen and comply. People make their decisions about how they will respond to you based on what they hear. If what you say makes sense to them, they will generally cooperate with you. Making sense, of course, means giving people a reason to do what you ask them to do. We are often dismayed to see frauds and charlatans talking people into destructive and foolish acts. But people are not really talked into them. When you see people obviously conned, it is because they want to be conned and are not applying their good sense of analysis to what they hear.

In addition to helping you overcome your shyness, this chapter can be used to help you defend yourself against foolish and unethical persuasion. It will help you discover flaws in the requests other people make of you.

To be effective with others, you don't have to be passionate or histrionic. You don't have to tell funny stories and you don't have to know everything about everything. Mainly what you have to do is make sense to the person with whom you are speaking. You must be responsive to his or her responses. You can do both by applying the categories of organization to your talk.

RULES FOR THE USE OF THE CATEGORIES

Occurrence. It is imperative that steps be presented in order. If someone is offering you a set of instructions or a narrative and something seems to be missing or the flow of talk seems illogical, test it by thinking through the steps. If something seems to be missing, ask. For example:

- "I got off the train and went to my hotel."
- "Did you take a cab?"

The questioner is asking about a missing step. Your questions will help the talker make sense. In your own preparation you can anticipate the questions that might be asked or you can try out your talk with a friend, who can ask you questions to help you make sure no details are omitted. In general, using the categories to ask questions is most effective if you stay within the organization the speaker requires. If the speaker is telling you what the car looks like, don't inquire about where it was purchased. Ask about the hood ornament or the accessories. If the speaker is explaining how to operate the machinery, don't ask if other models are available, ask which way to set it, start it, or use it.

There are four main requirements for using *Occurrence*.

1. Use it whenever your goal is to cover a span of time.
2. Make sure the steps are in order. Edit your talk to make sure that nothing is omitted.
3. Don't digress. Complete the sequence before going on, even if it is tempting to talk about some detail.
4. If you are telling a joke, remember that laughter is contingent on getting to the punch line properly. An effective joke has all of the steps in perfect order. If you telegraph the punch line or leave out an important detail in sequence, your joke will fall flat.

Description. Descriptions are used when you want to talk about how something looks or how parts are joined together. When you describe something, work in sequence from top to bottom, right to left, or whatever sequence you choose. However, once you decide on a sequence, you must stay with it, or you will confuse your listener. Description is a rich source of questions. When you want a conversational turn, take advantage of the break in the flow of talk to ask a description question.

- "What does the organization chart look like?"
- "How is the shipping department laid out?"

There are three things to keep in mind when using this sequence.

1. You can describe concrete things or abstractions.
2. You have not done your job if you omit a major component.
3. You can decide where you will begin and end your description, but once you start, you must stay within the sequence.

Components. Putting ideas in terms of components or categories is perhaps the most basic way of making sense. It can be applied to almost any topic.

- "The government is divided into executive, legislative, and judicial branches."
- "This city faces five major problems."
- "There are three things that might be fun to do tonight."

Organization by components will provide you with headings, and each of the headings may be further subdivided. For example,

- "The hospital consists of three major divisions—outpatient, inpatient, and emergency."
- "Procedure in the emergency room is as follows. . . ." (Occurrence).
- "The outpatient division is divided into three categories. . . ." (Components).
- "The inpatient rooms look like this. . . ." (Description).

By using organization by components you will be able to offer clear definitions. If, for example, someone is talking about her job as a counselor, you can ask, "What kinds of cases do you handle?" Or you can ask a specific question, such as "Do you handle depressed clients?" Furthermore, sensible questioning signals to the other person that you are interested and paying attention.

There are three important ideas to remember in using this organization pattern.

1. Whatever categories you use, for the purposes of your talk, they will describe the whole topic. Once you have laid out the categories, you cannot add anything without the risk of confusing your listeners.
2. You must take care to avoid overlapping categories. "Inpatient," "outpatient," "emergency," and "kinds of doctors" would be overlapping categories, since "kinds of doctors" would cut across the three other categories. Adding "administration," however, would not be overlapping since it is a separate division of the whole hospital.
3. Categories should be about equal in importance. If you are mentioning unusual occurrences or exceptions, you must make it clear that they are not as important as the main components.

Comparison. Once you have explained the steps for doing something or described something or divided it into its categories, you can compare it with something else to show similarities or differences. You can compare things that appear similar to show that they are different.

- "Jerry Ford was a very different kind of president from Richard Nixon."
- "You cannot operate a two-cycle engine the same way as a four-cycle engine."

You can compare things that look different to show how they are similar.

- "*The Odd Couple* makes just as serious a statement about relationships as *Who's Afraid of Virginia Woolf?*"
- "There are some psychological similarities between poker and chess."

When you use organization by comparison, you should be alert to three things.

1. The items you compare must be in the same sequence. You can compare two occurrences, two descriptions, or two sets of components, but you cannot compare occurrence and components.
2. Whatever the patterns of organization, you must also compare similar features.

3. There is no point in comparing two familiar things that appear similar in order to show that they are similar, or two dissimilar things to show that they are different.

Standards. When you want to evaluate something, you must compare it to some standard in order to demonstrate the reasons for your judgment. You must, of course, select a set of standards that make sense and be prepared to defend your selection of standards. Very often we permit people to slip their standards by us without questioning them. For example, "Joe Smith would make a good governor because he is honest, experienced, and a good family man" implies that you believe that quality as a governor can be predicted from these three characteristics. Similarly, "*Chicken Roost* is a good play because it is suspenseful, contains sharp character development, and has a great number of funny lines" implies that the three characteristics you cite are qualities of a good play. Your respondent might question you by citing other characteristics—quality of theme, for example. You would be required to show why this quality was not as important or agree that the play met this standard also.

When you declare that something is better than something else, you imply that standards exist. Your intent may have been only to explain why you chose what you did. If, however, you seek to convince the other person to make a similar choice, then you must be prepared to argue on the two levels just mentioned, that is, that the standards you are using are sufficient to justify the judgment and that the thing being judged does indeed meet the standards better than available alternatives. There are three things to keep in mind when employing this method of organization.

1. Be sure you understand what standards you are using. Many people seem to make value statements without understanding what they are committing themselves to.
2. Be prepared to explain why the standards you choose are most relevant to the issue.
3. When you compare two or more things, be consistent in the criteria of evaluation.

Association. This is the most complicated method of organizing material. It is more useful to a scientist seeking to make connections than it is to a conversationalist, but often we attempt to make statements of this kind and frequently find ourselves in trouble when we do, so you ought to be thoroughly familiar with it. The order of Association is used when we say things such as "That restaurant will give you heartburn," "People who buy that model car are generally satisfied," or "The Smedley Law will cause an increase in crime." When we attempt to explain by making connections, we are associating.

If you seek to explain how one thing causes another, you leave yourself open to considerable questioning and argument. If, for example, you wish to claim that one event causes another, you must demonstrate that there is no other possible cause, that the two events are connected all the time, and that there is no exception that cannot be explained by something lying outside the two events. Those people who claim that "delinquents come from bad homes," are vulnerable to anyone who provides an example of a person coming from a "bad home" who did not become delinquent. They are further vulnerable to those who demonstrate that a great many delinquents come from "good homes." Finally, they are open to argument about the standards they use to identify a "good" home from a "bad" one, as well as those that define what being a "delinquent" means.

We will not attempt to teach you the subtleties and complexities of reasoning by association. It is important for you to understand, however, that statements of this kind are virtually always arguable and that there is a tendency for all of us to make them off the top of our heads without having a basis from which to argue them.

Rather than give you a list of things to remember about this method of organization, we ask you to keep only one point in mind: Things are rarely as simple as they appear. One event can cause many events, and two events that appear to be connected can be, themselves, separately caused by a third or each caused simultaneously by different events. If this seems complicated to you, it should stand as a warning to you to take care when trying to make associations.

Argument. Many people believe that they should not argue. As a matter of fact people must argue all the time, and those who do not believe in argument or are afraid of it often sacrifice their share of influence on the decisions that are made about them. Shy people often avoid making any statements they believe to be controversial for fear of being challenged or contradicted. But actually argument can be exciting and productive, and it is much easier to handle than association. Argument is nothing more than offering reasons for your choice or proposal. If there is an expert around, his or her reasons might carry more weight than yours, but by and large, when laypeople are involved in argument, one persons reason's are potentially as logical and persuasive as another's.

Think of a simple argument, such as when more than one person makes a proposal of a movie to attend. If there are four people planning to go, there could be four proposals. Somehow agreement must be reached. In most groups each person makes a proposal and offers reasons, and the group agrees on a preference.

Argument is a simple process in which one person claims that something ought to be done, some idea ought to be accepted, or that some course of action is preferable to the alternatives and someone else disagrees. The argument is carried on until some third party decides who wins. Argument is never carried on to convince the opponent. Attempts to convince the opponent are called combat, and they are generally fruitless. Argument is conducted when there is a need for a decision, some legitimate authority to make the decision, and some rules of order that everyone follows. In close personal relationships, it is imperative that some method be arranged to resolve disagreements, otherwise arguments invariably become combat and the relationship is put in danger.

The person who proposes the course of action or idea carries what is called the burden of proof. That means that things are presumed to be all right until someone demonstrates that they are not all right. It comes from the legal principle that a person is innocent until proven guilty. The person who opposes the idea does not have to propose a counteridea, merely show that some essential component of the proposal is false, fallacious, or poorly reasoned. The arguer has four obligations any of which can be knocked down by an opponent.

1. The arguer must show that there is some problem that must be remedied. Either something is going on that shouldn't be going on or something is not going on that should be going on and someone or something is being injured by it.
2. The arguer must present the details of a plan or proposal that addresses itself to each component of the problem.
3. The arguer must show how the proposal will eliminate the problem and that the proposal can be brought into existence (including a demonstration of how it can be financed).
4. If challenged to do so, the arguer must demonstrate that the proposal will not create a worse problem.

The person who opposes the proposal may claim that there is no problem, that what is happening or not happening does not cause sufficient injury to warrant a proposal, or that the facts as stated by the arguer are simply wrong. He or she may also claim that the proposal will not solve the problem, cannot be brought into existence, is too costly, or will create even greater problems. Finally the opponent may propose an alternative course of action, but if so he or she is obligated to assume the same burden of proof as the original arguer.

By carrying out an argument within the framework of rules, those who listen and judge are able to follow the thread of the argument without becoming confused. By applying rules, arguers are restrained from offending or injuring each other. There is enormous potential for fallacious argumentation, commonly used when two people are doing combat. When people go head to head, it is possible to inflict injury through personal insult, corruption of logic, plays with words, lies, intimidation, bribery and pleas, or threats of physical force. When this happens, the strongest party usually wins, unless, of course, the weaker party has some protection at law. In close relationships this kind of protection is generally not available, and shy people are often pushed around badly by overpowering partners. Their best alternative is to get some skill at parrying unethical argument and, when possible, get the argument transferred, by agreement, to a third party—a counselor or a lawyer—who can adjudicate, question, and resolve. Another alternative is for both parties to the relationship to learn the steps of cooperative problem solving.

At any event, when an argument and counterargument have been offered, each of the patterns of organization can be used to present ideas. For example, one person argues that sanitation service in the town is bad enough to warrant a change while the other person argues that there is an even better idea. Here is how it might develop.

- "Sanitation in our town is terrible. We have the following problems. . . ." (*Components* is used to list and explain the problems.)
- "On the contrary, our problem really consists of. . . ." (*Comparison* is used to contrast one list of components with the original.)
- "At any event, it is not good enough. . . ." (*Standards* are employed to show what "good enough" is, and present conditions are compared with those standards and judged.)
- "We ought to adopt this plan, which would operate like this. . . ." (*Occurrence* is used to provide step-by-step details for the plan.)

- "But the plan will not eliminate the problem. . . ." (*Association* is used to examine the effect the proposal will have on the conditions alleged and to predict the future.)

And so on.

Remember that it is very unlikely that the person with whom you are arguing will change his or her mind. Argument is customarily directed to an "audience" or judge, some agency that can decide. In industry this may be the boss or it may be the board of directors. In private relationships, in order to avoid the necessity of submitting arguments to a neutral third party, the couple may apply cooperative problem solving, which consists of the following steps:

1. A problem is identified by one or both of the parties. The problem may be feelings, events, or acts inside or outside the relationship that cause discomfort or difficulty to one of the parties.
2. Agreement is achieved with the proposition that something is wrong and that something must be done about it. The couple agree on what is wrong. (Joe is hanging around the house too much. Sally is excessively fatigued because of responsibilities at home and on the job. Their budget is not carrying them through to the end of the month.)
3. The couple agree on some tangible end state or goal to be achieved. (Joe comes only once a week. Sally gets some help with the housework. There must be some money left at the end of the month.) A problem question is phrased based on this goal statement. ("How can we tell Joe not to come around?" "How can Bill be more effective in helping Sally?" "What expenses can be cut?")
4. The couple search for facts that indicate the nature of the problem. Sometimes the facts require that the couple rephrase their problem question.
5. The couple examine their assets and limitations. They take into account practical, moral, legal, and financial barriers to their solution and then they set a goal for themselves that lies within their limitations.
6. They propose a number of solutions and inquire, first, about whether each one violates the limitations and, second, about each one's chances of accomplishing the goal.
7. They select a solution or construct one. They decide on some ways to check its effectiveness once they put it into operation.
8. They develop an operation plan and decide what each is to do.
9. They check back periodically to make sure things are working well.

Argument is frightening and often destructive when it becomes combat. It almost always becomes combat when there is no referee or neutral third party to make a decision. Couples who go head-to-head, each expecting to convince the other, put themselves on a collision course in which the final alternative is breaking up the relationship. It is possible to engage in heated discussion, to express emotion, and even to yell at each other without disrupting the relationship so long as there is agreement on the procedure to follow and the outcome desired. Combat offers neither of these protections. The techniques of cooperative problem solving offer an alternative to combat that permits argument within a framework of rules that might lead to a productive solution to the problems.

QUESTIONING AND CRITICIZING

The seven organizational patterns can be used to examine critically what other people say. In fact, they serve as a basis for training yourself in effective listening. As you listen to someone speak, you ask yourself, "Which pattern of organization is most appropriate to the idea being offered?" If the speaker is giving you instructions, you can listen carefully to discover missing steps and you can ask about them. If the speaker is describing something, you can ask yourself if you could recognize it from the description. If not, you can ask for missing details. If the speaker is offering components, you can check to see if major components are missing or if the components provided overlap. If the speaker is providing a comparison, you can make sure that he or she is comparing two objects with the same pattern of organization. If the speaker is criticizing, you can discover the standards used, and if they are not obvious, you ask about them. If the speaker is making an association, you can apply the relevant tests of logic and ask for missing details or connections. If the speaker is arguing, you can put yourself into the position of an opponent and ask about the nature of the need, the details of the plan, the steps in implementation, and you can raise questions about possible hazards if the plan is accepted. The patterns of organization help both in the preparation of talk and in the reception of it.

DEVELOPING AN IMAGE OF COMPETENCE

There is nothing wrong with taking a hand in the building of your own image. You will have an image anyway. You will be what people think you are. If people think you are shy, you will have an image of shyness. You can alter your image of shyness by acting in ways that are not shy. We have discussed many of your options with you already, and in the following chapters we will offer you some suggestions for your performance on the job, with your loved ones, and in the ordinary situations of your life. Regardless of how you feel inside, you can change the way people see you merely by changing what you say and how you say it. If you speak competently and effectively, gradually people will come to see you as competent and effective.

Most people do not look as incompetent as they think they do anyway. Most shy people are excessively concerned about the way they look to others. Some books advise people to learn to improve their speaking by practicing in front of a mirror, and some courses use videotape in order to show people their "mistakes." It is dangerous to look at yourself too closely, however. You are a biased observer and you will generally see what you set out to see. The only way you can see how you look to others is to examine how others respond to you. You can then ask yourself what kind of a person you must be to receive that kind of response. If you can get people to listen to what you have to say, then you can regard yourself as an interesting person. If you can get them to agree with you, then you can regard yourself as a leader. And so on. Other people are the mirror that provides you with the only accurate image you will get of yourself.

It is dangerous to see yourself as more competent than you really are. There are some people who have an exaggerated image of themselves. They think they are attractive, charming, and brilliant. Generally they are bores, but they manage not to see themselves as others see them merely by ignoring others.

Shy people make their own trouble by trying to find a mirror inside themselves. They look into themselves and see tension and fear, and then they believe that the people out there can also see the tension and fear. They get an impression of how they must look if others can see their tension, and then they see themselves that way. By seeing themselves as tense and fearful, they maximize their tension and fear and they prevent themselves from acting.

Shy people tend to see others as more competent than they really are. They see others as handsome, articulate, slick, smooth, poised, self-confident, while they see themselves as apprehensive, tense, withdrawn, cringing. Once they have made comparisons based on these fantasies, they have provided themselves with a powerful argument not to try. After all, how could a fearful and cringing person manage to talk to a poised and articulate person like that one over there? But you are only shy if you behave shyly. Thus, learning principles of controlling your own behavior will alter your self-image considerably.

Shy people also tend to concentrate on physical attractiveness. They tend to believe that there is some relationship between beauty and competence. But all of us know physically attractive people who are totally vapid when they open their mouths. As a matter of fact, physical attractiveness is often a trap, because attractive people tend to get an exaggerated notion of their competence and often fall flat on their faces when their beauty begins to fade. We all must cope with the media, of course, which constantly present us with images of extraordinarily beautiful people acting in heroic ways. Sometimes excessive attachment to media heroes can make people feel very small. Please keep in mind that media people are actors, carefully selected for their attractiveness. They spend much of their time tending to their beauty. It is a profession for them, and they get paid for it. You are not competing with them and need not compete with them.

What is most important for you is a "good reputation." More than two thousand years ago Aristotle pointed out that there are three ways to persuade: through logic, through emotion, and through a good reputation. The most powerful of these, he said, was reputation. You can acquire a good reputation by acting in reliable and competent ways. If you can identify the components of a good reputation, you can act in ways that will convince others that you are that way. Reputations, after all, are made, not born. The best way to get a good reputation is to say credible things. This is easy. All you need to do is to think about what you are going to say, prepare yourself, and then say it. Shy people tend to believe that credibility is somehow connected with their mood or their inner state. It is not. It is connected with performance and the way other people see it. Reputation is a judgment made by others, not an inner state you are born with. You have the power to control your words so that you can control the way you are seen by others.

A good reputation is earned. A phony is a person who makes promises to us that are not kept. All of us have encountered phonies. We learn to identify them and to compare their actions with their words in order to trap them or train ourselves to avoid them. They may be glib and they may be attractive, but if they deceive us, they lose credibility. People who are taken in by phonies allow themselves to be conned. They are not paying attention or they are so desperate to have someone pay attention to them that they are willing to believe anything. Shy people are easily victimized because they are so attentive to their own frailties that they are unable to see the weaknesses of others. We are trying to convince you that if you learn nothing more from this book than what has been offered in this chapter—how to examine the words others offer you—you will be able to spot phonies and avoid them. Once you learn to listen to the words a person says and note the content of his or her remarks (not the facility with which they are said), you can spot phonies and take action against them. Once you decide to control your own words so that they represent what you honestly believe and help you accomplish what you want to accomplish, you can become a person of good reputation.

Reputation is built over time. Your friends will not treat you differently the minute you change your communication style, although they will notice it and probably ask about it. It will take a while for them to adjust to your new behavior, because it has been comfortable for them to have you the way you were. If you have been shy and subservient, it will be threatening to them (no matter how much they love you) when you throw off your subservience and start asking for your fair share. Sometimes it is necessary to find some new acquaintances in order to convince yourself that you are doing all right. In the following chapter we will offer some suggestions for doing this.

Shy people sometimes break loose emotionally and demand credibility by shouting or crying. This is not effective. People respond strongly to emotion, and their response is usually negative. Shy people tend to believe that if someone says something vehemently or loudly, it is an indication of strength. Overuse of emotion is one way that phonies build themselves up into people with charisma. They speak so strongly and assert themselves so vigorously that others are afraid to contradict them. Many shy people fall under the spell of such people. They see the people with charisma as persons with special powers, which is just what they want them to see. They comply with their wishes, thus making them feel even more powerful by becoming subservient to them. The people with charisma in turn reinforce their shyness by claiming to have the power to provide them with rich and happy lives. Many of our contemporary cults are populated with shy people trying to escape the responsibility of social interaction and surrendering their humanity to powerful, charismatic others, who run their lives to their own advantage. People who are voluntarily silent—shy people—submit to control by everyone around them and sometimes submit so thoroughly that it is virtually impossible to come back to a normal life in a social world. That is the ultimate tragedy of shyness.

Charismatic people often write books. They promise readers that by following the simple instructions offered they will lose weight, make a million dollars, win power and glory, or become physically fit. They offer magical systems to cure physical and emotional ills, make you a better person, provide you with success on the job, become a leader of people and nations, all based on a simple formula or ritual.

There is no formula. It offers you information that you can use to alter your social behavior in the ways you seek to alter it. Everything offered has been tried by other people and used effectively on their own. There is no organization you can join that will provide you with perfection by using what this book teaches. You are on your own to use the book as you see fit. This book offers you a chance to change gradually, in small ways, and to achieve your goals for your own purposes. The only demand it makes on you is that you check what you do against reality. If nothing else, this book should make you a bit suspicious of people who may have been pushing you around. We hope that it will make you chary about following what they direct you to do, and at best we want it to help you take your own stands on behalf of your own interests.

ADMONITIONS

Before going on to the following chapters, which offer you specific advice about social situations you will encounter in your life, we offer you some recommendations for listening to the others around you and deciding on the amount of credibility to give to what they say.

When people tell you about things they have seen and done, ask yourself whether their report squares with other reliable reports. If there are differences between the way they see it and the way you see it, do not immediately assume that you are wrong and they are right.

When people draw conclusions or present arguments, ask yourself if they are distorting information in order to get you to believe what they are saying. Ask yourself if they are hiding behind a title or position. Find out whether their reputations are earned and legitimate or merely claimed. Examine the reasons they offer to see if they make sense. Try to discover whether you are being assaulted with a barrage of words that make no sense.

Remember: The little boy who saw the emperor without his clothes is the model for the informed social critic. Anyone who is trying to get you to do something or believe something is obligated to give you a good reason for doing it or believing it, a reason that makes sense to you! Just because the other person says so or wants you to is not a good enough reason for you to agree. Look out for some of the tricks people will try to play on you:

- Look for references to obscure authorities that you can't check out. Just because a person drops a name doesn't mean it is so. Just because it is in the book doesn't mean it is so.
- Look for refusal to answer questions. People have a responsibility to answer questions, and you have every right to demand it of them. Refusal to answer questions is a sign that the speaker is trying to hide something important, either a crucial fact or his or her own ignorance.
- Look for long strings of technical words given without definitions. Speakers are obligated to make things clear to their listeners. They must speak in language you can handle, and you have every right to demand that they do so.
- Look for disorganization, which hides the reasons or advantages they will gain if you believe them. People try to hide their motives, but you have the right to protect yourself by looking for motives. If you can't get it clear in your head what a speaker will gain if you comply with him or her, then you should avoid complying.
- Look for unwillingness to admit error. There has never been an infallible person. People who insist on being right all the time must be wrong some of the time, and you have the right and obligation to discover those times. You needn't point out that they were wrong, because that sometimes triggers vigorous outbursts. You simply need not comply with what they want when you discover their errors. Unwillingness to admit error is a sign of weakness.

- Look for references to mystical forces you cannot understand. This is not meant to be an irreligious statement, but sometimes people use religious belief as a means of forcing others into compliance.
- Look for premature pressure to get you to agree. If the other person won't let you take the time to consider his or her statements, you should be rightfully suspicious.
- Look for loud and bullying talk. If people feel they have to yell at you, it is a sure sign that something is wrong. You have the right to insist on being treated respectfully.
- Look out for the argument that because something worked for the other person, it will work for you. People are different. You have the right to seek your own way, so long as you do not injure others.
- Remember that the people who make a proposal have the burden of proof. Insist that they assume it.

You owe it to yourself to be just a little suspicious all the time and very suspicious the more the other person asks from you. Remember: Your obligation when you talk to others is to take their needs into account. You may also demand that others take your needs into account. You cannot expect them to sacrifice their interests on your behalf any more than you will sacrifice your interests on their behalf, but you can ask for a reasonable bargain that will benefit both of you.

Now we can review what we have told you thus far in the book so that you can approach the next chapters with a real prospect for change.

- Shyness is the result of believing that you can lose more by participating than you can gain.
- It is costly to you in your vocational and personal life when you are not competent in dealing with others.
- You have control over your own participation by controlling what you say and do. You cannot control others.
- When you do not control what you say to others, you are not effective, and when you are not effective, you tend to become anxious and depressed.
- If you focus on your feelings, you will never try to change your behavior.
- You will never become effective with others until you change your behavior.

There are no guarantees in human social life. However, within the range of the possible, the best guarantee you have is to control the words that come out of your mouth. When you can do that, you have power, and when you have power, you can become the person you want to be—so long as that person doesn't jeopardize others. When you control your words, you can be an interesting and effective participant in life. Others will enjoy you and you will be able to enjoy them.

- Set your goals with other people in mind. You can't have everything, and neither can they. It is better to try for small goals that can be attained than to fail gloriously by not attaining impossible goals.
- Base your selection of what to say on the reality of the situation, not your personal dream. React to what is said and done. Learn to spot phonies and do not let yourself become one.
- Select your ideas by searching your own mind and resources. Don't let others force you to accept their ideas without offering you good reasons in your terms.
- When you express ideas, put them together in ways that other people can understand. Honor their questions. When you listen to others, make sure you can follow their organization and remember that you have the right to request clarification.
- When you make requests of people, make sure that they know what they will gain by complying, even if it is nothing more than your gratitude.
- Prepare yourself for contingencies and remember that anytime you fail, you can put part of the blame on the other person. There are reasons for the behavior of others over which you have no control.

You cannot read other people's minds, and they cannot read yours. It is reasonable to respond to what you see and hear. As a matter of fact, much of what you believe is based on inference. If you see and hear a person behaving competently, it is not a fact that they are competent, it is an inference based on what you observe. If you can draw that inference about someone else, others can draw it about you—if you give them a chance to by behaving properly.

Remember that there is ineffective behavior, not necessarily ineffective people.

Leave a bookmark at this point so that you can review these summaries as you read through the final chapters.

RECOMMENDED READINGS

Gerald M. Phillips and J. Jerome Zolten, *Structuring Speech* (New York: The Bobbs Merrill Co., Inc., 1976).

Monroe C. Beardsley, *Thinking Straight*, 4th ed. (Englewood Cliffs, N.J.: Prentice-Hall Publishing Co., Inc., 1975).

A. H. Chapman, *Harry Stack Sullivan: The Man and His Work* (New York: G. P. Putnam's Sons, 1976).

chapter 10

Talk and Daily Living

Most of us get a little annoyed with the daily business of living because we do not think we are getting our fair share. Doormen and clerks seem to ignore us, cab drivers seem to take the long way around, service in the restaurant is too slow, and our friends seem to ignore us when we need them.

It is hard for us to understand how unimportant we really are to everyone but ourselves. But, the long and short of it is, when we are concentrating on accomplishing our goals, everyone else is concentrating on accomplishing theirs. The world seems to promise us a lot. Magazines tell us we can have good marriages, raise happy and successful children, earn enough to buy the good things in life. The media tell us how to be beautiful and romantic. Meanwhile, we face a world filled with shortages, threats of war, inflation. We are in a constant state of tension between our desires to do well and our fears that we won't.

It is, therefore, not surprising that some people try to avoid trying. Many shy people believe themselves to be realists. They are so frustrated by what they are not getting in their daily lives that they give up trying. One of the most important things you can do is learn how to handle your daily life effectively. You can do this by paying attention to normal social routines, by trying to become effective at behaviors designed to make daily life go smoothly.

For example, in a store, where you are "customer," you play your role against another person, who is "clerk." If both customer and clerk do what is expected of them, customer benefits by receiving a fair chance to make a purchase and clerk benefits by receiving a fair chance to do the job properly. Neither can be hurt. Customer need not buy, and clerk need not sell, yet both can be all right. However, customer cannot demand personal information from clerk or service that is not included in clerk's agreement of employment. And supervisor has the power to punish clerk if clerk exceeds a proper role. If customer pushes clerk to exceed his or her proper role, then customer is taking unfair advantage. On the other hand, if clerk takes undue liberties with customer, is insulting, perfunctory, or crude, then clerk earns punishment from supervisor. Safety for both persons demands adherence to prescribed public roles. What they may think about each other is their own business.

It is important in overcoming your shyness that you accustom yourself to playing standard social roles. You can discover how to play these roles by observing common social situations. Watch diners in restaurants, shoppers, people meeting each other at cocktail parties. Listen to what they say and do. Look especially at those whom you think are doing well. Notice how simple their behavior is and how uncomplicated their conversation. They almost look like stereotypes. They must keep these stereotypical roles, or they will upset the fragile balance required for people to meet each other and do business. Even the lines are stereotyped. Even though we know that every contact with others is unique in its own way, we have public ways to ease into the contact so that we can explore it for the special features of a situation. This saves us from plunging into contacts we might not be able to handle. Standard lines are directed toward accomplishing whatever limited goals are possible in the situation. In a restaurant, for example, the best you can hope for is a good meal courteously served. There are standard ways to request this. You can always encounter an inept waiter who does not respond to standard lines, but generally, if you say what you ought to say, the waiter will do what ought to be done. You cannot ask for more.

In a store you can demand proper service, minimal waiting, and fair prices. At a party you can hope for standard small talk and decent refreshments. There is little a meal or a trip to the store can offer besides what is expected, but a party may offer some special human contact that can be developed. To discover this, you must appear to be an acceptable human being, which is simple enough to do, so long as you stay within conventional behavior.

People who play routine roles make specific and limited information available. It is perfectly legitimate to ask a clerk to explain something about the quality of the merchandise, but it is not legitimate for the clerk to investigate to discover whether you have the money before showing the merchandise to you. It is also unreasonable for the customer to hold the clerk responsible for violations made by the company. If merchandise turns out to be defective, it is not necessarily the clerk's fault. Redress must be sought from the appropriate person. By the same token, the clerk cannot demand that the customer put the merchandise to any particular use. Once paid for, the customer has the right to do what he or she pleases with the merchandise. The clerk no longer has any stake in the matter.

At social gatherings strangers may exchange names, occupations, locations, and simple statements of interest. Anything beyond this routine disclosure is voluntary. If you elect to provide voluntary information, you may find yourself building a private relationship. Those who violate the rules by giving too much information too quickly may find themselves locked into a relationship they did not expect. The process of negotiating relationships is delicate and complicated. We will discuss it in detail in the following chapter.

Sometimes it is necessary to object to the way routines are performed. If reasonable service is not provided, it is proper to seek correction of the behavior. However, once a simple request is made, there is little that can be done. If proper service is not provided, you have the right to refuse the merchandise. If service in a restaurant is poorly rendered, you may leave. A complaint to the hostess or a request to see the manager are also legitimate. Shy people often put up with abominable service because they do not know the extent of their rights. So long as complaints are made in proper form to responsible persons, they are legitimate. No one has to put up with persecution.

Some clerks delight in harassing quiet customers, and some customers get joy out of persecuting shy clerks. The antidote is simple. Learn to play proper roles and stay within them. Every proper role has a built-in protection to being bullied. As a customer, keep in mind that competition is the cogwheel of our economic life and that you are not obligated to buy where you are not treated well.

Prepare yourself to accomplish the following goals:

1. To provide instructions clearly to clerks, waiters, and other service personnel so that they cannot mistake what you expect of them. If they cannot do what you expect, they may say so, and you may then bargain for lesser service. If you do not make your requests clear, you cannot hold the service person responsible if you are not satisfied. Be prepared by practicing your request in advance.
2. To register complaints reasonably to the proper party with proof of inconvenience. It is perfectly legitimate to prepare your remarks if you seek to complain about defective merchandise. If you are asking for an exchange or your money back, prepare yourself to assume the burden of proof by presenting evidence of the defectiveness of the product.
3. To ask questions in a way that evokes useful answers. Don't ask questions for the fun of it. Be sure of the information you want. Be sure that the person you ask has the information. Then prepare your question in such a way that you will receive a useful answer. Be sure you know what a useful answer would sound like.
4. To answer questions so that you provide necessary information. Sometimes this is difficult to do, since not everyone is trained to ask good questions. If you are asked a question, listen to it carefully and try to figure out what the other person would do with an answer if you gave one. If you discover that the other person would put the information to use on your behalf, answer the question. If not, remember that you are not obligated to answer anything beyond what is expected in the normal situation.
5. To resist attempts to bully you. Shy people have long been patsies for super salespeople, since they are not prepared to say no. If you know the most that can be expected of you as a consumer, then you will find it easy to refuse to purchase what you do not need or want no matter how hard the salesperson tries to make you do so.

You can apply these goals to virtually every routine public situation—to doormen, cabdrivers, sales clerks, waiters and waitresses, hosts and hostesses, receptionists, information givers, complaint receivers, office clerks, and safety personnel, such as firemen and policemen. Clerical personnel are, themselves, often shy people. They appreciate consideration and respond well to it. On the other hand, they have the power to make your life miserable if you treat them badly.

The situation is somewhat more formidable when facing medical personnel. Physicians' receptionists are notorious bullies. Sometimes a simple protest to the doctor that the receptionist is exacerbating your illness helps. Sometimes you may have to find another doctor. The problem is that when you are a patient, you are often helpless. Hospital patients, for example, while protected by the Constitution and the Bill of Rights, are at the mercy of nurses, ward personnel, and the various therapists who work on them and often deal with them in depersonalized ways. Fighting back sometimes does little more than bring even greater discomfort and neglect. Sometimes intervention by someone from the outside can make a difference, and if your doctor is reasonably sympathetic, a clearly stated complaint might bring about a desirable change.

If the doctor is the person you are having trouble with, you will probably have more difficulty, since doctors' position seems to give them authority over almost everyone. Generally, it doesn't help to antagonize people whose services you need.

Sometimes people try to mystify you by using technical language. You are entitled to ask questions. People are not entitled to respect simply because they use complicated language. When you are seeking service from them, you are entitled to ask them to be clear. That means you can ask questions about what will happen to you, what the fee will be, and what other choices you have.

TRY THESE EXERCISES

Proceed through these social situations. Try at least one. Follow the instructions carefully.

ASKING QUESTIONS OF A STORE CLERK

Think of some object you normally buy in a department store, one for which you have a legitimate need and you can afford if you can find a good one for a good price. Inquire into the nature of the situation in which you normally buy this object. For example, if you are buying a sweater, take note of the fact that most of the sweaters are in glass cases, and that service is needed in order to examine them. Make a list of questions you could legitimately ask the clerk. Make sure they are questions the answers to which will help you make a decision. For example, "Do you have a blue sweater in my size?" (Wait for the clerk to ask you what your size is. If you know, tell him. If you do not know, ask for a measurement or a good guess. The clerk may ask you what some of your other sizes are, or he or she may produce a tape measure and take the proper measurements. Notice how you have developed a good deal of conversation out of this question. It is all legitimate?) Or again, "What is the difference in washing procedures for wool and synthetics?" (This question seeks some useful information. The clerk may not know the answer to this, but sweaters must have little tags that give washing instructions, and the two of you can talk about it as you examine the tags.)

There are a number of other questions you could ask. For example, "Why is wool so much more expensive?" "Will this sweater produce those little balls when I wash it?" "Does this fabric gather static electricity?" Make sure you have several questions to ask. If you are not seriously thinking of buying, two questions will be sufficient. It would not be fair to take much more of the clerk's time. If you are seriously going to buy, proceed through your list of questions. Try this exercise with three or four different products in different circumstances. Make sure you have a closing line, such as "Thank you for your time," so that you can excuse yourself conveniently. You do not owe the clerk an explanation of why you are not buying.

You can vary this exercise. In the supermarket you can ask, "What is the difference between the national brand, the house brand, and the generic brand?" "How would you identify a good soup?" Remember to say, "Thank you for your time," when you get the information.

IMPROVING SERVICE IN A RESTAURANT

Remember that waiters and waitresses receive very low hourly wages. They rely on tips. If you do not intend to leave a sizable tip (more than 15 percent), do not try this exercise.

The main idea of this exercise is to discover the ingredients in some dish you are thinking of ordering. This works best in a restaurant that serves ethnic food, but only if the service personnel speak English. You must prepare your lines. You can check the posted menu outside the restaurant and select an item.

- "Can you tell me the ingredients in your wine sauce?"
- "How is the Chicken Kiev prepared?"
- "What are the ingredients in the house dressing?"

The waiter may reply that it is not the policy of the house to give out recipes. You reply, "There are some foods I do not care to eat," or, if you are legitimately allergic, "There are some foods I cannot eat. I do not want the recipe, I merely want to know the ingredients." The waiter may then ask what you cannot eat. Be prepared with an answer. "Monosodium glutamate," is a good one since a great many people get headaches when they eat it. In most cases you will find the waiters and waitresses cooperative. They may have to go back to the kitchen to inquire. It is at this point that you had best start inflating the tip.

Once you have mastered this line, you can add, "Is there a specialty of the house?" "What would you recommend?" "Why would you recommend it?"

REGISTERING A COMPLAINT

Most of us can find something legitimate to complain about in a store or in a cab. With a cab, for example, the statement, "I think you are taking the long way," could evoke a real hassle. However, by planning your discourse in advance, you can say, "I want to go to West 117th and Clifton via the Shore Drive. Please get on the Drive at Ninth Street." It is often sensible to check city maps before using a cab anyway. It is not that cabdrivers always try to take advantage of you, but many of them are new and know even less about the city than you probably do.

Another way to handle cabdrivers is to ask three different drivers at a cabstand, "What is the cost to the airport?" They will probably all give the same information, but if one is different, ask, "Why are you more expensive (or cheaper) than the others?" If you do not have access to a cabstand or the price of a cab and you don't know where you are going, there is very little you can do to defend yourself. It is at times like these that we wish Saint Christopher was back in office. Incidentally, this exercise will probably not work with bus drivers. Bus drivers are commonly too harried to give much information, although some of them try very hard to be civil. You can, however, try your hand at phoning the transportation office of the city you are in and asking what bus routes to take to various places. Keep your organization patterns in mind, because you will need to get very accurate sequences of occurrences.

To register complaints in a store, your first step is to prepare, in writing, a statement of the nature of the complaint. Make a copy for yourself and have a copy ready to hand the person in charge. The statement might read, "The lever that operates the slicing mechanism came off in my hand the first time that I used it," or "According to the advertising claim, I should be able to focus the jet stream on any part of my body, but there are no instructions about how to do so, and I cannot get it to work properly."

You can read your complaint if you want to. Make sure your complaint is specific, "It just doesn't seem to work" will accomplish little. Prepare for the following routine:

Step 1. Go into the store and return to the department in which you bought the merchandise. If possible find the clerk who sold it to you. Then ask, "Are you authorized to handle customer complaints?" If the clerk asks what your complaint is, do not say, but reply, "I want to register my complaint with a person authorized to handle it. Are you authorized to handle customer complaints?" If the clerk says no, then ask, "Where can I find the person who is?" Make sure you get a name if you can. If the clerk doesn't give the information, close with, "Thank you, I'll register my complaint to the manager," and move on. If you get the information, close with, "Thank you for your time."

Step 2. Once you find the person authorized to handle customer complaints, use the opening line "I would like to complain about some merchandise I bought on (give the date and produce the sales slip). This is my complaint." Read what you have on your prepared sheet. Then make your request.

- "I would like it repaired."
- "I would like it replaced."   (Pick one)
- "I want my money back."

You may be satisfied with any of the three, but only ask for one. Your respondent might settle the complaint then and there. That happens a good deal of the time. Some managers, however, will try to make you feel guilty. They will accuse you of breaking or misusing the merchandise. They may claim you did not buy it in that store. (That's why you need the sales slip.) They may try to show you that nothing is wrong with the merchandise. In any case, do not waste time arguing. Repeat your request. If you do not get satisfaction, ask the individual for the name of his or her supervisor. If you do not get the name, close with, "Thank you. I will present my complaint in a registered letter to the manufacturer, in which I will name this dealer." Then exit. Another possibility,

"Thank you. I shall take my business elsewhere in the future, and so will my friends." Then exit.

We are assuming, of course, that your complaint is legitimate, that you are not seeking to harass anyone, and that you are willing to accept some reasonable settlement. *If your complaint does not fit these criteria, do not do this exercise.*

What all of these exercises have in common is that

- You must be specific about the service or information you want.
- You must have a prepared line with which to request it.
- You must be prepared for alternatives.
- You have a closing to use in any case.

You can rehearse each of these components. You can also apply them to any service you seek and in any kind of store. By learning these standard lines you should equip yourself with enough strategy to get reasonable service anywhere you go.

SOCIAL SITUATIONS AND SMALL TALK

Most people feel awkward when they try to make small talk with people they have just met. Routine social situations are designed to be pleasant ways for people to meet one another and to expand their contacts.

The development of friendships and intimate relationships starts with small talk in routine social situations. There is a pattern to small talk, and it is possible for you to set goals within that pattern in order to improve your ability to acquire human contacts. Initially all you need to do is to handle basic conversation. Once you spot someone who looks interesting and who seems to be open for contact, you can set out to engage that person's interest and perhaps attempt a trial outside the social situation. ("Take me home?" "Join me for coffee?" "Let's walk to the subway together." "How about a drink?" "Let's get together next Tuesday.") Your goal would be to make enough small talk to make the extending of an invitation comfortable and reasonable.

In order to handle these routine social situations you must have the following skills:

1. You must have a few lines with which to open conversations.
2. You must have a closing line to use when necessary.
3. You must be able to ask and answer some basic questions. ("What kind of work do you do?"
4. You must be able to express some opinions on some relatively noncontroversial issues.
5. You need to evade attacks on you and your ideas when someone else is crude enough to level them.
6. You need to be able to change the subject away from controversial or personal issues.
7. You must be able to contribute something when the group is discussing a common topic.
8. You must be able to talk much of the time with either a glass or a plate in your hand and at times with both hands filled. This means that you must avoid spilling and breaking wherever possible.
9. You must be able to listen courteously to what other people are saying.

If you can manage to do all this, you can probably manage to lead the conversation to the point where you can make a request for future contact if you care to.

However, there is no guarantee that everyone at a routine social gathering will know the rules. When others do not conform to reasonable expectations, all you need to do is listen until you can make a gracious exit. Even when people around you are behaving like fools, you can improve things by managing your own behavior. Be sure that you have three or four exit lines mastered so that you can use them whenever you need to.

REHEARSE THESE LINES

Of course you will have to fill in your own name and occupation, specify the books and movies you have read and seen, and refer to events in your own city. These are blank forms you should commit to memory.

OPENERS

"My name is ———————— and I do (work at) ————————."
If the other person does not respond with some identification, reply, "Nice talking to you," turn, and leave. Once the other person responds

with at least a name, you may proceed to ask questions, respond to talk, or answer questions. If the other person opened the conversation and asked about your occupation or other basic information, return the courtesy by asking him or her the same questions (although you may vary the wording).

SUSTAINERS

Be prepared with questions that will sustain the conversation. Organize your questions according to the seven patterns. For example:

- Did you see the movie?
- What was it about?
- Did you like it?
- What did you like about it?
- What was its message?
- How were the individual stars?

And so on.

Be prepared to answer similar questions about something you saw or did, so that when you introduce it into the conversation, you can talk about it.

Do not ask, "Are you going to the game Saturday?" unless you are soliciting an invitation or are about to extend one.

Try to avoid questions that can be answered yes or no. If you are asked such a question, offer an additional line, for example, "Did you see the movie?" "Yes, I liked it very much."

Avoid questions about personal details. It is legitimate to ask about occupation, hometown, favored recreations, good books and movies, or what to do in town. It is not legitimate to ask about illnesses, social encumbrances, or family (unless you know the family). It is relatively dangerous to talk about mutual friends, since either party might pass on an unfortunate comment and jeopardize the relationship.

Do not expect the conversation to be "heavy" or scholarly. If you find yourself discussing capital punishment or abortion too early, you may be making more of a commitment than is reasonable. Many shy people complain about the superficiality of conversations they hear at social events, although they are not prepared to do anything about it. They use it as an excuse to avoid trying. Small talk may not deal with major topics, but when skillfully handled, it is fun.

In fact, it is sensible not to editorialize about groups, individuals, or commitments. If your conversational partner is a member of the group you are inveighing against, you may have more than you can handle. Furthermore, one is willing to put up with disagreement from someone one cares about, but in someone one has just met, disagreement is a signal that the relationship is going nowhere. It is better to build some kind of reasonable relationship before moving on to emotional topics.

It is useful to read a newspaper daily, keep posted on events in the arts, and have a passing acquaintance with new books. Television is also a good source of topics for discussion, since it can be praised or blamed without stirring up much wrath.

CLOSERS

You must be equipped with closers so that you can move on when things do not seem to be working out. You also need response lines when other people excuse themselves. The standard, nonthreatening closing lines are the following:

"I think I'll refresh my drink, excuse me." Notice that nothing was said about coming back. Do not say, "I'll see you in a moment," unless you plan to come back.

"I see Agnes over there. I haven't seen her for a while. Excuse me." Note the speaker did not say that he or she was going to talk to Agnes.

"I have to leave now, excuse me."

If you and the other person have exchanged names, be sure to say, "It was nice to meet you." Do not say, "I hope we see each other again," or "See you around," unless you are working for an invitation.

When you give your closing line, turn and leave quickly. Do not stay on the fringes and try to drift off. Departures must be crisp.

When other people excuse themselves, all you need to say is, "It was nice to talk to you." Not, "It was pleasant," "See you around," or "Oh, let me go with you." Just, "It was nice to talk to you." Make no further conversation. Let the person escape. There are probably good reasons. Simply assume you were spared several minutes of what could have been an unpleasant encounter.

CHANGING THE SUBJECT

Standard lines are available if someone introduces a topic you do not care to discuss. The lines are clichés. They should be uttered flatly, and if the other person persists in the conversation, you may use a closer and depart. This is somewhat difficult if there are only two of you talking, but since there is a considerable potential for distress if you allow yourself to talk about topics you find unpleasant, too personal, or threatening, you must simply offend the other person and thus make your point. Here are some "changers."

• I don't care to discuss that on a Sunday afternoon.
• This is not the time of day for politics or religion.
• The only people to whom I would give that information are my analyst or my priest.
• I don't know enough about that topic to have an informed opinion, nor do I care to have one. Excuse me.

The last option is the most definitive and the most effective. It is a changer and an exit line in one, and it is instructional for the other person. A great many people are not sensitive to the interests of the people they meet. Every so often they need to meet someone decisive enough to let them know that not everyone approves of their social performance.

EVADING ATTACKS

If someone attacks you or something you said, it is appropriate to use an exit line. You need not defend yourself. It is not appropriate for someone to attack you at a social gathering, and you have the right to refuse to discuss anything you do not care to discuss. You are entitled to an opinion. If, for example, a group is discussing *A Clockwork Orange* and you found it offensive, you do not need to say anything at all. You can make your exit if you care to. On the other hand, if someone demands your opinion, you are entitled to say, "I didn't like it." If you are then berated for not liking it, you may use an exit line like "Thank you. I liked it so little I'd prefer not to discuss it. Excuse me." People who try to force you to express opinions that they can attack are rude. You do not have to spend time with them unless you are living with them or working for them, in which case you can nod politely while you contemplate making other arrangements.

CONTRIBUTING YOUR SHARE

If you do not care to contribute or you do not understand what is being discussed, either use an exit line or ask a question. If you do not receive a satisfactory answer to your question, exit. If you want to participate, use your questions to make an entry for yourself into the flow of the conversation. Make sure your questions are well timed. Some shy people spend so much time phrasing questions that by the time they ask them, they are out of phase.

If you cannot break into the conversation even with a question, or if someone jumps on what you say and begins a monologue, use an exit line. You are entitled as a consumer of conversation to shop around until you find a conversation group that suits you.

MANAGING

You need skill to manage the refreshments at social gatherings. Some events have chairs and tables arranged, although rarely do you find anyone using them. What you have to keep in mind is that it is not customary to try to make the hors d'oeuvres into dinner. You eat sparingly and drink even less. Those who come to social gatherings to gorge or get drunk are probably not the people you want to talk with. The best rule to follow is, When you are eating, eat, get it over with, and then move back into the mainstream of conversation. When you drink, make sure your intake is light. Nurse your drink, and if you do not drink, you will find that a glass of ginger ale looks like a highball.

Everyone feels a little klutzy at large social gatherings. Protect yourself from accidents as best you can by doing only one thing at a time.

DATING

Extending the relationship is what it is all about. We will discuss this in detail in the next chapter.

SPECIAL CONCERNS

AVOIDING SHAKEDOWNS

You have the right to refuse to be harassed by people who solicit you on your own time. When you are in a place of business, there is some reason to believe you are there on business purposes. If you are accosted on the street or if someone calls your home or knocks on your door in order to sell you something, solicit funds, get information, or convert you to his or her religion, you do not have to listen. You are entitled to walk past street solicitors, hang up on phone solicitors, and close the door on anyone who comes without an invitation. You do not have to give an explanation, you do not have to excuse yourself by explaining that you gave elsewhere. If you care to listen to what they have to say, that is your business. There are some solicitors for reasonable causes who will seek you out, but keep in mind that you are in control of the situation and that you are donating your time for only as long as you like. It might be helpful to master some closing lines for your own convenience in extricating yourself.

- For the phone solicitor, "Good-bye," then hang up.
- For the street solicitor, "Excuse me," or "You are in my way." Keep walking.
- For those who come to your door, "I choose my own charities, thank you," or "I'm sorry, I do not carry on transactions with people who come uninvited."

In each case, close the door. Do not apologize, even if it is raining. There are some religious sects that purposely come to your door with small children on miserable rainy days. You need not invite them in for tea. They know what they are doing and they do so at their own risk.

DEALING WITH PROFESSIONALS

Marcus Welby and the crusading lawyer who has no other case but yours are fictions of the media. Most professional people have very little time and an extraordinary urgency to get paid. You will have to face both of these issues when you deal with them. Through enlightened consumership and advance preparation, you can make the most of the time allotted you.

Since you are paying the professional for the time, make it clear that you know what you want. "I want a complete physical including lab tests." "I have been having sharp pains in my (fill in the proper word and point if possible) for about a week." "I need advice on the consequences of signing this contract. What does it obligate me to?" "Please draw up a simple will and tell me what I can do to take advantage of estate possibilities in this locality." If you do not have a specific request, there will be a great deal of muddling around at great cost to you. It is perfectly all right to make lists.

It is also useful to keep yourself informed about the professionals whose services you seek. While it is not sensible to try to practice medicine or law based on information you read in magazines or newspapers, stories and articles about medicine and law can alert you to topics you can use to engage interest in your case. "I read about something similar to this in . . ." will usually get the professional talking, even if for no other reason than to correct the information.

Remember that you can shop around. You do not have to commit yourself to a doctor, dentist, or lawyer who does not give satisfactory service. It may not be smart to shop for price, but if things do not go well in the first few visits, you must keep in mind that this is the person you have selected to help you in time of serious trouble. If you lack confidence, there will be little possibility of help. Professionals are obligated to transmit your records to a subsequent practitioner.

When you first meet your professional, be sure to inquire about rules and method of payment. There is nothing quite so dismaying as receiving a bill about three times larger than you can possibly pay. Be sure to explain what kind of insurance coverage you have, if that is relevant, and answer all questions carefully. Particularly in giving a medical history, it is not at all helpful to avoid talking about your bathroom habits because that embarrasses you. The physician doesn't care to embarrass you, but the information is important. With your lawyer, do not conceal the dangerous and offensive things you did. They will come out in court, if you ever get into court, and your attorney is better off when not surprised. Remember that you have the right to a second opinion (or third or fourth) when something drastic is suggested.

Be aware of the stress under which most professionals work. If they are any good, great numbers of people demand their time. You are entitled to your share but not to someone else's. That is why it is good to be prepared when you make your visit. Don't try to get chummy. Most professionals have all the social contacts they can handle, and they have learned that it is not a good idea to socialize with their clients or patients. If they make overtures to you, you can consider them in context, but remember that once your professional becomes your friend, you may have to seek out a new professional.

SMALL-TALK REVIEW

In general, what you say and do in routine social situations depends on what you want and how legitimate it is to want it. Most routine business is conducted through clichés, and you must obtain skill in saying cliché lines. You can overcome your shyness sufficiently to handle most situations merely by memorizing and practicing clichés in advance of the situations you will encounter or by preparing standard lines for situations you encounter regularly. Don't be afraid to sound like everyone else. It is that quality that will make it possible to get what you need out of such simple situations.

Small talk can be handled best if you regard it as the oil of conversation. It must flow smoothly enough to lubricate people so that they can move into subsequent conversation. Small talk is the audition for future contact. At the beginning everyone can move in and out as he or she sees fit, and most social gatherings are organized so that this happens.

Plan your openers around standard topics. Avoid getting personal. Do not disclose or ask for disclosure. Do not ask for advice from strangers. Try to avoid the appearance of an interview in your small talk. If you ask two questions in a row, it is smart to fall silent and let someone else in for a moment. People do not like to be grilled.

Sometimes you must be a little rude when you try to break into conversation. You must virtually always interrupt someone or interrupt his or her thought at a pause. On the other hand, if a group of people seems intensely locked into a conversation, it would be excessively rude to break in. Even if they seem very desirable to you, if you forced your way into their group, they would reject you. It is better to wait until some or all of them seem free for contact and make your approach then. Stay gracious and most important of all keep alert to the cues the other people are offering.

MOVING FROM SMALL TALK TO CONVERSATION

Asking and answering questions is stress evoking, even if you are not shy. On the other hand, it is the normal way through which people get to know one another. The reason it is stressful is because we all know that the judgments people make of us are based on our conversation. Sometimes we fear asking questions because we think they will make us look foolish or stupid. The intriguing thing, however, is that people are alike in a great many respects. The question that is on your mind has probably occurred to someone else in the group, and if you ask it, that other person will be appreciative, since you spared him or her the necessity of asking.

The only way to appear stupid when asking questions is to ask one that someone else has already asked or to time your question poorly. If you listen carefully, you can avoid the first pitfall, and if you move quickly, you can avoid the second. Even more important to consider, however, is that people normally do not spend their time awarding grades to the skill with which other people talk. As long as what you say and do doesn't threaten or bore them, other people will not react as vigorously to you as you think they will. They might get annoyed if you monopolize the conversation or ask a string of questions so that they do not get a turn.

When you are asked a question, make sure you can give the answer succinctly and in a straight line before you begin to speak. You can always say, "I'm sorry, I don't know," or "Maybe I can check it for you and get the answer later." Avoid saying, "Smith can tell you," because that puts Smith on the spot. Unless you are answering a question on the job, it is not necessary to give a complicated explanation of why you don't have the answer. However, it is not effective to use "I don't know" as an excuse for not talking. One of the problems shy people have is that they often say they don't know when they know perfectly well.

Before you answer a question, try to figure out whether the person who asked it had a legitimate reason for asking it. You do not have to answer questions like "What is your weekly salary?" or "Did anyone in your family have a nervous breakdown?" People who ask those kinds of questions are rude.

Social conversation goes beyond small talk because the people participating can choose a topic and stay with it as long as they like. The way people participate in social conversation gives you some idea of what they might be like in other situations. You can listen to their voices, observe the way they smile, pick up their views on simple matters, and get some information about the kinds of lives they lead to help you make a decision about whether or not you want to associate with them in another context. They are sizing you up in the same way. If you do not participate, they will not give you a positive evaluation.

Social conversation has as its first general objective sharing time in a pleasant fashion. The second objective is to give people a chance to size each other up, to get reacquainted or better acquainted if they know each other slightly, and to provide each person with a chance to show-case favorite ideas and behaviors. For this reason it is imperative to avoid head-on argument, personal attacks, private disclosures, and provocative stands. It is useful, however, to signal topics that might be offensive to you. If you have serious religious convictions, you can allude to them to deter offensive remarks or to discourage the attention of someone whose opinions differ drastically. Many minority group members clearly signal their minority status in order to discourage those who don't accept them.

You rarely get business done in social conversation. You do not get people to change their minds about very much, except of course about you. When something is said that interests you, make note and be sure to check back if you want to encourage attention from the person who said it. Be aware of the kinds of things people talk about, because if you are seeking to extend your contacts, you can use those topics both as openers of negotiation to get together and for topics when you are together.

The seven organization patterns outlined in the previous chapter serve as a basis for conversation-evoking questions.

- Where are you from? (Description)
- How did you come to get here? (Occurrence)
- What do you like to do? (Components)
- Which do you like more? (Standards)
- What's the difference? (Comparison)
- Why do you think so? (Association)
- What do you think we should do? (Argument)

Social conversation is carried on in staccato fashion. Ideas and topics seem to flit around like insects near a lamp. It is hard to say anything substantive and have people react to it seriously, so it is not productive even to try. You must be content with offering small advertisements about what a worthwhile person you are. This is most effectively done by combining a question with a conversation-evoking statement.

- "I am from Hannibal, Missouri, the home of Harry Truman. Where are you from?" The speaker offers the other person a cue to the next line, a statement of origin, and a statement about location.
- "I had a funny experience the first day I arrived here. . . . Did anything interesting happen to you?" The speaker tells a little story and asks for one in return.

- "I enjoy jogging and Mel Brooks films. What do you like to do in your spare time?" The speaker offers a choice. The respondent can talk about jogging or Mel Brooks films or introduce a new topic.
- "I think we ought to pay more city tax. What do you think?" The respondent can either express an opinion or ask the speaker to justify the opinion expressed.
- "I didn't like the film because it overemphasized sex. What do you think?" The respondent can express personal evaluations of the film or discuss sex in films. Introducing the topic of sex is a bit risky, however.

Some people lace their small talk with names of celebrities they have known or try to display their intellectual acumen or sensitivity to the arts. These are signals to avoid further conversation, for example:

- "I was talking to Dexter Winthrop the other day." You needn't inquire about who Dexter Winthrop is unless you care. You can infer that Winthrop is important to the speaker, and that may give you a cue to the kind of support the speaker offers for an argument.
- "I remember the time I was talking to Gary Cooper." It may be threatening to ask the speaker how he came to be speaking to Gary Cooper.
- "Well, I think both Jurgen Habermas and Gunter Grass aptly capture the new mood in Europe." Interesting statement and probably provocative in a seminar. You can ignore it.
- "I think Bernstein's rendition is immensely more sensitive, particularly in the way he integrates the strings." Okay, so stay off the topic of music.

When speakers attempt this kind of talk, you needn't respond in kind or challenge the speaker. If you think the speaker genuinely knows important people and you find this interesting, you can encourage the talk. If not, you can excuse yourself and find people who provide you with more manageable conversational entries.

Some people engage in sallies of wit and punning. This is very interesting, but for most people a spectator sport. It is not advisable to try to be witty or funny unless you have cultivated some skill at it. Most funny people have been at it for a long time. They are social performers, often doing their act because they find themselves infinitely more interesting than the people they meet. You can use what they do as a brief interlude from conversation. It is particularly important not to tell jokes unless you can do them skillfully. Most good joke tellers rehearse and try out their material in various conversational groups. Another important consideration in joke telling is that a great deal of humor is offensive, since it capitalizes on human adversity, minority group membership, sexual activity, or bathroom habits. You probably should be pretty sure of your company before trying your hand at this.

Another possible conversational ploy is called cutting people up. Often social conversation becomes a vehicle for the sharing of gossip. When you encounter a group of strangers who seem to delight in tearing apart someone they know in common, you might conclude that you might be a topic of conversation if they got to know you and act accordingly. If they are tearing apart someone you know and are tempted to defend, be sure of your ground. If you plunge in with a stirring defense, you risk alienating the people, who may well know more about the situation than you do and hence have the power to embarrass you. When you encounter this kind of talk, your best recourse is to move elsewhere. It is also important to try to ignore what you have heard, since most gossip is unfounded anyway, and it is dangerous to hear gossip about someone you do not know and then meet that person later on. If you blurt out, "Sam Smedley, you're the guy who was grafting from the company and didn't get caught!" you may prejudice future relationship possibilities, not to speak of risking a slander suit.

SAFE TOPICS

Expert conversationalists are prepared with several safe topics and provoking questions. A provoking question is one that tends to evoke an answer, such as

- "The dip is delicious. I wonder what it is made of?"
- "They have Bombay gin. Can you tell the difference between that and regular gin?"
- "That's an incredible punch bowl. I wonder if it is an antique?"
- "I notice from the bookshelf that the hostess likes mysteries. Read any good ones lately?"
- "Did you have the same hard time getting a cab that I did?"

Provoking questions seek an answer somewhat broader than yes or no. They are used to invite the other person safely into conversation.

The safe topic is one that the speaker can use to introduce interesting information to which another person can respond. The safe topic should not include items that can threaten or bore. For example, parents do not talk about their children with people who do not have children, although childless people can inquire, if they are interested, about someone else's children. It is helpful to know a little something about the person with whom you are speaking in order to help you avoid threatening topics, such as the Chrysler loan with someone who has just been laid off by Chrysler. Using provoking questions and safe topics should get you through at least fifteen minutes of conversation in virtually any company.

Many people have prepared statements on safe topics. Often they do not do this consciously. It just develops over years of conversation. You can, however, prepare yourself for social conversation by preparing about a minute's worth of talk on various topics. You can use the patterns of organization to help you.

DANGER SIGNALS

Look for danger signals in social conversation. When you spot them, it is time to use an exit line.

PERSONAL TALK

When talk becomes so personal that you find yourself getting uncomfortable, you can leave. You are not obligated to get into group therapy at a social gathering. Don't get drawn into discussions of your love life, your private opinions on sex or religion, your attitudes toward various people. If someone from your place of employment is present, avoid talking about the job. Don't ask for private information, don't give any that you don't want to give, and make sure your ginger ale glass is always half empty so that you always have an excuse to fill it.

ARGUMENTS

When an argument breaks out, it is smart to leave, even if you are not involved. People who get into arguments in public are often embarrassed later on by things they did or said. If you are not around to witness them, you will not be a source of embarrassment. They will be eternally grateful if you spared them the necessity of being foolish in front of you.

If you find yourself challenged vehemently, don't be afraid to back off. Use an appropriate exit line and get out quickly. If people follow you to continue the argument, they will look foolish, and if you attach yourself to another conversation group, they will have to leave you alone. Some people go to social gatherings spoiling for a fight, and it is best not to get mixed up with them. Let them find someone of their own kind and play *King Kong versus Godzilla* without you. You can't win one of those social arguments.

MONOLOGUES

There is no future in standing around and listening to someone recite a monologue. Often at social gatherings one person will take the floor and drone on and on, while listeners either wait their turn to talk or shift nervously from one foot to the other while they wait for a gracious way to exit. The best option is simply to decide that the person who holds the floor is paying attention to herself and doesn't need you. You don't need an exit line. If you have waited for five minutes or more and can't get a word in edgewise, it would probably take too long to wait for your exit line. Either mumble a farewell to another onlooker or just move away. Chances are the monologuist will not even know you are gone.

INTERVIEWS

If someone seems to be interviewing you about details of your life ("Where do you work? What do you do? Do you like it? Who works with you? How much do you make? Do you belong to the union?"), you needn't stay around. If you get more than two questions in a row, reverse the third question. If the questioner doesn't give you a straight answer, it is time for a refill.

INVITATIONS

If someone extends an invitation to do something outside of the social gathering, you are on your way to a potential friendship. We will deal with this situation in the next chapter.

Do This! It Will Help You the Next Time You Attend a Social Gathering. Arm yourself for the next social gatherings by preparing some thirty-second conversation makers. Following are some topics that seem to work at most social gatherings. Prepare yourself with a brief statement and a return question for each of them.

1. The worst snowstorm you ever experienced.
2. The future fortunes of the local athletic team. (Pick the most obvious.)
3. The relative merits, or lack thereof, of your car.
4. The quality of public transportation in the locality.
5. The latest exploits of Doonesbury (or any comic-strip character people would be familiar with).
6. The best movie you have seen in the last three months.
7. The funniest thing that happened recently to a relative of yours. (Pick one that no one knows.)
8. What I miss most about my hometown.
9. How I would like to spend my summer vacation.
10. What you intend to do about changes in fashion this season.

End each statement with a question that will get the other person started talking. Make sure it is not a question that can be answered simply yes or no.

This is a simple exercise. Your statement should be slightly less than one-third of a double-spaced typewritten page. You will have, all told, about five minutes worth to memorize. Remember that skilled conversationalists prepare these topics without even being aware of it. By having something to put into a social conversation, you will escape the evaluation of "shy" that you will surely earn if you say nothing at all. Once you have used these topics a few times, they will become part of your repertoire, and you will begin to add topics to them so that you will become more and more adept at social conversation.

ARRANGING FUTURE CONTACTS

If an individual seems sufficiently appealing that you would want to get together with him or her again, there are a number of ways to introduce the topic. First you must realize that there may be many good reasons why other people may not want to get together with you. They may not have the time, or they may have encumbering arrangements that do not make room for you. They may not be as impressed with you as you are with them. They may not understand your cues.

Most of the time you will not get immediate acceptance anyway. People like to think it over. The best you can hope for in most cases is a walk to the subway or bus at the end of the evening or perhaps a ride home—during which time you can discuss other possibilities. Phrases like "Let's get together sometime" or "I'll give you a ring" are usually rejections. When they are used on you, drop the subject. When you want to disengage from someone who is trying to arrange further contact that you do not want, you can use those lines. Don't even offer, "Give me your number and I'll call you," because that is too much of a promise.

In trying to make a date it is best to be explicit. "I eat out every Tuesday. Would you like to join me this week?" Do not say, "Would you like to join me sometime," because it is too indefinite. If the other person agrees to join you, prepare to be flexible about the place.

"The touring company of *Elephant Man* will be in town next week. Would you like to go with me if I can get tickets?" You may not be able to get tickets, but if you get a yes, you can bargain about another event.

"How about doing the museums with me next Sunday afternoon?"

"Would you like me to take you to the next meeting of the Coin Club?" Phrase your question specifically. When the invitation is specific, other people have options. In the first place they know it is a firm offer. They can accept the substance of the offer, although they might not be able to accommodate themselves to the date or place. If they want to get together and cannot do it on your terms, they are free to make an alternative proposal that you can then evaluate. They can stall for time and keep it open by saying, "Let me check my date book and give you a call." If you can't work something out, it is appropriate to exchange phone numbers and agree to try again. Sometimes the opportunity simply never arises again. A great many people pass through our lives. They look attractive at the time, but somehow things just don't work out.

The idea behind being casual throughout this whole process is to spare feelings if a rejection is necessary. Furthermore, you should take care, if you are starting this kind of negotiation, to step away from the main group of people so that you do not involve them in your date making. It is awkward to stand around and listen to two people trying to make arrangements for further contact.

A CAUTION

The following paragraphs are going to sound very moralistic. They are particularly important for shy people. Sometimes when we are very shy, our stomachs rebel at the thought of making contact with other human beings. When we face a social encounter, we are uneasy, frightened. It is very easy to calm ourselves with a shot or a joint, but it is simply not wise to try to deal with other people while under the influence of alcohol or pot. Although most social gatherings seem to emphasize alcohol of one sort or another, and group smoking is becoming more and more popular, the important thing for you to do is to keep your wits about you and your mind working. Contrary to popular opinion, neither alcohol nor pot is particularly useful in stimulating the mind or the tongue.

A great number of people get out of control at social gatherings. They destroy their prospects for constructive social contact by drinking or smoking too much. Often they do not even know the damage they have done to themselves. The alcohol and pot dull their senses sufficiently so that they see themselves as the smash hit of the party. We have already cautioned you to pay careful attention to reality. You cannot do this if your mind is muddled.

PREPARE YOURSELF
FOR POSSIBLE DATING

Before going on to the next chapter, prepare yourself with a list of topics you can use to introduce offers of dates to someone else. Select about five that you can use for same-sex dates and five for opposite-sex dates. If you are part of a couple, work this out with your partner. You can do this simply by writing the answers to the following questions:

- What restaurants do you enjoy eating at? Write down one good reason why someone else would enjoy each of them.
- Is there an interesting exhibit at one of the local museums? Describe it briefly.

- Are you having friends over in the coming weeks? Could you use another person or couple? Write down one reason why they would like to come.
- What sporting events are coming up in the next two weeks? Are any of them particularly promising? Why?
- What movies, plays, and concerts will be in the community? Why would you like to see each of them? Why would someone else like them?
- If you were inviting someone over for dinner what would you serve?

Make sure you know how to get tickets for those events for which tickets are required. Dining out is probably the most effective starting point for a new relationship. Eating together provides a relatively brief contact, and you have a common topic, the food, in case other topics fail. Going to events is also nonthreatening, since you spend a good deal of the time together watching in silence, and afterward the event itself is a discussion topic. However, tickets are sometimes hard to come by, and if you get tickets for a particular evening and the person you invite is not free that evening, you are stuck with an extra ticket and the possibility of spending the evening with someone not quite so desirable. Keep yourself regularly posted on the possibilities for recreation in your immediate vicinity.

RECOMMENDED READINGS

Peg Bracken, *I Try to Behave Myself* (Greenwich, Conn.: Fawcett Publications, 1963).

Ellen Langer and Carol Dweck, *Personal Politics* (Englewood Cliffs, N.J.: Prentice-Hall Publishing Co., Inc., 1973).

Stephen Potter, *The Complete Upmanship* (New York: Holt, Rinehart & Winston, 1970).

Eric Berne, *What Do You Say After You Say 'Hello?'* (New York: Grove Press, 1972).

chapter 11

Building Friendships

There are as many possible goals for friendships as there are pairs of people who become friends. A friendship is an intimate society, and the participants can create their own world within it. A true friendship reflects the personalities and goals of the friends. Friendships are not magic. When you become close to someone, it is because you have made an effort. The attraction that drew you together is not sufficient to keep you together. Every marriage counselor knows countless loving couples who came apart at the seams once they discovered that they had to transcend the relatively irrational emotion that accompanies falling in love. Friendships are not romantic; they are common enterprises built by people who want to be together and who are, therefore, willing to find ways to accommodate themselves to the other. Friends do not try to make each other over; they do try to curb their own annoying behaviors in order to earn the same accommodation from the other person.

We do not believe in magic. We believe that relationships can be built by people who are willing to take the time to work out the rules together, each caring about the other's needs and wants. Close relationships are the result of bargaining, of give and take. In a real friendship you know who you are because your friend helps you to be it.

Shy people often feel used in relationships. They are so uncertain about their ability to form new relationships that they tend to cling tenaciously to some very unsatisfactory relationships, unable to improve them and fearful that if they were to abandon them, no other relationship would be possible. That is why the most important step in overcoming your shyness is to learn how to make new friends. If you understand how friends are made and have some skill in meeting and developing new people, you can free yourself from the pain of an unsatisfactory relationship.

The aspects relationship that can be learned are talking, listening, and evaluating what you hear from others. We can offer little advice about your personal feelings, except that you should be careful about acting on them. However deeply you may think you feel about another person, if there is no tangible evidence of mutuality in the relationship, there is no relationship. Whatever the other person declares about the intensity of feelings for you, without behavior that confirms the words the relationship must be regarded as phony. Words, however poetic, are not the relationship. They are the currency on which the relationship can be developed. Building close relationships is a process of talking, acting, testing, evaluating, and extending, done mutually by people who choose to relate. A close relationship doesn't ever just happen.

Developments in our society over the last thirty years have changed the way people carry on relationships. Families are shrinking in size, and relatives are no longer influential. Now there are new rules everyone must learn. For example, marriage is not the only way men and women can relate. Living together is becoming more and more common and generally accepted. And because people move around a great deal, rules of extended family cannot be relied upon. Today we must build our relationships from scratch and negotiate with others for our personal security.

This has serious repercussions for people who are not skillful at relationship building. Shy people have difficulty getting their fair share in relationships. They are often bullied into relationships and quickly cast off. They are usually unable to defend themselves against the unilateral decisions of their partners. Shy people are sometimes amazed at the ease with which others can cast them aside, and they are sometimes embittered by their treatment. The case of the young woman who helps her husband through college and is then discarded when an attractive fellow professional comes along is not unusual. Many men also find themselves pushed aside as their wives seek fulfillment through a career and meet other men who are more attractive to them. It is usually the quiet and shy partner in a relationship who is left behind when the more aggressive one decides that a major change is necessary. It is amazing how many major changes fail to include the old partner.

Furthermore, sex is not necessarily a binding and restrictive activity. People may now define their own limits. Society's norms no longer seem to prevail, although there are groups of people who are still fiercely monogamous. People begin participating in sexual activity shortly after puberty, before they have a chance to think of the relationship aspects of sexuality. It is used initially as a source of personal gratification, and many people use it narcissistically, regarding it as useful only when their standards of pleasure are achieved. Consequently when people make a sexual relationship, there is the possibility of great disparity in the meanings each assigns to the act. In addition, the popular media fan the fires of discontent by placing emphasis on gratification and how it can be achieved, and professional sex clinics offer therapy to people who are not "getting enough" or not "getting enough out of what they are getting."

The idea of personal expectations seems to be central to the whole business of intimate relationships. Contemporary social messages place great emphasis on personal fulfillment, and they seem to promise people much more than they can possibly achieve. Shy people are particularly taken in by these promises. They come to expect fulfillment even though they haven't the vaguest idea of what fulfillment would be like if they got it. The notion that one can be fulfilled, however, automatically plants the seeds of discontent, since if one sets goals for fulfillment, there are no testing points and no particular behaviors associated with the accomplishment. There is clearly no choice except to wait for magic.

The fact that egocentric norms impel some people to highly aggressive seeking makes shy people all the more vulnerable. Those who cling to "old values" find themselves in a position where they must materially distort what they see in the other person in order to convince themselves that they are getting something of value. It is not the purpose of this book to advise shy people to become like the aggressive people with whom they associate. There is nothing especially positive in this. However, we do advocate that shy people develop critical discretion, so that they are able to monitor what they are receiving from others and are able to make choices on behalf of their own needs.

One way to cope with new styles of intimacy is to become consciously aware of what is possible in relationships. There are many promises made, but the only thing that matters is the reality of the partner's behavior. People who can perceptively evaluate potential partners in order to discover productive exchanges may lack a bit of romance at the outset, but they have the distinct prospect of developing permanently rewarding relationships.

People want the same thing from each other. They want someone

- With whom it is fun to pass time.
- With whom to share joys and triumphs.
- To support them when they are down.
- With whom to share home, work, money.
- With whom to raise a family.
- With whom to share common goals.
- With whom to talk about serious matters.
- With whom they can laugh and cry.
- To depend on in times of sickness or catastrophe.
- With whom to share their wealth.
- To reassure them about their personal worth.
- Whose promises they can count on.

No one person can provide all of these "services."

In recent years many messages have been offered to unhappy and frustrated people. Promises have been made about how a perfect relationship can be had with a perfect person who will provide for all needs. Shy people fantasize, and they daydream, and they distort the realities of their life to make it come out better, though all the while they know they are nowhere near where they could be.

A noted psychiatrist commented recently that most people speak very loosely of ideas such as "love." He advised people to avoid believing that saying the word means anything at all. Love, he pointed out, is an exchange of mutually supporting acts. Love cannot exist in one direction only.[1] The same holds true for the word *friend*. A person called a friend ought to act like a friend and not be merely "friendly." Friends have obligations to one another, sometimes as intense as a loving male-female couple.

To love or to be a friend demands obligation and commitment, quite contrary to the contemporary message that these states just happen if you "leave yourself open" to them. What happens when people take each other uncritically is momentary pleasure and long-term hurt. Shy people can spare themselves considerable pain by keeping an eye on the reality of relationships and avoiding myths that lead to hasty conclusions about what can be expected from others. Seeking evidence of love and friendship as opposed to verbal expression requires patience and just a bit of temporary loneliness, but in the final analysis the reality is infinitely more important than the words. The final blow to your shyness will come when you can control your behavior so well that you are no longer taken in by promises and respond only to delivery.

THE MYTH OF THE VIBE

We find most of our associates by accident. Despite computer matching, which doesn't seem to have caught on in most localities, our selection of associates is more random than anything else. In fact, we think more consciously about selecting a car than about selecting our friends. We tend to accept the people around us uncritically as good friendship risks, despite behavior to the contrary. As for "love," we are a bit more edgy. We believe that we ought to feel something special. The myth is that if two people are supposed to be together, they will feel the proper "vibes." A "vibe" is a vital force between people that tells them what ought to be.

Sadly, we must report that there is no such thing as a vibe. There are feelings at the outset of a relationship. Two people come together and have an impact on each other. Often the feeling is intensely sexual (in opposite-sex relationships). They like each other's physical appearance; mannerisms seem to suggest great wonders. We have already discussed this process and identified it as transference, the irrational belief that if a person looks like a loved one from the past, that person will behave like the loved one. Even worse is the belief that if a person resembles a media hero or heroine, he or she will have those same heroic qualities and be worthy of love. This process is nothing more than wishing, however. Sometimes people are attracted to others because they perceive them as beautiful or handsome. If they discover them to be unpleasant or unreliable, however, they tend to alter their perception and see them as ugly. By the same token, a person who looks unpleasant at first sight can become attractive after experience demonstrates them to be good and decent people.

The matching of two people in a friendship or love relationship is a fragile enterprise. If we think of the incredibly large number of people who cross our paths in our lifetime and how few we have ever come together with, we get an idea of how difficult it is to form a friendship. One authority suggests that the average person will only have room for four or five real relationships in an entire lifetime.[2]

It takes considerable concern and action to build a productive relationship. Shyness is often self-defeating because it impairs taking such action. Each failure makes the shy person less able to act and more willing to depend on some magic to bring about an improvement in his or her condition. It is when you learn to take action on your own behalf that you can finally claim that you are no longer shy.

A friendship is the result of mutual decision and commitment. There is no such thing as a one-sided friendship. When one person sees the other as a friend but the feeling is not reciprocated, the stage is set for exploitation.

People who share experiences often regard themselves as friends. Those who share common interests often spend a good deal of time together. A person who shares your interests, however, is not necessarily a friend, in the sense of having a commitment to you. Commitment must be made and tested under a variety of experiences. We do not have in the English language words that can indicate degrees of difference between the people with whom we have regular contact. We can discriminate friends, relatives, enemies, acquaintances, and business contacts of various sorts, but we cannot discriminate persons with shared interests, persons with shared geography, persons we see regularly with whom we do not fight, people who greet us pleasantly, people of whom we are a little suspicious, people who seem to need us more than we need them, people we'd better watch out for, people we do not like, people who would hurt us. In fact, most people will not concede that they could possibly have any enemies.[3]

It is useful to have your friends catalogued so that you have some idea of what you can expect from them. To expect the person you chat with at the Philately Club to be available when you are in serious need is unrealistic. Shy people often expect too much. They so much expect rejection that when they receive a kind word from someone, they attach a good deal more to it than is warranted.

We do not advocate paranoia, but we do advocate periodic inspection of the people around you. Check out their motives. Are they after the same rewards you are? How badly do they want it? What would they do to get it? How does this affect you? Often you will discover that people who are "on the move" do not think much about what they do to the people around them. They bribe, intimidate, and use people as they move ahead, and when they reach their goal, they sometimes wonder who would be their friend if they had no power. Shy people sometimes respond very strongly to the urges of those who are moving ahead, associating themselves with the "campaign" and believing that they have found someone who really cares about them. When they are abandoned, they have discovered one more reason not to try again. The notion that other people can hurt you badly is important to keep in mind when you evaluate the people you meet as potential friends.

Finally, shy people have a tendency to "put all their eggs into one basket." They expect a great deal from their mate or their good buddy back home. They expect one or a very few people to meet all their relationship needs. Unfortunately for them, there are few people, if any, who can meet all of those needs, and most people become very frustrated when someone expects more from them than they can deliver. The pressure shy people place on their friends rapidly becomes intolerable, and the beautiful relationships that are so sustaining have a tendency to come apart. This sometimes seems very sudden to shy people, whose tendency is to block out any negative information.

EXERCISES IN FRIENDSHIP BUILDING

HOLD AUDITIONS!

It is fun to audition for new friends. It is a real test of creativity in making social contact. What you try to do is to develop a program of social gatherings that you sponsor, varying the personnel and the theme so that you have a good time regardless of whether you meet anyone who might later become a friend. When you go to someone else's party, you are required to choose among the people they invite. It is a good experience to hold your own party. For one thing, you have the experience of setting goals to invite people. You gain experience working with tradespeople as you purchase refreshments and make arrangements. You can keep control over the number of people who come, and you need only pick people who are interesting to you. You can mix couples and singles, people of both sexes. You can accommodate your gatherings to the size of your living quarters. If you live in a studio apartment, you can probably manage about four or five guests. You can also take people to lunch.

All of this is expensive, of course, but there is probably nothing more worth an investment in both time and money than the search for friends. One thing we often forget is that we spend money on recreation anyway. These days, with the price of theater and movie tickets being what it is, you can probably have a pleasant evening in your home with a few people and still come out even. The idea is to follow a sensible plan while doing it.

1. Write out invitations. Provide the details. If you want to serve a sandwich buffet early Saturday evening, your party can probably run from about 4 P.M. until well into the evening. Some of your guests may have commitments for later on, perhaps tickets to a show, but most people are quite satisfied with one social event for the weekend, and if you do not put a cut-off time on your invitation, they will plan to stay for a while. Sandwich buffets are relatively inexpensive and satisfying. You will need a variety of beverages, but you needn't serve hard liquor.

2. Issue your invitations early enough to block out other possibilities but not so early as to seem excessively eager. About two weeks lead time is usually enough. You will get some refusals, of course, and if you are scheduling your event for a major holiday such as the Fourth of July or New Year's Eve, invitations should come very early. On the other hand, Halloween and Valentine's Day are also good excuses for a gathering. People sometimes wish they had made arrangements, but they rarely do. If you plan for minor holidays, you can think up some unusual motif, for example, a late-night TV-watching party on Halloween to watch the horror movies together. Selection of refreshments fo fit the theme will be an interesting exercise for you.

3. Don't be hypercritical in developing a guest list. Don't invite people you think are enemies, but it is entirely proper to invite the

couple you have been chatting with in the apartment elevator. ("Say, we have been smiling at each other for a year now. I'm having a little gathering a week from Tuesday and I'd really like to get to know you better. Would you folks like to come?") You needn't be deceptive or cute. A straight invitation accompanied by a reason that need be no better than "I'd like to get to know you better" will do. Most people are very flattered when someone wants to get to know them enough to stage an event for them.

4. Using written invitations gives you practice with phone follow-ups. Do not put R.S.V.P. on your invitations. Say, "I'll be calling you to find out if you are coming." Wait three or four days from the time you sent the invitations and then make some calls. You'd be surprised how these follow-up calls can fill an evening. Call early so that if you get turndowns, you will be able to plug in replacements. Have an alternate list of people you will invite by phone. If you send out invitations two weeks early, make your phone follow-up ten days from the event; you will still have more than a week to fill vacancies caused by people who had previous commitments. And, incidentally, if people say they have previous commitments, they may be telling the truth. You can try them again. On the other hand, if you get turned down twice, it is probably sensible to scratch the person from your try-out list. If they really want to get to know you, they will feel sufficiently guilty to invite you when they have a gathering.

5. Try to include on your invitation list some people who seem to remind you of yourself, quiet people who do not claim much attention. They probably would be very eager to come, and they would also probably be eager to reciprocate. What you want to avoid is inviting a lot of people who think it is their right to be invited, the social royalty who are so popular that they expect homage from everyone who knows them. In general, you need to avoid people who seem to have heavy commitments. The man who talks a lot about what he does with his relatives on the weekend is probably a poor risk, since he is no doubt heavily encumbered. Incidentally, you might have considerable luck with midweek card games. Males generally welcome contact with others in a loose situation. Generally, males do not take the initiative in making such arrangements, so when an opportunity comes along, they usually seize it. Trips to sporting events are also appealing, although you must take care not to get stuck buying all the tickets. A good way to handle this is to issue "after the game" invitations. ("Before the game" invitations are not

so profitable, since everyone has to leave at the same time and will not return, and thus anything you started will be aborted. You want to have events so that there is some loose time at the end that you can use to get better acquainted with someone.)

6. Have plans for your event so that the pressure to talk is not too heavy. If you invite other shy people, they will be very uncomfortable if too much pressure is put on them to socialize. They may not, after all, be working their way through a book like this. However, you should note that in the Reticence Program, when groups are formed in which all of the people are shy, talk starts fairly quickly, and most seem to do very well at it once they discover there are no skilled people to "push them around." One good activity is an attractive jigsaw puzzle at a table with four chairs around it. Make sure you do the border first, since people will not attempt the border if it is not done. Leave the box lid out so that they can see what the final picture will look like. Make sure it is interesting, not scenic "schlock" or one of those geometrics that only aficionados can do. You will find that people will sit down and play with the puzzle and begin to talk while they do so. It is an excuse to be with people. Games that require concentration are not so useful. An evening of chess would not stimulate much conversation. Games like backgammon that draw fanatics also would not work. A great many shy people turn to duplicate bridge because the game is engaging and does not require conversation. That would rule bridge out as a pastime. Some of the new computer games and topical board games are useful conversation pieces. Board games are cheaper. A good one costs around ten dollars and can provide a real evening of fun. Even if you never use it again, it will have done its work. You can always donate it to some charity when you are finished with it.

7. Make sure you have records available for your stereo, but protect yourself from the stereo taking over. Put out different types of music so that people can discuss the relative merits of their choices. Country, Gilbert and Sullivan, musical comedy, and light classical seem to work best. Talk records, comedians, heavy rock, and classical do not work well, since people tend to pay more attention to the records than to the others around them. Fix your stereo so that it cannot be turned up too loud. This is another escape technique used by people who don't want to talk much.

8. Don't make your refreshments too complicated. Serving unlimited alcohol is expensive and tends to disrupt a gathering as people

ingest too much of it. Those who are serious drinkers (or pot smokers) are probably not good risks for friendships anyway, so if they are uncomfortable without hard liquor, they can go elsewhere for refreshments. White wine and beer along with a variety of soft drinks represent your best bet. Don't try to get enough wine and beer for the entire evening. When alcohol runs out, provide coffee and tea along with the soft drinks. You do not have to have a drinking party. This would defeat your purpose. Be sure not to put too heavy a catering responsibility on yourself. Keep it simple and you will not threaten your guests. Some people are edgy about extending a return invitation when the service was more ornate than they could match. Cheese and crackers are simple to provide, sandwiches, salad vegetables, and fruit for dessert will do in most cases. When you get to know people well enough to count on return invitations, you might want to get into a cooking exchange, which is a good way to regularize contact with people you like very much.

9. Keep the number of people manageable. When people have to stand around, conversation usually remains on a small-talk level. You are using your gatherings to get to know people, so you want extended conversations that you can get into. Make sure there are enough chairs around so that your guests can sit comfortably. Arrange chairs in threes and fours to discourage couples from forming dyads that exclude others.

10. As hostess or host you have an advantage. You get to move around at will, to participate where you choose, to arrange conversational groups. You can also accompany your guests to the door as they depart. Departures are an excellent time to do subsequent business. You are alone with each person or couple as they leave and if there are to be new invitations exchanged, this is the time to do it. If you have picked up information during the evening, don't hesitate to use it. If Eddie has indicated that he knows something about the museum in town, inquire when he would like to go with you. If you casually mentioned lunch to Susan, make your arrangements as she leaves. Make sure you develop a "departure goal" for each guest, except, of course, the ones you decide that you do not want to see again.

To prepare for these events, you will need to organize your thoughts about each of your guests. You must show concern about "mixing and matching." If you have three or four people from work you are interested in, you do not want them all on the same evening. True, they have something in common, but there is nothing more boring or threatening than an evening of shop talk. Try to figure out which of your contacts from elsewhere they would fit best with. For these kinds of parties select people you know casually but are not yet willing to risk being alone with.

I LIKE NEW YORK IN JUNE.
HOW ABOUT YOU?

This is an exercise to do with someone whom you would like to get to know a little better. We do not advocate private sessions in people's apartments until there is some reason to believe that a sexual advance will not be made or until there is reason to believe you are ready for one. Private same-sex encounters are sometimes a little awkward, too. Thus, regardless of the sex of the person you want to know better, this is an exercise that is best conducted at a quiet restaurant where the music is not too loud, where celebrities do not go, and where the service personnel do not try to push you into the street as soon as you have finished dessert.

The exercise starts as you discuss the menu and concludes when you decide to leave. It virtually guarantees that nothing unpleasant will come up, since at worst you can always discuss the food or the decor. The cost is often considerable, since dining out is not exactly a poor person's pleasure these days. Therefore, you should be reasonably certain that you are interested in the person you invite to join you.

Prepare for the evening (after your invitation) by making a list of things you would like to know about the other person. Write down similar things about yourself, What you are trying to do is figure out what exchange you are willing to make. If there is a bit of information you don't care to give, then do not ask the other person to give it. You see, this social event will start out like an interview. What happens is that you make a statement and follow it with a question.

- "My favorite musical group is _____. What's yours?"
- You follow with a probe: "What other kinds of music do you like?"
- You wait for a question to be addressed to you.

You can keep the questions and answers flowing. If things go well, the other person will pick up on the theme and begin to ask questions also. Listen carefully to those questions, for they will be a guide to what is important and interesting to the other person. Look also for questions that the other person evades, for they will be a guide to information the person does not wish to disclose. Your task is to keep the conversation on topics your guest wants to talk about and to avoid topics that you have reason to believe he or she wants to avoid. You also have the obligation to yourself to avoid topics you don't want to talk about. For this evening keep the talk on what the other person is interested in and take note of whether that person tries to explore to see what you are interested in. This is a guide to the level of interest the other person has in you. Get your statements (about twenty seconds in length) and your questions in order, and make sure you have at least one probe question for each topic.

- "The best play I have seen this season is _____. What did you like? What kinds of entertainments do you like the most?"
- "I read this fascinating story in _____ magazine. . . ." (Wait for a return story.)
- "I really enjoy playing tennis (golf, etc.). What do you enjoy?"

List about ten topics and prepare about three comments of your own about each. You may get the impression that if you want to make friends, you need to read books and magazines, go to the theater, listen to good music, and fill your head with interesting ideas. If you have received this impression, you are correct. The best way to get people interested in you is to be interesting.

Introduce the conversation as if it was a game. You might even open with the statement, "Remember that song, 'I like New York in June, How About You?' Well, I like to look at my stamp album on rainy days in the fall. How do you spend your rainy days?" With any luck at all, your partner, even if shy, will take the cue and begin talking.

The worst that can happen with this exercise is that you pay for two good meals. If you can get your lines out, however, your chances of failure are very slim. If things have gone far enough that the other person accepts an invitation like this, you are probably on safe ground. (Although you should not rule out the possibility that you have hit on an exploiter who will eat your food and offer nothing back. It is customary after paying for such an evening to wait awhile for a reciprocal invitation lest you give the impression that your role in a subsequent relationship is to be paying all the bills.)

A WORD ON SELF-CONSCIOUSNESS

If you are not used to planning your social engagements and preparing your talk, some of these exercises will seem awkward to you at first. Shy people are not terribly experienced at playing host or hostess, and because they are so concerned about the impression they make, they often hang back from trying. You will find, however, that the more you have control over the situation, the more confident you will feel. Once you have designed and run a few social gatherings, you will find yourself a pro.

As far as people accepting your invitations is concerned, it is amazing how many people have little or nothing to do during their time off. There are not that many swinging discos, the bars are not that crowded, and the number of people who seem to be waiting on movie lines alone should give you an indication that a lot of people are sitting around watching Saturday TV wondering whether their mouthwash failed. You will find that most people will accept your invitations with considerable eagerness. Incidentally, when this starts to happen, you will no longer be the "shy one" in their eyes. You will be the "host" or "hostess."

SOME TIPS ON SAFETY

One of the things we discovered about shy people is that they are very edgy and uneasy about sexual contact. They do not know how to manage it, what it could possibly mean, and how to get their fair share out of it. For that reason we offer some cautions to people who do not wish to get involved in sexual contact prematurely.

Sex is extraordinarily valuable in relationships between men and women. The problem of mutual respect after the fact is still terribly important. It cuts both ways. Many men are inordinately concerned about their performance. These kinds of tensions impair the possibility of a real relationship growing. In fact, if sex is too much of an issue, then no further relationship is possible. One authority noted that sex is the ultimate intimacy and ought to be bestowed once it has been ascertained that the couple have a considerable amount in common.[4] Sex that comes too easily without critical examination of its meaning in the relationship makes both parties suspicious. Worse, premature sex can drag one partner into an exploitative situation, in which the person comes to believe that his or her only worth is as a sexual being. Our advice goes something like this:

1. Stay out of singles bars. People go there because (a) they are hustling; (b) they want people to think they are hustling; or (c) they want magic to happen. About all that happens from singles-bar contacts is what is known as a "roll in the hay." Of course, if this is what you think you are after, the singles bar is a proper place to look, but you must reckon with the possibility that once you find a willing partner, he or she may be unable to deliver.

2. Participate in hobby clubs and group activities. Work for a candidate or join your neighborhood block association. It is somewhat easier to start friendships with people with whom you have some binding interest or shared activity. At worst, you will spend time pleasantly with people who might be able to tell you something you don't know about something you are interested in. Furthermore, at such activities you can get to observe people in action before making a decision about whether to encourage further contact. Hobby clubs and group activities are good sources of people to invite to your parties. They might also invite you.

3. Do not engage in private tête-à-têtes with potential sex partners unless you are ready for the consequences. A recent survey showed that men regard a dinner invitation to a woman's house as an invitation to sex. If a woman comes to a man's apartment, there is also a presumption about her motives.[5] We are not discouraging sex, merely telling you that if you get involved before you are ready, you may find yourself in an exploitative relationship.

4. It is useful to have a "line" you can use to turn down unwanted invitations and to recognize when other people really do not want to accept invitations from you. Deferring lines like "I'll let you know" can cause trouble later on. "I'd rather not" is a simple way of turning down someone without offering the possibility of another try. When people want to associate with you, they will turn down your invitation if they have to with some offer to negotiate. "I can't come, please call me the next time," or "How about next week at my house?" Leave the matter open.

GAMES, GAMES, GAMES

If you'd like to get to know someone a little better and you are not yet self-confident enough for an evening of conversation, you can schedule a formal activity, a game. Intense games such as bridge or backgammon, tend to discourage talk, but games of the Risk or Monopoly variety encourage interaction and still provide the participants with a refuge from talk in the game itself if they choose to take it. Inviting three other people or another couple for a specific game is a good way to spend a nonthreatening evening getting to know one another. Alcohol costs are minimal and refreshments can be very light. It is considerably less expensive than a night on the town.

DINNER WITH THE FAMILY

When you get to know someone well, it may be necessary to meet the family. Shy people are not the only ones who feel stress in this situation. It is very much like being a prize heifer put out on display. You are expected to be on your good behavior, and the family can disapprove of you for any reason they choose. This is an excellent exercise for anyone who wishes to test his or her interpersonal skill. You are, of course, in greater control if you have the family visit you at your house, but this is generally difficult to arrange. Thus, if you choose to go, here are some ways to prepare yourself:

1. Have your friend tell you a little about the people who will be present. Get some stories about regular family events. Prepare yourself with at least one comment to be directed to each particular family member who will be there.

2. Be prepared with several thirty-second speeches about yourself, including where you work and what you do, what you hope to be doing five years from now, interesting experiences on the job, your past summer vacation, what your family is like (just light stories, please, no discussion of skeletons in the closet), and where you went to school and some interesting things that happened to you there.

3. Look out for commitment questions. Any answer you give can get you into trouble. Rehearse, "I am not certain enough to comment now. What do you think?" If they ask you about Billy Graham, the draft, the coming election, living together without benefit of clergy, abortion, the prospects for the nuclear family, or similar questions, be prepared to be noncommittal and try as hard as you can to get them to express their point of view. Their ideas may clash with yours. Say nothing. You can always mutter under your breath about it on the way home. If they ask you about your taste in literature, the arts, or athletic teams, be prepared to comment.

4. Meeting the family is very much like a job interview. You will be asked a number of questions similar to those an interviewer might ask.

People are inordinately interested in the financial prospects of people with whom their sons and daughters are associating intimately. If you are just coming out of a divorce, you will need to be prepared to say something superficial about it. "Sally and I couldn't work things out. We are still on speaking terms, though." "Fred and I broke up two years ago. It helped me grow." Try to find a statement that will close the conversation. And try to avoid looking depressed. That customarily stimulates a third-degree, both for you at the moment and for your loved one afterward.

MEETING THE FOLKS NEXT DOOR

When people move into a new house or apartment, they are ripe for contact. We all want to be welcome when we come to a new place. You may not be interested in anything more than superficial contact, and just because people happen to be your neighbors doesn't mean they are automatically worth associating with, but it is comfortable to know who they are and to be on speaking terms with them. Make contact with them as soon as you see them coming. "Hello. I'm your neighbor from over there, Beth Turner. If your phone isn't connected yet, feel free to use my phone for emergency calls. Would you like some coffee? I'll bring some over." Keep the patter straight till you say your whole speech. You are setting the rules for the initial contact. Don't let people get into your house too easily. Be sure that the phone calls are legitimate emergencies and stand by when the phoning is going on. Bring the coffee over in a pitcher you won't miss if you never get it back. Include some crackers and throwaway cups.

Be equipped with information that the neighbor would like to have, for instance, location of stores, what to do about emergency fire and police service, where to get information about schools. Do not offer recommendations. Your doctor or dentist may not be satisfactory. Don't praise the community too much, or you may sound like a bore. And remember, people who are in the midst of moving are easily depressed. Keep your visit short, keep yourself open if they need you, don't offer to lend too much since you do not know whether they are the kind that tends to take advantage. By making the initial contact, you will have the upper hand in controlling the relationship and you can extend it or turn it off as the evidence indicates.

If you are moving in and no one approaches you, you can take matters into your own hands. Prepare small statements to your neighbors about simple requests you wish to make. "May I use the phone? I have to find out when they are coming to connect me up." "I haven't unpacked my dishes yet, where can I get a cup of coffee?" There may be no store nearby, and this is an obvious play for an invitation, but so what? Who would want to be friendly with someone who wouldn't give a cup of coffee to a new neighbor? No matter how your neighbors respond to you, you cannot lose, since your contact will give you information about them. If no one in the vicinity is willing to pay any attention to you, consider the possibility that you made an error in your choice of residence.

SOME GENERALIZATIONS ABOUT FRIENDSHIP

Based on a study of 511 pairs of friends,[6] there are some generalizations that can be made about friendships. First, people who seem really secure in their friendships keep tight controls on the number of people they see regularly. They have no more than five or six couples or individuals whom they see regularly, although they have a great many people with whom they are on friendly terms.

Most people with satisfactory relationships maintain membership in some formal groups where they can be with people. They do not necessarily participate fully in the organizations, but they have a place to go when things become boring and none of their close friends are around. The social organizations give them a place where they can audition new people. Many belong to hobby groups, some to church or political groups. On the other hand, people with difficulty making friends seem to avoid places where they can make friends.

Furthermore, the study showed that everyone has serious concerns about privacy. Those with the closest friends can explain what they keep private and why they do not want even their close friends to know about it. Few with long-term friends believe in complete openness, while those with difficulty making friends advocate complete disclosure. They seem to believe that a person is not a friend unless he or she is in full possession of the deepest secrets. Experienced friend makers seem to believe that the details of their lives are boring to others and they try to develop shared experiences with their friends so that there is plenty in common to talk about.

Long-term friendships are not only characterized by familiar exchanges, but the friends know exactly what they are getting. There is very little mystery in long-standing friendships. The partners remember services rendered, emergencies in which the friend helped out, and shared moments of joy. Those with few friends have inordinate difficulty figuring out what other people provide for them or what they do for others. A number of them express magical notions, that is, that they are looking for people they feel good with. Shy people seem very impatient, almost urgent to push their casual relationships into immediate friendships, and thus they have a tendency to alienate people by being excessively cloying.

Hardly anyone is aware of using criteria to select friends, yet it is clear that people do use such criteria. Sometimes the criteria are sensible, and sometimes they are foolish. The most frequent criterion mentioned is seniority ("We have been together a long time and we have done enough for each other so that we can count on each other"). Those who have the longest standing relationships are more likely to talk about specific behaviors in people they meet. While they would not admit to "auditioning" new people, they can give solid reasons for rejecting overtures from one person and seeking contact with another.

Based on the survey data, here are some "tips" about seeking friendships that you will find useful.

- Avoid excessively popular people. They do not need you in the way you need to be needed. Enjoy them when they are around, but remember, your best service to them is to be part of their admiring audience. Their service to you is to amuse you.
- There is no correlation between personal appearance and human decency, although you can count on the fact that people who look sad are probably sad.
- People often get themselves trapped into premature commitments. If people come on strongly with you, keep yourself reserved and see if the attraction wears well. Give them the luxury of discovering they made a mistake. If you find yourself wanting to push your attentions on someone, put on the brakes and analyze the reasons for your feelings. If you find that the person reminds you of someone you cared for in the past, be very cautious.
- Have a clear idea of the behavior you want from others and make sure you do not act until you get it.
- Move slowly and keep lines of contact open. Do not plunge into intense relationships quickly, even when they are offered. Once

you get involved in an intimate relationship, you must sacrifice a great many other possible contacts. This fact is particularly significant if you want to overcome shyness. Making a premature commitment can put you in a position where you must remain shy.

- It is important to have friends of both sexes. Relationships that offer the possibility of sexual contact may be a little difficult to manage, but you can socialize with the opposite sex in public places and avoid premature sexual contact.

The act of building a friendship is a skill that can be learned and perfected. What is more, you can forget how to do it. One of the hazards of middle age is that people sometimes get involved in work and professional activities and forget how to make friends. Married women often devote extraordinary amounts of time to their families. Once the families are grown and the nest is bare, they find themselves overwhelmed with boredom but uncertain what to do about it. Professionals and dedicated executives have similar experiences. Most of their contacts are derived from their work. They do not have people with whom they can spend time just for the fun of it, and as a result as they face retirement, they find the time to do a great deal but no one interesting to do it with. They may have to learn the skills of making friends all over again.

TESTING THE WATER

Here are some ways to test whether or not a relationship is growing into a friendship. When you have had considerable experience with another person, it is sometimes useful to discuss the nature of your relationship. This does not mean that complicated disclosures need to be made, but it is good to touch base and talk about what you think you are getting and what you think you are giving to see if the other person sees it the same way. The survey of pairs of friends indicated that most people do not like to open this kind of talk for fear the relationship is so fragile it will blow away if it gets discussed. However, virtually all said they would have appreciated it if their friend had brought it up. Everyone, it seems, needs confirmation of his or her value, and when you are reasonably sure of the affection of another person, it is simply good sense to tell that person how valuable the affection is.

Step 1. Plan a special evening in which discussion can start but can terminate graciously if it does not seem to work out. The perennial quiet restaurant is probably best, because if things get awkward, it is easy to change the subject.

Step 2. Make sure your goal is clearly phrased. Rehearse your remarks carefully. Prepare an introduction on a topic such as "some mixed emotions I have about my family" or "problems I am having on the job." Talk a bit about it and ask your friend for a response. The response could either be commentary on what you said or it could be some personal statement about similar problems. The idea is to check whether the friend is willing to talk about some serious and personal topics. If that goes well, then it is possible to introduce the idea of the importance of the friendship. Don't get maudlin about it. A simple statement like "I certainly appreciate the time I spend with you. It is important to have someone to check things out with."

Step 3. Have an exit line prepared when the friend signals that no more discussion of the topic is possible. The best thing to do is to plan another event. The idea of the whole process is simply to flash a signal and get a response. It is not necessary to make a night of this kind of talk. By testing the water periodically, you spare yourself from making excessive commitments to one-sided relationships.

SHYNESS AND POPULARITY

Shy people are attracted to popularity. They think the popular person has all the qualities they would like to have. When given the chance, the shy person would be willing to stand in the third ring around a popular person rather than try to build a relationship with another lonely person. Shy people also often regard public expressions of goodwill as being privately and exclusively directed toward them, even when they are clearly publicly given and clearly given to several people all at once. Shy people are often so starved for a kind word that the "hale fellow" routine of the popular person has great appeal for them. They go home and daydream about their wonderful relationship and then are dismayed to discover the next time they see the popular person that he or she does not even remember their name.

Analyze your own behavior. If you find that you are mostly a spectator, listening to the same person run through the same monologues, then you need to make some other choices. Friendships must be reciprocal, and you are getting nothing except sore hands from the obligatory applause you must give the popular person in order to hold your place in court. You are actually a vassal. While you are around popular people, however, use a little of the time to your own advantage. Notice their style. Notice how they *seem* to be considerate of others, how they take care to adapt their remarks to the people they are addressing and to the occasion. You can use some of their style in your own efforts to build strong interpersonal relationships.

Popular people shake hands firmly and look people directly in the eye. Most have a good memory and can remember others' names and faces and can recognize them at a second meeting. Popular people know how to tell a story well. They do not get steps out of sequence and they can modulate their voices to "punch" a punch line. In general, the people we call "popular" are those who have the ability to amuse others. They do not necessarily have close friends, though they often live their lives in a fishbowl.

A relationship should provide equity for both partners or at least a fair chance for equity. When a relationship starts off with a wide disparity in power, it is almost impossible for the weaker party ever to catch up. That is why it is important for shy people to be sure of their ground before committing themselves to an intimate relationship. There is no point to getting into a relationship on the chance that things will improve when the other person "gets to know me better." Beware of charisma. Shy people sometimes offer themselves as followers of people who appear powerful and protective. When you become this kind of follower, you lose your own identity. If you find yourself in a relationship where you are expected to perform services for the other and receive nothing in return except permission to be around, then you are in an unproductive relationship. You should try to find a way out.

FINDING SOMEONE WHO NEEDS WHAT YOU HAVE

Many people report that they are fearful and miserable at social gatherings. They don't know how to meet people, how to make small talk, how to take advantage of the obvious opportunities. Their eyes are on the popular people who are obviously enjoying themselves. For some reason they do not see the roomful of people very much like themselves yearning for someone to make a move toward them.

Some people are lonely because they are essentially unpleasant people. But for the most part the world is filled with bored and lonely people who are all right. They are not geniuses, charmers, actors, or heroes. They are trying to make it as best they can in a world that seems stacked against them. They feel sorry for themselves some of the time, for they know they are good people and they can't understand why the world doesn't notice their decency and invite them to participate. If you can learn to approach people like that, virtually the whole world can be the pool from which to choose your friends, and you will be the fortunate shy person who brings personal sensitivities to the service of others like yourself.

SELECTING FRIENDS

Friendship is no accident. Friends select each other. If you pick the people you associate with according to foolish criteria, then you get unreliable friends. But you do pick them, and they pick you. If you can find a way to isolate behaviors that predict solid friendships, then you have a first-rate opportunity to improve your social life. Start seeking friends with the steps you used for any social encounter:

- What does this person have that I need?
- What would I have to do in order to get it?
- Is it worth the effort?

If you decide it is, then prepare a plan to contact the person you have selected. Monitor each stage of the relationship to reassure yourself that it is reciprocal. Make sure you do not push on and expect more than the other person is prepared to deliver. Some friendships "freeze" at a particular stage. You have some friends whose company you enjoy and who would lend you money but in whom you cannot confide. You have others who are very supportive but with whom it is very difficult to socialize. You will have specialized friends for all occasions, some for recreation, some for advice, some for exchanges of services, some for common interests, some because you simply feel comfortable together.

Once you have discovered your needs and a person by whom they may be fulfilled, detail your strategy.

- I am sick of eating out alone. I'd like to get someone to eat with me at least one night a week.
- I have seen Tom Smith eating alone. I was always afraid to join him. I think he is shy also.
- I see Tom mostly on Thursday nights. Tomorrow is Tuesday. I will walk past him at the water cooler and say, "How about joining me for dinner at Benjie's Thursday? You set the time."
- The way I say it will suggest that we each pay, but at worst, it will cost me a dinner, and I can find out whether eating with Tom is an improvement over eating alone.

Once you have consolidated Tom as an eating partner, it is relatively simple to suggest other activities. Through trial and error you and Tom will learn what you have in common. It may well be that eating together is the best you are going to do. Your interests may be so diverse that you cannot accommodate yourselves to each other. On the other hand, your eating together may give you an opportunity to share some confidences and to discuss some personal problems that will put each of you in a position to help out when the going gets tough. You will have created one kind of friend.

Don't push too hard. Don't try to make Tom a constant companion. If you try to push even a very lonely person into too much activity too fast, the relationship will rip apart. Furthermore, you do not want to make Tom too reliant on you, because you are going to try to find more than one friend. You may be trying to develop a relationship with Susan. You can't let Tom generate obligations that would keep that from happening. Keep tuned in to what Tom is doing and saying so that you can keep tabs on how the relationship is going.

OPPOSITES ATTRACT, BUT SOMETIMES BIRDS OF A FEATHER FLOCK TOGETHER

Some of your friends may be very much like you and some may be very different. There is no way to figure out which of the two proverbs is correct, although the evidence tips slightly on behalf of the "birds" hypothesis. But your selection depends on what you need. It may be very important for you to know someone so different that each encounter will test your dearest premises. It may be equally important to have people around you who are experiencing what you are experiencing and with whom you can test reality and exchange advice.

The study of 511 friendships reported earlier showed that most people who have passed middle age and retained good and close friends have one friend from youth (high school or college), one friend from the job, a neighbor who is a close friend, and usually a "strange" friend, one met by accident who is very different in beliefs and life-style. This pattern suggests some principles about where you can seek friends.

- Some of the people with whom you work can be friends, so long as they are not potential competitors.
- Friends can be selected from people who share your hobbies and interests.
- Some of the people who live near you can be friends.
- Sometimes friends or relatives can introduce you to people who can become good friends.
- Sometimes people you meet by accident can develop into friends, but don't count on it.

A LOCATION EXERCISE

To make sure that you employ your full resources in your search for friends, supply the following information.

Name three people in your apartment building whom you would like to meet. Provide one reason each why you would like to meet them. It doesn't matter whether you know their names yet. An identification like "the man in the cap" or "the woman with the scottie" will do.

Do the same for people at work. Don't worry if you get more than three names. Check each name and cross off anyone who is a direct supervisor of yours and anyone with whom you might compete for advancement.

Develop, for the six or more names, a plan for an initial meeting. For those whose names you do not know, write a scenario in which you will greet the people and offer your name in exchange for theirs. The reason you want to meet them might serve as a good opener. "My name is Jane Anderson. I really like your dog." "My name is Bill Smith, you look like you have the same hours off that I do." Hold out your hand. You are now implicitly offering three choices: (a) they can turn around and walk away (a very unlikely prospect); (b) they can offer their name and excuse themselves (the most likely prospect); or (c) they can pick up on the cue you offer and make small talk for a while (which is the prospect you must prepare for).

Once you have the names of the people you are interested in, prepare an invitation to an opening encounter. A conversation during coffee break, an invitation to the coffee shop in the neighborhood, or an invitation to lunch would all work. You can also include them, one at a time, in your social gatherings. It is not productive to invite too many complete strangers at the same time, since they may all prove to be dull. You want to have them when you have some people you can count on.

Keep this information available. Whenever you find yourself uneasy about your rate of making social contacts, pull out your notes and start developing a new acquaintance.

EXTENDING THE RELATIONSHIP

If one partner in an intimate relationship wants to extend contacts with other people and the other partner does not, there is a potential problem of jealousy. This is particularly sticky if the new friend is of the opposite sex. Without expressing a moral judgment, it would appear that this kind of extension is so potentially threatening that it should probably be avoided. At any event, it is sensible to discuss the situation openly.

Get some information about the potential new friend. Find something about the person that would appeal to your partner. Don't be phony about this, for there may be nothing appealing about the other person as far as your partner is concerned. In that case, have a statement ready about why the new person is very important to you.

Prepare a social event in which your partner has a chance to meet the new person in a nonthreatening atmosphere. Be particularly attentive to your partner's needs at this event. If you give the impression that the new partner is going to preempt time and attention reserved for your partner, your partner will probably resist. Be prepared for a refusal to participate by your partner. The new person may appear so unpleasant and threatening that no amount of persuasion will work. In this case, you may have to work out some arrangement for time alone with the new person.

Introducing a third party into a relationship is often the cause of the relationship breaking apart. Third parties who demand time and attention from one partner generally cause the alienated partner to rethink the relationship and to take compensating action. Although it is fairly easy to handle work and professional contacts with people of the same sex, contacts with the opposite sex are particularly threatening to on-going intimate relationships. Despite some advice to the contrary, it is very difficult for males and females to maintain close contact without sex becoming an issue at one time or another. Infidelities are very difficult to handle. They often result in termination of intimate relationships. If it is necessary and desirable to be friends with a person of the opposite sex, the more open the relationship, the less likely it is to threaten existing intimacies.

Intimate partners cannot provide for all of each other's needs. Friends of various kinds are necessary for a full social life. If a commitment has been made to be a partner, part of honoring that commitment means openness in building other relationships.

THE MALE-FEMALE RELATIONSHIP

There is considerable disparity in sexual goals between people. Today there is no operational moral barrier to "one-night stands." Sexual experimentation is common and not only confined to the young. There are a number of men and women who appear able to handle casual sexual contact without any visible emotional stress. Others, however, stampeded into easy contact, find themselves consumed with guilt and apprehension about the meaning of the act, what it does to their self-esteem, how they will be regarded by the partner, and what it says about them as a person if they are unable to enjoy it thoroughly. Furthermore, if one partner is casual and the other attaches meaning to the act, there is the possibility that the overinvestment will later result in a highly emotional disaster for both parties. Shy people are often sexually dominated because their urgency for social contact may force them to make sexual concessions that are not necessarily compatible with their moral structure and that cause them feelings of guilt, despite the fact that the acts help them cement social contact in other dimensions.

Any kind of male-female relationship carries some sexual contact. Even the most casual contact requires consideration of the possibility that the sexual issue may arise. A sensible caution is to reserve sexual contact until other matters have been disposed of and a basis for intimacy has been established. This may or may not mean "saving oneself for marriage." More realistically, it may mean managing social situations so that sexual threats do not arise. If necessary, social contacts between potential sexual partners can be managed outside the privacy of the home until it is established that both people have similar sexual goals. Then you can just ease back and "let it happen." Sexuality clearly is not gratifying if one has to haggle about it in the same fashion as buying a used car. By the same token, it is sufficiently emotional to warrant a good deal of consideration of its potential meaning before indulging.

Both partners must understand what they are after in sexuality. Frequency of sex, the way gratification is achieved and shared, the method used to get started, what happens afterward, all contain considerable emotional potential. It is hard for people to know exactly what they believe if they haven't had experience. This means that everyone is confronted with the paradox of potential injury from a bad experience without knowing what a bad experience is. All of this argues for some security in the relationship before sexual efforts are made. Remember, this issue is a practical one!

The idea that sexual relationships can be carried out with "no strings attached" is a myth that has injured a great many shy people. They get talked into a commitment only to discover that there are strings in that they want to retain the relationship. They often want more from it than sexual contact, but their partner offers nothing more than physical contact. When the relationship comes apart, the dominant partner goes on to new arrangements, while the shy partner is devastated, often unable to attempt new relationships. Thus the most practical advice to shy people is to avoid making arrangements until the *facts* convince you that there is more to it than an attempt to achieve physical pleasure. When you can discuss possible meanings with your partner and can be reassured that there is sufficient evidence of intimate exchange, then physical intimacy can be granted. Managing your own sexuality is one of the strongest capabilities you can have in social relationships with the opposite sex. It can be maintained at the outset by managing situations. The quiet restaurant, the long walk, sitting in the park, a quiet bar, or a coffee house, can provide ample opportunity for talk. Fine moments are possible. As the relationship matures and there is more talk about personal feelings and commitments, access to privacy can be granted, and nature can take its course—modulated of course by sensible goalsetting.

SOME CAUTIONS
IN STRIVING FOR INTIMACY

Foremost in setting your goals to achieve intimacy is to understand how little power you have over the decisions made by the other person. All you can do is attempt to control your own actions and to design them so that they test sensible hypotheses about the other person's reactions.

Sometimes we get ourselves into exploitative relationships because we fly in the face of the facts and extend our hand and service to someone who is willing to relate to us only in a limited way. Unwilling to accept the limitations imposed, we distort reality until we convince ourselves that the intimacy is genuine, but when we have to test it in reality with an important request, we find ourselves closed out.

Attempts to make your relationship fit some standard are foolish. The television generation believes in easy and speedy resolution. After all, television dramas get all their business done in ninety minutes. Soap operas show life closer to the fact, however: The stories drag on and on, and just when things look good, something awful happens. Life is sometimes like that. We all have our personal soap operas—a sick person in the family, an aging relative, the prospect of unemployment. We all need to work our way through them in our own unique fashion with the people we care about. Thus each pair of people must make decisions about how they will conduct their personal business based on their needs, the kind of life they are living, and the kind of life they want to live together.

Another important point in relationship building is to keep moving. Some shy people try for a single relationship, and when it does not work out, they freeze. When they do form a relationship, they stop trying. Everyone needs alternatives and variety. To demand that one person, however loving and dedicated, fulfill all your needs in unreasonable, and that person will soon become exhausted from the sheer effort. In real intimacies, partners can handle adversity by sticking together, but normal stress such as a new job, new interests, and new people often pose insurmountable threats when one partner does not have sufficient variety in his or her social contacts to accommodate changes in the other. When couples begin to get intimate, some of their old friends must be cast off to find new associations. On the job, a promotion may mean severing contact with those who now become employees. When people move, they are confronted with the need to find a whole slate of new associations. It is not sensible to allow your skill at making friends to atrophy, however firm your association with your partner is.

Relationships sometimes end. Sometimes they end because of the death of a partner, sometimes because the people no longer like each other. It is not only shy people who suffer the pain of broken relationships. However, people who have skill in relationship building have the ability to come back quickly and form new supportive associations when they are needed most. Everyone keeps meeting people and everyone must keep open to the possibility of some new person becoming a part of his or her life. Even such mundane events as the birth of a child or a parent coming to live in a couple's home can drastically affect relationship patterns. As one partner's attention is distracted toward the new need, the other partner may need to find compensations in the form of outside activities and associations.

What sustains male-female relationships is considerate goalsetting. Accommodations by one party to the needs of the other permit flexibility in arrangements. It is rigidity on the part of one or both partners that customarily leads to the destruction of relationships. Egocentric demands by one person upon the other may temporarily get big returns in one direction, but when demands become excessive or there is no return, the deprived partner either seeks to break loose or is so browbeaten that he or she loses value. Whatever is obtained from another person must be paid for either in reality or in potential, and potential must be like a bank account, available for withdrawal whenever needed. Returns need not be immediate nor need they be one for one, but they must be present if the relationship is to last. Most important is maintaining communication links so that difficulties can be dealt with.

People need to remind themselves that talk is exchange. Sometimes when relationships begin to come apart, one partner dehumanizes the other by refusing to talk or provide ordinary attentions. Such actions are incredibly destructive, for to withdraw communication is to reduce the value of the person. Shy people who entered painful relationships only because the stronger partner paid attention to them are often completely destroyed when the stronger partner decides to withdraw communication. Partners who wish to remain together need to listen to each other talk directly. We do so much in relationship based on inferences about what our partner wants and needs that it is sometimes startling when we get a direct request.

Relationships are fueled by talk. Shy people suffer because they do not talk enough or because they read the popular magazines and then try to "communicate." The late Eric Berne once commented that communication is really terribly boring.[7] He deplored communication and expressed the wish that people could learn to talk to one another. Talk is useful because it is directed at real issues and circumstances. What is referred to as communication is usually devoted to accomplishing some unattainable goal generated by panacea salesmen.

Remember also that not every male-female relationship you have needs to proceed to intimacy. There are some relationships that can stabilize on levels of interest or activity. Shy people are often frustrated because some of their relationships don't seem to be "getting anywhere." Interestingly enough, it is precisely those relationships that seem locked at a particular level that become prime pools for intensification when needs and opportunities change.

All of the preceding may seem cold and unromantic to you. It is intended to be so. There are so many romantic myths that it is hard to convince people that romance is nothing but a state of mind. An antidote to romance is important for those people who wish to sustain their relationships. Relationships go along nicely until one party needs surgery or gets gastritis. Love is a marvelous sustaining force until the first overdraft at the bank or until the first cockroach invasion starts. It takes more than love and romance to run a relationship.

Love in its effective sense is an enduring state of deep commitment between two people. It has its romantic aspects as well as its physical ones, but it is more than an occasional orgasm and a dream. It does not happen "at first sight," no matter how powerfully two people may be attracted to each other. It takes time to develop love, and often it is built around extraordinarily mundane bits of business. We can hear the romantics out there sighing, "Ah, but what does it matter? A wild, passionate romance will leave memories even if it fails." Sadly, most wild, passionate romances leave nothing but pain, and even nice memories are useless when surgery is required or you lose a lawsuit.

Everything in this book that you learned about talk can be applied to intimate relationships and close friendships. You can set goals to discuss whatever you need to discuss. So long as you keep your partner's interests in mind and adapt your concerns to his or hers, you will probably be able to attain realistic goals.

There is little we can advise about pathological relationships. This book is not addressed to sick people or people with sick partners. People sometimes have special needs and must solicit the services of "specialists" to help them handle them. If you have tried ordinary means of improving your relationships and have failed, it may mean that either you or your partner or both need the services of a counselor of one type or another. There are relationships in which one party is entirely free from guilt while the other is a complete villain, but most of the time the sickness in a relationship is shared. Shy people sometimes take more than their share of blame, and if it is your habit to blame yourself, you may need the services of a counselor to help you understand that you are probably not capable of messing up another person's life all by yourself. In fact, the person whose life is messed up probably worked very hard to accomplish it. While you must tolerate the "peccadillos" of the people you care about, there is no rule that you have to do social work with emotionally disturbed or pathologically selfish people. This book can be used as a source of goalsetting to help you extricate yourself from such relationships.

Finally keep in mind that the unpleasant fact that people sometimes hurt other people. Everyone is not moral, pure, and good all the time. People sometimes try to be decent, and sometimes they consciously set out to injure others. Most of the time they just fumble along trying to get what they are after, and sometimes other people profit by it, and sometimes they are injured. You are entitled to defend yourself against potential exploiters as well as against accidental damage. The person who injures you by accident can be dealt with; the one who does it on purpose is to be avoided or defeated but can never be dealt with. You have the obligation to have realistic expectations and to resist exploitation, threats, bribes, and intimidations. You must control your own behavior, directing it toward your own goals and basing it on sensible analysis of other people's behavior. On this basis, managing relationships uses the same tools and techniques as getting service from tradespeople. Only the stakes are higher.

REFERENCES

1. Richard Rabkin, *Inner and Outer Space* (New York: W.W. Norton, 1970).
2. John Silber, "Masks and Fig Leaves" (audio tape prepared for the Center for the Study of Democratic Institutions, Palo Alto, Calif., 1972). This matter was considered in detail by Dr. Patrick de Mare, St. George's Hospital, London, in a paper delivered to the National Conference about the Teaching of Group Psychology, Philadelphia, March 1980.
3. Gerald M. Phillips and Nancy J. Metzger, *Intimate Communication* (Boston: Allyn & Bacon, Inc., 1976).
4. Murray Davis, *Intimate Relations* (New York: The Free Press, 1973).
5. Phillips and Metzger, *Intimate Communication*.
6. Phillips and Metzger, *Intimate Communication*.
7. Eric Berne, *Sex in Human Loving* (New York: Simon & Schuster, Inc., 1970).

RECOMMENDED READINGS

Gerald M. Phillips and Nancy J. Metzger, *Intimate Communication* (Boston: Allyn & Bacon, Inc., 1976).

Murray Davis, *Intimate Relations* (New York: The Free Press, 1973).

Elaine Walster, G. William Walster, and Ellen Berscheid, *Equity: Theory and Research* (Boston: Allyn & Bacon, Inc., 1978).

Elaine Walster and G. William Walster, *A New Look at Love* (Reading, Mass.: Addison-Wesley Publishing Co., Inc., June 1978).

George Gilder, *Sexual Suicide* (New York: Quadrangle/The New York Times Book Co., Inc., 1973).

Edward Albee, *Who's Afraid of Virginia Woolf?* (New York: Atheneum Publishers, 1962).

chapter 12

Getting and Keeping the Job

There are two purposes for using talk in your vocational life: to get the job and to keep the job. Shy people have trouble with both. It is difficult for them to appear competent when they take interviews for jobs, and they have trouble making their accomplishments known when they are on the job. Recent studies indicate that oral skill is a very important criterion for advancement on the job, for it is often the only way for employees to display their competence.[1]

Effective talk helps you, of course, only if you are otherwise qualified. It is not a *substitute for competence but a method of displaying competence*. There is the tendency for supervisors to assume that people who do not speak up are not fully confident, but it is equally simple for them to use your talk to identify your shortcomings. Thus there is considerable risk on the job both in talking and in keeping silent.

MANAGING INTERVIEWS

Shy people tend to select occupations that keep them from contact with others. Many base their vocational selection on their projection of the amount of human contact it will require. They do not understand, of course, that there are few jobs, if any, that are devoid of human requirements, and even worse, they do not understand what is at stake in job seeking. Most jobs are acquired through skillful talk, in the interview. The more challenging and lucrative the job, the more crucial the interview. Thus all decisions to avoid people notwithstanding, getting a job that enables you to avoid people requires considerable skill with people.

Job interviews allow candidates to display themselves so that interviewers can decide whether or not to recommend employment. The job seeker must demonstrate

- Competence by confirming information on the application blank and in the résumé,
- Competence by talking intelligently about the job for which competence is claimed,
- Social skill by talking reasonably and intelligently with the interviewer,
- Interest in the company and its activities, and
- The contribution the applicant can make to the company.

There is no way these goals can be attained without skillful talk. The candidates must adapt not only to the circumstances of the interview but also to the demands of the interviewer. In addition, the candidates must defend themselves by getting sufficient information from the interviewer on which to base their eventual decision about whether or not to take the job if it is offered.

Everyone, shy or not, is relatively powerless in an interview situation. You have been invited at the convenience of the interviewer to a place he or she has chosen. The interviewer knows what he or she is looking for, you do not. Questions have been prepared. You may have prepared answers, but not necessarily to those questions, so you have the problem of adapting to contingencies. You are "one down" right from the start. Fortunately most interviewers are trained to make you feel reasonably comfortable, and few will patronize or insult you. Still, you are at a disadvantage, and the interview will work to keep it that way. The interviewer has a job and has a job to bestow. You do not have a job and you want one. Thus you are insecure and the interviewer is secure, and he or she will use that security to find out how you manage insecurity. And there is no appeal if you have been misjudged. You have one chance and you must do your very best with it.

There are ways to prepare for interviews. If you understand how to prepare and you rehearse carefully, you ought to be able to represent yourself well. If you have engaged in orderly preparation, you will have a jump on most candidates who enter interviews, shy or not. Interviews are not spontaneous happenings. They are sales experiences. You are selling your services to a potential employer. You have a limited amount of time to convince that potential employer that you are superior to the competitors for the position, and you don't even know who they are.

Your interviewer usually has a completed application blank or résumé in advance of the interview, so you are not a total stranger. He or she is a stranger to you, however. The interviewer has had a chance to figure out what he or she wants to know about you, and it will be very difficult for you to conceal important information. As a matter of fact, you do not really want to conceal it, merely to present it well.

COMPETENCY ASSESSMENTS

Most people undersell themselves. Shy people are particularly skillful at hiding their competencies. They are accomplished at snatching defeat from the jaws of victory. Before attempting to fill out an application blank or prepare a résumé, you ought to have a plan to represent yourself well in writing. Your application or résumé should contain information that will convince the interviewer of your competence. The idea is to have a real sense of your own capabilities and, without apology, to say what you can do well, what you can do well enough, and what you are willing to learn. It is equally important to rule out what you cannot do and what you do not want to learn to do. Almost as bad as not getting the job is getting the job for which you are not qualified. Fill out the following checklist as a guide to your competencies.

COMPETENCY CHECKLIST

INSTRUCTIONS

In column 1, rate your competence on the following scale:

- 1 = I can do it really well.
- 2 = I can do it well enough to get started.
- 3 = I am willing to learn to do it.
- 4 = I am not interested in learning to do it.
- 5 = I don't know enough about it.

In column 2, note how you can prove your competence with the following code:

- 1 = I have a diploma or certificate.
- 2 = I took a course or am participating in a training program.
- 3 = I interned or apprenticed.
- 4 = I did it on a previous job and have a reference.

You can use more than one number. Fill in this column for every item you coded 1 or 2 in the first column. In column 3, note for yourself a reason why you are not interested in learning to do whatever you coded 4 in column 1. When you are done, you should be able to make a series of statements about each of the occupational categories that will explain to your potential employer what you can or cannot do. This can be translated to the appropriate place on the application blank or résumé or discussed orally with your interviewer.

BASIC SKILLS	1	2	3
Arithmetic (level _____)			
Reading (level _____)			
Listening skills			
Writing skills			

(BASIC SKILLS *cont'd.*)	1	2	3
Speaking skills			
Discussion skills			

PERSONAL SKILLS	1	2	3
Sewing and mending			
Making clothing			
Child care			
Home nursing			
Household management and food preparation			
Obtaining loans and credit			
Outdoor management and gardening			
Auto repair and maintenance			
Entertaining			
Furniture repair			
Sports and games			
Music			
Dance			
Theater			

(PERSONAL SKILLS *cont'd.*)	1	2	3
Art			
Other:			

VOLUNTEER SKILLS AND HOBBIES	1	2	3
Planning and managing meetings			
Committee work			
Organization secretary			
Organization treasurer			
Community action			
Fundraising			
Hospital volunteer			
Fraternal service			
Service to the disadvantaged			
Religious organization or Sunday school			
Hobbies and crafts (list):			
Youth leadership			

(VOLUNTEER SKILLS AND HOBBIES *cont'd.*)	1	2	3
Coaching sports (list):			
Camping			

JOB EXPERIENCE AND VOCATIONAL TRAINING	1	2	3
Typing w.p.m. _____			
Shorthand w.p.m. _____			
Speedwriting/notehand			
Speedreading w.p.m. _____			
Information storage and retrieval			
Keypunching			
Card sorting			
Computer programming: languages			
Office procedures			
Traffic control			
Shipping and receiving			
Market analysis			

(JOB EXPERIENCE AND VOCATIONAL TRAINING *cont'd.*)	1	2	3
Machine operation (specify):			
Receptionist			
Switchboard			
Duplicating machines			
Letter and memo writing			
Technical writing			
Editing			
Copywriting			
Research			
Layout			
Graphics			
Photography			
Clothing design			
Food service (list):			
Maitre d'			
Bartender			

(JOB EXPERIENCE AND VOCATIONAL TRAINING *cont'd.*)	1	2	3
Sales: Door to door			
Store clerk			
Manufacturer's rep			
Real estate			
Banking (specialty):			
Stocks and bonds			
Insurance (specify):			
Cashier			
Driving (list vehicle):			
Vehicle repairs			
Maintenance and custodial			
Appliance repair			
Radio/TV repair			
Electronics			
Construction (skill):			
Credit and collections			
Phone solicitation			
Other:			

Make a list of everything in which you have professional training, certification, or school training. For example, engineering (specialty: civil, mechanical, aeronautical, industrial, electrical, etc.); business (management, advertising, merchandising, logistics, planning, etc.); human services (social work, gerontology, health services, planning, etc.); public administration; labor relations; agriculture; and so on. Be sure to distinguish training from instruction and list types of training and types of instruction. Do not list courses you have taken such as history or philosophy.

If you can tell your interviewer what you can do well and what you would like to learn, you will have an edge on the other candidates. Use this list to prepare statements to your future employer.

APPLICATION BLANKS AND RÉSUMÉS

Use this information and gather together everything you need to fill out an application blank and résumé. It is very much like preparing your autobiography. You will be looking for facts, not feelings, and you will have to be careful to document everything you put in writing. Many candidates for jobs lose out when the information they provide cannot be corroborated. If you anticipate what you might be asked, you can prepare yourself to give accurate information. Following is a master application guide that you can use as a basis for any application you must fill out and also as an outline for your résumé.

APPLICATION BLANK KIT

The following form contains questions taken from a great many application blanks. It would be useful if you would make a copy and fill it out carefully. Have it duplicated and keep one in a safe place and another with you when you go job hunting. Make sure you have everything on it spelled correctly. Check addresses, phone numbers, dates of employment. Make sure you have contacted all of your references and obtained permission to use their names. If former employers are out of business, note it. This is a compendium of all the information you will need to fill out application blanks and, together with your Competency Checklist, you will have all you need to prepare a résumé.

Full name _____
Present address _____
City and state _____Zip_____

Permanent mailing address if not the same as above _____
Name and address of person to notify in the event of an emergency
Phone number _____ Phone number to call to leave
messages _____
Social Security number _____ Type of citizenship _____
NOTE: It is against the law for prospective employers to ask you to
provide information about age, marital status, race, religion, national
origin, or physical condition. They can ask for personal statistics such
as height and weight. They may not ask you for an arrest record, but
they can ask for convictions.
Height _____ Weight _____ Hair _____ Eyes _____

Military Service
Branch _____ Date entered _____ Date
discharged _____
Type of discharge _____ Disability _____
Type _____
Reserve status _____ Rank at time of discharge
_____
Reserve rank _____ Technical assignment _____
Overseas experience _____

References
Personal character (name) _____
Address _____
City, state _____Zip_____
Phone _____ Date of permission _____
Educational reference (name) _____
Address _____
City and state _____Zip _____
Phone _____Date of permission _____
Work reference (name) _____
Address _____

City and state _____ Zip_____
Phone _____Date of permission _____
Provide one work reference for each job you have held.
Don't ever write, "References provided on request." Most employment managers will reject your application if references are not immediately available. Do not provide reference letters unless requested.

Education and Training
High school and address _____
Name of confirming person _____
Diploma date _____Rank or average _____
Type of program _____Honors _____
Activities _____
Vo-tech program (name and address) _____

_____
Competencies and certificates _____
Date of completion _____ Name of confirming person _____
College (undergraduate school name and address) _____

_____
Name of confirming person _____
Degree _____ Honors _____ Rank or average _____
Majors _____Activities_____
Graduate school (name and address) _____

_____
Name of confirming person _____
Degree _____ Honors _____ Rank or average
Thesis or dissertation title _____
List all schools attended. Be sure to provide complete listings including the names of persons who can confirm your attendance. Check with schools to find name of current records supervisor. Be sure to give all ZIP and area codes where needed.

Work Record (List present or most recent employer first. List all previous employers working backward. There is no need to include part-time work during school if you have had three or more jobs since. Be sure to provide complete and accurate details as specified.)

Employer _____

Street address _____

City, state, _____Zip _____

Supervisor's name _____Title _____

Personnel department phone _____

Your duties _____

Date employed _____ Date terminated _____

Reason for termination _____

Salary at time of termination _____

What does this organization do or provide? _____

Additional Information

Account for missing time, illness, marriage, childbirth. You need not put this information on your formal application, but you may need it to explain gaps in your employment. If you are claiming a disabling illness, report name of doctor who can verify.

Self-employment and names of persons who can vouch for it _____

List volunteer activities, community service, civic honors, elected positions. _____

List publications, art displays, performances. _____

If relevant, list grants and financial awards obtained. _____

From your Competency Checklist, list the professional competencies and certifications you have. _____

From your Competency Checklist, list the skills you can document and wish to have considered. _____

From your Competency Checklist, list the skills you would most like to learn. _____

List bonding history (if relevant) _____

List convictions (Not arrests or charges; do not list summary offenses)
_____

List your past three addresses _____

_____

Write a fifty-word statement beginning, "The type of work I am looking for is . . ."
Write a fifty-word statement beginning, "What I hope to be doing five
years from now is . . ."

Keep this blank application up to date and readily available so that
you will have all the information you need when it is time to seek employment.

RÉSUMÉS

A résumé is a statement of your competencies designed to present
yourself in the best possible light. It is used to solicit interest in you on
the part of potential employers. Most professional positions require a
résumé. It is useful to have one available for any position. A good résumé should be simple and factual. Employers do not read long résumés
except for high-level administrative or professional jobs. In that case,
you may solicit the help of a professional résumé-writing service. Your
résumé can be built from your master application blank and your Competency Checklist. It should be divided into simple categories.

- *Vital statistics.* Your name, address, phone. (You need not provide
  information about race, age, sex, marital or family status, nationality, or physical conditions. If you are in doubt, check a summary of
  Title VII of the Equal Opportunity Employment Act.)
- *Educational record.* List all schools attended, dates, and a contact
  person who can confirm the information. If there is any other
  significant information, such as major honors, list it. Do not list
  junior high or elementary school. Do list trade and vocational
  schools.
- *Vocational record.* List all jobs, dates of employment and termination, reason for termination, supervisor's name, and type of work
  you did.
- *Accomplishments* when pertinent to the type of job you are seeking.

- *Community and civic activities*, but only when they will not reveal information forbidden under Title VII.
- *Major references*. List recent employers, important school references, and someone who can attest to your character. Be sure to give accurate addresses. Make sure that you contact your references for permission to use their names.

You needn't prepare a master résumé unless you are doing a major job search of companies to which you are applying for the same type of job. It is sensible to make a specific résumé for each company to which you apply. Head your résumé with a brief statement of the kind of work you are seeking. Make sure that your résumé is neatly prepared, and check carefully for errors in spelling, grammar, and punctuation.

Following is an example of a simple résumé. Note that it is not cluttered. If you can get your résumé to fit on one page (front and back maximum) you are at an advantage. There is no need to use fancy paper or multicolored ink, but a good-quality paper and sharp carbon ribbon should be used.

RÉSUMÉ

SALLY FORTH NICHOLS
1968 MARKET STREET
FOREST SLOUGH, ARK. 99999
PHONE: (555) 666-7777

I am seeking an opportunity to use my skills and experience in a human service agency. I am prepared to accept an entry-level job if advancement is possible.

Education: BACKPACK COLLEGE
12 COLLEGE ROW
EVANSVILLE, ARK. 99998   1955–58
DANIEL JONES, REGISTRAR

B.A., June 1958. Major in social welfare. Minor in business administration. Emphasis on application of sound business practices to human service agencies. President, Student Volunteer Association. Dean's List, 1957, 1958.

MUDSINK HIGH SCHOOL
ROCKY ROAD, R.R. 2
MUDSINK, ARK. 99997   1951–55
JIM-BOB HOOPLE, PRINCIPAL

Diploma, 1955. Top 20%. Women's varsity track. Senior-class treasurer.

Work   TRAVESTY REGIONAL AGENCY
Experience: ON AGING
866 COLONEL SANDERS LANE
TRAVESTY, ARK. 99996   1962–66
TOMMY-JOE HOPPER, SUPERVISOR

Supervised office staff of eight persons. Processed Title XX applications for senior citizens. Wrote and edited monthly community news bulletin.

HOUSE BAYOU MUNICIPAL
AUTHORITY
1929 CRASH STREET
HOUSE BAYOU, LA. 88888   1958–62
AL GIDWITZ, SUPERVISOR

Administrative assistant. Responsible for issuing compliance certificates for day care mothers. Kept minutes of city council meetings. Copy-edited proposals.

Volunteer   League of Women Voters, Forest Slough, Ark.
Experience: Member since 1966. Chairman, Candidates' Night Committee since 1973. Forest Slough Community Church. Board of Trustees, 1972–.

Skills: Type 55 w.p.m. Shorthand, 85 w.p.m. Office machines: xerox, multilith, keypunch. Simple bookkeeping. Child care.

References: Personal	*Education*	*Work*
Evan Slater, M.D.	June Jones, Ph.D.	Artemus Zook
		Flap County
929 Winston Rd.	Dean,	United Way
Slab Cabin,	Social Work	R.D. 2
Ark. 99944	Mississippi	Flapville, Ark.
	College	99944
	Euchre, Miss.	
	77766	

PREPARING FOR THE INTERVIEW

Once you have been notified that you are to have an interview, you must prepare yourself to say what you need to say. Your interviewer will know something about you at the start and will have some prepared questions that are asked of all candidates. It is a good idea to review your Application Blank Kit before going to the interview.

Make sure you arrive at the interview on time. Even if you have to wait, it is better to be there when called. As you enter the room, pay attention to the amenities. Wait for directions about where you are to sit. If the interviewer offers to shake hands, comply at once and make sure you grasp his or her hand firmly. Wait for the interviewer to start. Do not blurt out how eager you are to go to work.

DRESS CAREFULLY

Do not convey unintended messages. A great many decisions are made about people based on the way they dress. Generally, if you wear expensive clothing, you may plant the idea that you do not really need the job or that you live beyond your means. If your clothing is too shabby, you may suggest that you are not considerate of yourself and others around you. If your clothing is suggestive, the interviewer may conclude that your mind is on something else besides work. The best advice is to dress discreetly. A conservative suit for males or females is best. Females should take care that their skirts are whatever length is in vogue and to sit so that as little leg as possible is displayed. Male clothing should be loose but not baggy. Neckties should be conservative—solid colors or stripes. Jewelry should be kept to a minimum. Clothing should, of course, be clean and neat. It need not be new.

PREPARE YOURSELF IN ADVANCE
WITH INFORMATION ABOUT THE COMPANY

Many companies provide prospective employees with an informative brochure. If this is not available, check the company at the local library. Make sure you know what product they make or what service they provide. If these are not available, feel free to ask for information. You can legitimately ask about

- Location, size of company, and type of business.
- Types of jobs currently available.

- Type of job for which you are being considered.
- Conditions under which you might work.
- Nature of the training program, if any.
- Opportunities for education and advancement.
- Promotion and raise policies.
- Whether there is a union and, if so, how it would affect you.
- Fiscal history and job stability record of the company.
- Nature of the competition you will have to engage in to qualify to keep your job. What goes on in the probationary period, if any.
- Turnover rate and prognosis for permanent employment.
- Whether travel or relocation is required.
- Salary offered, job description, qualifications for position.
- Nature of the community in which the company is located.
- Employee benefits,

Be careful about asking about benefits. You do not want to suggest that you are more interested in retirement than you are in advancement.

PREPARE REMARKS YOU MIGHT MAKE IN THE INTERVIEW

Your interviewer will try to size you up to see how you will fit in with the company. Some estimate will be made of your personality. You can presume that if you are being interviewed, you have the basic qualifications. If there is any doubt, your interviewer will bring it up. Normally, however, companies do not spend time and money interviewing people who are not qualified on paper.

Given that you are as qualified as your competition, the interviewer will make decisions about you based on your behavior and appearance. People who are sloppy, inarticulate, excessively heavy, smoke, use drugs or alcohol, act blasé or lackadaisical, lip off to the interviewer, or cannot document what they claim do not get hired. The interviewer's judgment is final. There are, however, certain kinds of questions that cannot be asked legally. Any employer who asks such questions may be trying to discriminate, but most likely he or she is simply not aware of the law. Be careful of the following types of questions:

- Employers cannot ask you what your name was before you changed it.
- Employers cannot inquire about your birthplace or the birthplace of any member of your family.

- Employers cannot ask about your ancestry or national origin.
- Employers cannot ask for your age unless, for some reason, it is a *bona fide* criterion for employment.
- Employers cannot ask you to name your religion, the church you attend, or what holidays you observe. They can declare the days of work required so that you may choose to reject the job if it violates your religious commitments.
- Employers cannot ask your race.
- Employers cannot ask about the citizenship status of anyone but you. They may ask if you are a citizen and if not, what kind of visa you have, and whether you intend to apply for citizenship.
- Employers cannot ask questions about your relatives. They may ask for the name of someone to contact in case of emergency.
- Employers cannot ask for your national origin. They cannot ask you what kind of a name Smith or Goliembiewski is.
- Employers cannot ask about physical handicaps unless the job is such that persons with certain physical conditions would not be able to perform tasks required. In cases like this, companies customarily require a physical examination of all employees, during which the physician looks for the specific disabilities.
- Employers cannot ask you to report legal charges that may have been brought against you. They may ask you to report convictions. They can also inquire about parole and probation status.
- Employers cannot ask about your marital status, living arrangements, children, anything about your spouse, or whether you are "free to travel" or whether there would be anything that would keep you from work on a regular basis. They are entitled to stipulate what they expect from you.
- Employers are not entitled to ask you about memberships that might disclose race, religion, or national origin.
- Questions about sexual preference are legitimate. Employers may legally discriminate against homosexuals unless there are statutes to the contrary in the locality of employment.
- Employers are entitled to ask you about alcohol use, use of drugs, and whether you are under treatment for alcohol or drug abuse.
- Employers are not entitled to question you about your mental health unless it is specifically relevant to the job.
- Employers can question you intensely about your education, what you did on your former jobs, reasons for termination, and so on.

Under the Buckley Amendment you have access to all your personnel files. You may inspect the information kept about you at your previous place of employment or at the schools you attended. You can discover whether reference letters are favorable and you can request that unfavorable references be removed from your file. Some employers will ask you to waive your right of access or will provide a box to check on reference forms, waiving your right of inspection. This is legal, and you check the waiver at your own risk. That is why it is useful to be sure of the people whose names you give as references. Note that your prospective employer need not confine questions to the references you provide. Inquiry can be made about your work or educational performance or anyone in a position to know.

PREPARE FOR COMMONLY ASKED QUESTIONS

Most employers have a list of questions they ask of all prospective employees. Here is a list of the twenty-five most commonly asked questions. Prepare yourself to answer each with a one-minute statement you develop according to the instructions we gave in Chapter Nine.

1. My educational achievements in high school and college.
2. What I am most interested in.
3. My skills are . . .
4. How I can be motivated to do my best work.
5. The kind of criticism that helps me most.
6. How I have demonstrated leadership.
7. My vocational goals now, five years from now, ten years from now.
8. I am mature because . . .
9. My past work experience has been . . .
10. I am a creative person because . . .
11. How I can help your organization.
12. Why I am interested in your company.
13. My extracurricular activities qualify me because . . .
14. My volunteer activities qualify me because . . .
15. What I have learned about myself in the past few years.
16. I have read the following books recently, and they are about . . .
17. I read the following magazines regularly because . . .
18. How I have gotten along with my former employers.
19. What I have learned on my previous jobs.
20. My school grades do/do not estimate my ability because . . .
21. What kind of work I am most interested in.
22. I can get along with people of various kinds because . . .

23. I can demonstrate that I want to get ahead by . . .
24. How I get along with people of various backgrounds.
25. Why I am your best choice.

Do not talk about how badly you need the job. Do not run down the other candidate. Be responsive to the interviewer's questions. If you need a second or two to think things over, ask for it. If you do not understand the question, ask for clarification. Sometimes it helps to repeat the question the way you understand it and ask the interviewer whether this is an accurate paraphrase. Try to integrate your prepared remarks in your answers to the interviewer's questions. Be terse in response to or else ignore illegal questions, do not make a big issue about not answering them.

Employers will evaluate you on

- Communication skills. They will want you to be clear, organized, and direct.
- Definitive handshake. Employers do not like limp or clammy handshakes.
- Neatness in appearance and on the résumé and application blank.
- Promptness.
- Attentiveness.
- Responsiveness to interviewer cues.
- Directness in answering questions. They will expect you to stick to the subject.
- Good manners.
- Whether you appear to have a grip on your future.
- Whether you are seeking *their* job or just any job.

They will try to make estimates about your willingness to work, whether or not you are qualified for the jobs that are vacant, your courtesy to past employers, your interest in and knowledge about the company, your desire for a permanent position, your ambition, maturity, and social awareness, your sense of humor. They will tend to reject people who are excessively talkative, disorganized and nonresponsive, terse and uncommunicative, flippant, short-tempered and impatient, and influence seeking. Never drop names of company executives or people you know at the company. If the interviewer is concerned about whether you know anyone who works for the company, you will be asked.

Be sure to find out how you will be notified whether you got the job. If you are to be notified by mail or phone, find out the approximate date. Inquire about the company's policies about phone call inquiries. Ask if you will be told why you did not get the job if you are rejected. If the company does not notify you on the date specified, wait a discreet forty-eight hours before you try to make inquiries.

THE INTERVIEWER'S POINT OF VIEW

Interviewers are your audience. They will have criteria for judging candidates, but you will not know what they are. You must proceed from what you understand about the situation and by observing the interviewer's behavior during the interview. You may infer that all interviewers will try to discover how you respond to stress. While interviewers employ many different styles, the situation itself is stressful, and from time to time the interviewer is likely to probe and ask you questions that you do not expect. There is no way to prepare for these surprises except to recognize the possibility that you will be surprised.

The interviewer wants information from you that is useful in shaping a judgment about whether or not you get the job. If you know what you want to say to represent yourself best, you can plan how to deliver it in an attractive package. Stay succinct, and well organized and try to respond directly to the questions you will be asked. Interviewers are concerned about your honesty, so don't try to hide anything. If the interviewer asks something you think is none of his or her business, say so courteously. It is better to refuse to answer than to attempt to give a false answer. Remember also that many interviewers do not have a precise notion of what constitutes a good answer. Most of them will try to compare you with other people they have interviewed and rate your answers alongside theirs. Thus you cannot psych out what they want anyway, so your best bet is to do the best you can with your own plan.

Interviewers will generate some tight situations for you by occasionally challenging your conclusion. If they ask what books you have read, they may follow up with the question, "What did you like about the book?" If you express an opinion, they will often ask you to back it up with evidence. Be prepared to document any statement you make about yourself, your education, and your experience. Your Application Blank

Kit will help you keep this information straight. It won't hurt a bit to take it with you into the interview and use it for reminders and documentation if you need to.

Sometimes interviewers will try to find out whether you have a sense of humor by joking a bit with you. Don't get carried away by their good humor. Smile when you feel like smiling and laugh when you hear something funny. Don't try to top the interviewer. He or she may be trying to see how willing you are to waste time.

Interviewers have as their most important task weeding out people who would not work out. The final hiring decisions are usually made by someone else. Therefore, interviewers are looking for behaviors from you that they can use for legitimate disqualifications. Questions about whether you are willing to relocate or travel are sometimes designed for this purpose. So are questions about work you would find unpleasant.

Interviewers want to know whether you drink or take drugs excessively, and although they are not allowed to inquire into your marital status, they would like to discover whether you will use the office as a source of sex partners. People would prefer to avoid sticky situations in the office. Try to keep your answers honest. You may think that your personal life is none of their business, but they do need to know a lot about you to make an informed decision. If you refuse to provide information they are entitled to ask for, they may disqualify you for being uncooperative. You can also talk your way out of a job by volunteering too much information. If you think the interviewer is getting too personal, simply disqualify yourself and state that you would rather not be considered if the information he or she is seeking will be used to judge your competency. Often the interviewer will back off and apologize, but in any case you will still have your integrity.

Interviewers want to know something about your sociability. This is where your shyness can really hurt you. If you are prepared to make simple small talk, you pass the first test. Most interviewers try to exchange a few clichés before going on to the important interview questions. Your interviewer cannot spend too much time in small talk, however, because there are other candidates waiting to be interviewed. Regard your interviewer as a person you are meeting for the first time who can be impressed. It is worthwhile doing so. He or she is, therefore, entitled to some of your best chitchat if you are asked for it.

Most interviewers will give you a chance to explain inconsistencies in your record. If you left a job for what you think was a good reason, simply explain it. If you were fired and you think your dismissal was unjustified, say so, and give your reason briefly. The same applies to your school grades. Most of the time your references will be asked to explain if your grades do not accurately represent your potential. There is nothing that you can gain from concealing this kind of information.

By preparing for interviews as carefully as for any social situation, you have your best chance to get the job. You can overcome your shyness by rehearsing interview situations. Each interview you experience will teach you more about what to expect and what to get ready for. Furthermore, it may help you not to say too much. Interviewers are human and are as likely to be bored by long-winded people as anyone else.

Once you get the job, you will be confronted with a number of situations where you must participate in public activities in order to represent your competencies. We will discuss how to prepare for and handle major communication requirements on the job in the rest of this chapter.

COMMUNICATING ON THE JOB

Once you have a job, most of your communication will be relatively formal, and you will usually have a chance to prepare yourself in advance. Most professional and technical jobs require attendance at meetings and formal presentations, and participation in various committees and group problem-solving experiences. Skill in these situations will help you call attention to your competence and will move you forward in the company. Concern about your shyness could be a real advantage here, since it will impel you to prepare, whereas others may take their skill for granted.

It is important to understand that virtually all rewards earned on the job are earned competitively. Advancement may come with seniority in some kinds of situations, but genuine advancement on the job is the result of you demonstrating superiority over the other candidates. You are matched performance by performance, and your qualifications are compared. While there may be some element of office politics operating, for the most part companies are attentive to people who are moving ahead and appear to be competent. The way they demonstrate their competence is through their communication.

Formal speaking situations have three possible goals:

1. To present information so that others understand it and can use it.
2. To express and defend opinions, evaluations, and proposals.
3. To change behaviors.

Such situations almost never require small talk. There are some social obligations on the job, but they are so simple that they should not present a problem to you. If you are uneasy during social contacts, you need not make arrangements to see your colleagues off the premises except for legitimate business purposes.

The idea of socializing with colleagues is attractive but often dangerous. You can be sociable without getting involved in a sticky network of friendships that might interfere with your freedom to make choices on the job. If you keep your contacts casual, you will never learn too much nor give away important information. You will not have to sacrifice an intimate relationship because you were promoted and left your friend behind. Some people try to use friendships politically, for advancement on the job. By being friendly with as many people as possible but friends with none, you make yourself available to all in the service of the company, which is precisely the way it ought to be.

Many people impair their chances on the job by talking too much or at the wrong time. Spreading rumors or gossiping about fellow employees may sometimes satisfy prurient urges, but once you get a reputation as a gossip, you sacrifice credibility in more important areas. Keeping quiet except when it matters can justify trust put in you by others. Furthermore, most of the gossip you hear is untrue, so if it stops with you, you have done a service to your fellow employees.

To make yourself appear most competent, you must acquire the following skills:

- You must be able to present information clearly adapted to the level of understanding of your listener.
- You must be able to present documented evaluations based on sensible standards.
- You must be able to substantiate your arguments on behalf of various proposals.
- You must be able to contribute your "share" to group problem-solving efforts.
- You should be able to display goodwill by treating your colleagues, superiors, and subordinates decently.

Each of these goals can be attained by managing your talk. Most people know their jobs, but few can talk about their jobs effectively. Mainly, the situations you will find yourself in will call for presentational speaking or group discussion. *Presentational speaking* places you in front of an audience of one or more people to whom you are presenting information, advice, opinions, or proposals. Your listeners usually have the power to decide what is to be done. Customarily you will have formal time limits on your speaking, you will have lead time in which to prepare, and you will very often have formal written information from which to draw your oral remarks. *Group discussion* is less formal. It is used when a committee or task force is charged with the responsibility of examining a problem and proposing solutions to it. The content of group discussion is regulated by the questions the group is trying to answer, and you will have time to examine the questions carefully before you have to speak about them.

STAND UP AND SPEAK

Public speaking is easier than social conversation because you can plan what you want to say and be guaranteed a specific time in which to say it without interruption. Furthermore, most situations in which you would speak are sufficiently formal so that no one can change the subject. In addition, you will very likely be the best prepared person there.

Furthermore, public speaking offers a limited number of goals that are relatively easy to attain. It has long been known that lectures are not very economical ways to transmit information. Industrial speakers do not try to instruct people through public speaking. They may, however, try to instruct people on how to get instructed, convince them about why they must get instructed, and persuade them to act now in order to get the instruction they need. Usually when you are called on to speak in public on the job, you will have one or more of the following goals:

- *To introduce a new program or idea.* This kind of speaking hits the high spots, explains why the program is necessary, and explains where detailed information on the program can be obtained.
- *To orient or create a mood.* This kind of speaking seeks to instill optimism, improve morale, or energize the "troops." It is somewhat like a sermon or a locker room message from the coach. It is fo-

cused on some major change or rite of passage, such as the orientation of new employees or an explanation of responsibilities under the new union contract. It is often used to charge up salesmen about to start a major campaign or to introduce a new product.

- *To brief or present a digest of information.* A great many executives depend on briefings to keep up with what is going on. The standard briefing is an oral presentation in which an "expert" digests the information and hits the high spots briefly.

In each case, the speaker is the expert with more information on the topic than any listener. For this reason, the public can be easily managed. Your main concern is to select information that will appeal to the needs and sensitivities of your listeners and to organize it so that they will understand it. You can depend on your professional capabilities to guide you in selecting information, and you can depend on the information we gave you in Chapter Nine for your organization.

Actually, you will find that you work mostly with four of the seven patterns of organization you learned in Chapter Nine. The orders of Standards, Association, and Argument will guide your writing of the complicated reports that most of your oral presentations will be based on. Mainly you will use Occurrence, Description, Components, and Comparison for your presentations.

Instructions and up-date reports are connected by Occurrence. For example:

HERE'S HOW WE GOT INTO THIS MESS

1. 1978. There was a strike at the Hooper plant. Here are the details.
2. 1979. The economy of the town where Hooper was located became depressed. The branch manager proposed decertification of the union.
3. Early 1980. Market research discovered that the branch had to be closed.
4. Present. The union went on strike and refused to let the closing take place. That's where we are now.

HERE'S HOW TO FILL OUT YOUR DAILY REPORT SHEETS

1. Place carbons between the original and each of two copies.
2. Put your name and date in the space provided on top.
3. In the boxes in the left-hand column list the companies you visited on that date.

4. For each company follow through the columns to the right and note the amount of time spent, whom you saw, the purpose of the visit, what you accomplished, and any special information.
5. Sign your name at the bottom.
6. Send original and pink copy to the main office in the special envelopes in the pocket at the front of your report book. Keep the blue copy as your record.

Clarifications are handled through presentation of Components, that is, the main features. If your topic is "How Decisions Are Made," you might use this pattern:

1. The role of Research and Development in initiating ideas.
2. Where other ideas come from.
3. The role of task forces in screening ideas.
4. The role of specialized units such as Community Affairs and Market Research in testing ideas.
5. The role of the board of directors in passing judgment on ideas.

or,

1. How ideas are generated.
2. How ideas are tested.
3. How formal proposals are made.
4. How final decisions are made.

But, you would probably not want to divide the components into

1. The role of Research and Development.
2. The role of Community Affairs.
3. How formal proposals are made.
4. The role of the board of directors

because this would overlap categories.

Often you will have to define a thing or event. This can be handled by explaining

- how it looks,
- what it is used for,
- how it works,

- how it is made, and
- how you can get one,

but you would not include "the names of its parts" because that would fit under "how it looks."

The appropriate pattern of organization should be suggested by your technical skill or knowledge of your job. It is not constructed out of some magical pattern. You demonstrate your competence by taking what you know, by organizing it sensibly, and then by putting it into words your listeners will understand. Attention to what you learned earlier about organization will help you adapt your technical material so that you can do effective presentations on the job.

TIPS ON PRESENTATIONAL SPEAKING

1. When you prepare your presentation, you need not use the elaborate proofs you find in prepared written documents. You must select the supporting material that makes things clear to your listeners. Try not to distort your ideas, but recognize that when you talk to people, you cannot give them all the details you have. The reason you are talking at all is because it is an economical way of hitting the high spots for people who really do not have the time to dig into the details. If there are questions, be sure you have the technical back-up to handle them.

2. Connect your supporting material to main ideas with the "because," "for instance," or "I mean" system. "Because" is used when you are arguing.

You should adopt this idea

- *because* it will solve the problem.
- *because* it is inexpensive.
- *because* if we don't do it, things will get worse.

Notice how each of the supporting statements completes the main idea by the use of "because." You can go further with "for instance."

Here's how it will solve your problem,

- *for instance* it will facilitate traffic flow.
- *for instance* it will reduce costly errors.

And you can go on with "I mean."

By "facilitate traffic flow"

- *I mean* that it will get products to customers faster.

Notice how logical these connections are. These are the main tricks you need to make your presentation sound smooth and coherent.

3. It is useful to have introductions and conclusions prepared in advance. Shy people have the most difficulty getting starting and finishing smoothly. Don't be afraid to write your introductions and conclusions out on cards and read them if you have to. Every introduction should have some attention-getting story (not necessarily a joke) that will appeal to your audience's interests. This should be followed by a brief table of contents ("These are the three points I will cover."), which prepares your listener to follow your presentation. There should be a brief line that explains why the information in the presentation is important to the listeners ("This is the first notice anyone will get of the 1982 sales campaign.") The conclusion should repeat the points specified in your table of contents and remind the listeners once more why the presentation was important. The cliché is, "Tell 'em what you're gonna' tell 'em. Tell 'em! Then tell 'em what you told 'em."

4. If you have to answer questions, remember what you learned about social conversation. Try to anticipate what pattern of organization the answer demands and work it out according to the steps. If you do not understand the questions, do not hesitate to *repeat it as you understand it* and ask your questioner if this represents what he or she wants to know. Rephrasing the question will help clarify your pattern for an answer, and it will also give you a little time to get your thoughts together. If you do not know an answer, say so, but inform your questioner when you will have an answer ready. Keep in mind your written back-up documents and do not hesitate to refer questioners to written materials to "get a more complete answer."

5. You may need some help in learning to use your voice and body effectively. The voice is a powerful instrument for helping you get your meaning across to your listeners. Some simple vocal training will help you learn how to emphasize and punctuate with your voice.

Shy people do very well at learning to control their voices. Some authorities believe that one of the reasons for their shyness is that they never learned techniques of vocal inflection. Learning to control the voice helps you place your tension in ways that help you communicate. There are a number of courses available in university continuing-education programs where you can learn vocal skills. Exactly as neat printing is important to the contents of a book, good delivery is an important aspect of effective speaking.

6. As you select material to present, be sure to test each of your supports to see that it does not violate basic rules of logic. Here are some cautions:

- Eyewitness reports are often biased and inaccurate. It is not that these reporters want to deceive you. Often they do not know how to look or how to identify what is important to remember. Firsthand reports also rely on fragile human memories.
- Information from authorities can be biased and excessively technical. It is sensible to paraphrase in your presentation, rather than quote, but be sure that your paraphrase accurately reflects what the authority said. Be careful of distortions. If someone asks why you are referring to this or that person, be able to state the basic qualifications.
- It is easy to distort statistical information. Check any statistics you use to make sure they are not flawed or biased. It is useful to check this kind of material with a professional statistician. It is not effective to try to present statistics directly to your audience. You need to interpret and simplify them. Sometimes it is helpful to use charts and graphs to help your audience understand.

MASTER PLAN FOR REPORTS

Here is a master plan to help you prepare reports. When you put the report in writing, each section should be completely detailed. For your oral presentation, preserve the logic of your written presentation but simplify it. Be sure to attend to all of the following headings.

- Who requested you to prepare a report or to talk? What did that person seek to get from it? To what purpose will your report be put? The answer to these questions will shape the introduction to your presentation.
- What is the background of the problem? What triggered it? What was the sequence of events leading up to it? What caused it? Who decided it was a problem and why?
- What is the nature of the problem. What organizational component is defective? What is happening that should not be happening? What is not happening that should be happening? What is the nature of the injury, and why is it an injury?
- What must a solution accomplish? How would we know a good solution if we encountered it? What legal, moral, practical, and financial limitations must we consider.

- What are the details of the solution? Who is to do what about what when, and where, under whose supervision, and at what cost? Where will the money come from?
- How is the solution to be evaluated? When will we know we have solved the problem? When will we know things are not working and we'd better try something else?

Oral presentations can be no better than the written documents on which they are based. When you are sure of your written report, you can be confident that you have the substance of a good oral report. If you are ever asked to present an oral report that is not based on a written report do not hesitate to do the detail work that you would do for a written document. It is better to overprepare than to find yourself wanting for material at a crucial moment.

HOW TO PARTICIPATE IN A GROUP

Groups of various sorts (committees, task forces) are frequently used to solve problems in large organizations. Modern organizations are so complicated that they cannot rely on one person's opinion or research when important decisions are to be made. Groups are brought together so that various experts can pool their competencies to decide on what is wrong and what to do about it. You will probably be included in many such groups during your career, and you will be judged on what you contribute to the group.

Group problem solving tends to take a long time and is often boring. There is no substitute for it. It is both democratic and effective, so long as everyone participates. However, if the members of a group permit one or two members to do all the talking and to make all the decisions, the purpose for which the group was organized is defeated. Here are some problems that typically plague discussion groups, along with recommendations for what you can do to improve the group's performance.

- Groups are often not clear about their task. Sometimes the authority who asked them to do the task is also not clear. There is no way a group can come up with a satisfactory solution if it does not know what problem it is supposed to address. Use your influence to inquire about the precise wording of the problem with which the group is to deal. Find out what form the group's answer should be in. Find out when the report is due. The group should not begin working until all of this is clear.

- Groups often tend to hurry through the examination of the facts. Whatever the problem the group is dealing with, they must take time to gather some details. Sometimes the whole view of the problem changes. Furthermore, facts must be evaluated critically so that propaganda and falsehood can be weeded out. You can help the group by asking whether there is enough information of sufficient quality so that the group really understands its problem.

- Groups often do not follow an orderly procedure in problem solving. In the next section we will present you with such an orderly procedure that can be used in all organizational groups regardless of the problems they are dealing with. If you can keep the group proceeding in orderly fashion, you will be performing a valuable service.

- Groups tend to divide into factions. It is a lot easier to argue with one another than to cooperate in finding a solution to a problem. Sometimes people go on ego trips by monopolizing the talk, challenging the authority of the group leader, or demanding their own way. At times like these, the group needs a cool head who can stop the conflict by reminding the group of its task and reviewing what it has done and what remains to be done.

- Groups often get preoccupied with trivial details. They sometimes spend hours discussing paper clips, then go ahead and dispense thousands of dollars without sufficient consideration. That is because people feel threatened by serious issues and try to pass them by. Then they try to prove their worth with serious deliberations over trivia. You can help by asking questions about the relative importance of issues.

- Sometimes groups are bulldozed into inadequate solutions by aggressive people or those who have an ax to grind. Most people will not face down a really angry or dedicated person, and those who do not have great commitment to a point of view fold easily when they are attacked vehemently, even if they know they are right. Groups can also be snowed under by charismatic people, who promise to lead everyone out of the wilderness. You may not always be able to face down people like these or defeat them in combat, but you can always file a minority report if you think someone has led the group astray.

- Many groups get carried away with interpersonal issues. They think that a group meeting is a place to make friends and find fulfillment. You can render a real service to your group and to your company by raising questions about quick consensus and by playing devil's advocate if you have to, so that solutions do not come too easily because members are more concerned with personal affection than with quality solutions.

You do not have to be a skilled orator to be effective in groups. You have to keep your wits about you, know your subject, keep an eye on what is going on, and ask questions. That is not hard to do if you understand the process of group problem solving.

Many groups become preoccupied with interpersonal issues. It is easy to go along with what appears to be the group consensus. Shy people have a tendency to avoid conflict in groups and, thus, they contribute to the process called "groupthink," in which conflict becomes unacceptable and groups agree on solutions designed to avoid hurting anyone's feelings. You can improve your effectiveness in problem-solving groups by understanding the process and acquiring skill in its steps. An excellent book, which will provide you with a simple understanding of how to operate effectively in task groups, is *Group Discussion: A Practical Guide to Participation and Leadership*.[2] Each step of the group process contains opportunities for you to speak your mind. For example:

- The first phase of group problem solving requires the group to discover what the end product will look like. You can help the grouping by insisting that they get clear instructions from the person that established the group.
- The second phase requires the phrasing of a good discussion question. You can help by insisting that the question be open-ended so that it will avoid splitting the group into factions.
- The third phase requires gathering information. You can help by inquiring about the qualifications of the persons from whom information is obtained, questioning authorities, and examining statistical information carefully.
- The fourth phase requires realistic goalsetting. You can apply what you have learned about your personal goalsetting to the goals of the group.
- The fifth phase requires careful examination of a solution. You can help by holding the group back from a premature commitment.
- Finally, the group must prepare arguments on behalf of its solution. You can help by testing the reasoning and evidence the group uses to make its case.

There are not many people who have real skill at group problem solving.

By cultivating such skill you can change from a quiet member to a real leader.

UNDERSTANDING HOW ORGANIZATIONS WORK

You can do an effective job of managing your behavior if you understand some of the basic conditions that exist in every organization. This understanding will prevent you from setting unrealistic goals.

Organizations are not cold and heartless. They are made up of people, each doing tasks that presumably help the organization. Some do them well, and some do them poorly. Everyone wants to be thought well of. Everyone wants the company to prosper, because if the company prospers, they prosper, but no one wants the prosperity to be at their expense. For that reason one of the main purposes people employed by organizations see the organization serving is to maintain their job. People have a great deal at stake in their work. They are easily threatened. If you can keep your eye on some exchange principle as you deal with them, you will be on the most solid ground. Make sure that you give when you get.

Every organization operates according to some chart that explains who is responsible to whom for what. You must understand who has authority and what the chain of command is. No matter how good an employee you are, if you violate the chain of command, you threaten someone and you earn an enemy. Many employees get into trouble because they don't know whom to please. Understand who is responsible for evaluating your work and give that person your prime service.

Enlist the wisdom of old and competent employees. Folks who know their way around the organization can be invaluable allies for you. They love to give advice and they will admire you for asking for it. However, be careful about accepting favors. There are those in organizations who seek to advance themselves politically. They will do favors and then expect a little more in return from you, often when it is very inconvenient for you to give it. If you accept a favor, make sure you return something equally valuable at a time when it is convenient for you to do it.

Try not to borrow from or preempt other people's work. Give

credit when you use someone else's ideas or material. Make sure you get proper credit for what you do. If you tell someone about your bright idea, make sure you have a memo dated before the time you made it public.

Beware of unethical operators. Not everyone in the organization would do you good. You can have enemies. Hanky-panky goes on in strange places. The less you know about who is sleeping with whom, the better off you are. The less you fraternize with your fellow employees off the premises, the less likely you are to implicate yourself. This is exceedingly hard to do, because there are so many nice people at the office and you will probably need friends. The more you can control your tendencies to become intimate with your fellow workers, the more independent you can be in your moves inside the organization.

Experts are the most powerful people in organizations. Bosses come and go, but experts remain eternally. If you are interested in job security, become an expert in some procedure or process that is important to the company. For the shy person, this is the most convenient path to organizational success. However, in order to demonstrate that you are an expert, you will have to find a way to communicate your expertise.

There are no important differences between communication on the job and communication in your personal life. Keep in mind what we have been telling you all along—you cannot control other people, only yourself. Take only your share of the blame, and keep your goals centered around behaviors. By this time you should be ready to take advantage of the innumerable courses available to you in continuing-education programs or perhaps in employee-training programs that seek to improve your communication skills. Courses in public speaking and group discussion will be helpful to you on the job and in your personal life. Beware of courses that make promises about how they will improve your life. They are more often than not designed to make money for the operators, and they will do you little good. Dale Carnegie Courses and Toastmasters Clubs usually provide useful programs, as do many colleges and universities. The way to identify a useful program is:

1. Make sure it deals with real events.
2. Make sure it does not ask you to believe in a person or a mystical system.
3. Make sure it addresses teaching you skills rather than problems in your psyche.

REFERENCES

1. For detailed information write: Speech Communication Association, 5105 Blacklick Rd., Annandale, VA 22003.
2. Gerald M. Phillips, Douglas Pedersen, and Julia Wood, *Group Discussion: A Practical Guide to Participation and Leadership* (Boston: Houghton Mifflin, 1979).

RECOMMENDED READINGS

Jean L. Rogers and Walter L. Fortson, *Fair Employment Interviewing* (Reading, Mass.: Addison-Wesley Publishing Co., Inc., 1976).

Richard Nelson Bolles, *What Color is Your Parachute?* (Berkeley, Calif.: Ten Speed Press, 1978).

Tom Jackson and Davidyne Maylens, *The Hidden Job Market* (New York: Quadrangle/The New York Times Book Co., Inc., 1978).

Amitai Etzioni, *The Active Society* (New York: The Free Press, 1968).

Gerald M. Phillips, Douglas J. Pedersen, and Julia T. Wood, *Group Discussion: A Practical Guide to Participation and Leadership* (Boston: Houghton, Mifflin, 1979).

Edwin Newman, *Strictly Speaking* (New York: Warner Books, 1974).

Dorothy Sarnoff, *Speech Can Change Your Life* (New York: Doubleday & Co., Inc., 1970).

Thomas E. Pearsall and Donald H. Cunningham, *How to Write for the World of Work* (New York: Holt, Rinehart & Winston, 1978).

Index

A

B

C

D

E

F

L

M

N

O

P

R

S

V